French Politics

French Politics presents basic information about the French political system and analyses in detail the most important debates and controversies concerning French politics today. This accessible study explores the numerous ways in which French politics can be interpreted, concluding that the study of French political life is being transformed in response to a changing global, European and domestic environment.

Elgie and Griggs provide an overview of contemporary controversies in French politics, examining key topical issues of the late twentieth century. Subjects covered include:

- the changing parameters of state intervention
- the relationship between the president and prime minister
- interpretations of voting behaviour
- the nature of interest group politics
- the impact of moves towards European integration.

French Politics highlights the disagreements between those who write about French politics, and argues that these disagreements are often based on radically conflicting interpretations of the French political process. It examines the opposing viewpoints held by these writers and identifies the differences between them, thus providing the student with a comprehensive introduction to the study of French political life. This thorough and concise study is an essential resource for students and scholars of French politics.

Robert Elgie is Senior Lecturer in Politics at the University of Nottingham. He has published widely in the field of French, European and comparative politics. His previous publications include *The Role of the Prime Minister in France* and *Semi-Presidentialism in Europe*.

Steven Griggs is Senior Lecturer in Public Policy at Staffordshire University. He has published widely in journals including *West European Politics*, *Parliamentary Affairs* and *Modern and Contemporary France*.

French Politics
Debates and Controversies

Robert Elgie and Steven Griggs

London and New York

First published 2000
by Routledge
11 New Fetter Lane, London EC4P 4EE

Simultaneously published in the USA and Canada
by Routledge
29 West 35th Street, New York, NY 10001

Routledge is an imprint of the Taylor & Francis Group

Typeset in Sabon by Taylor & Francis Books Ltd
Printed and bound in Great Britain by St Edmundsbury Press,
Bury St Edmunds, Suffolk

British Library Cataloguing in Publication Data
A catalogue record for this book is available from the British Library

Library of Congress Cataloging in Publication Data
Elgie, Robert
French Politics : debates and controversies / Robert Elgie and Steven
Griggs.
p. cm.
Includes bibliographical references and index.
France–Politics and government–1958–   I. Griggs, Steven,
1962–   II. Title.
JN2594.2.E54 2000
320.944–dc21   99-056248

ISBN 0-415-17478-3 (hbk)
ISBN 0-415-17479-1 (pbk)

This book is dedicated to the memory
of Vincent Wright

Contents

List of illustrations

Tables

Figures

Preface

This book is designed to be a textbook on French politics unlike any other. There are already a great many very notable and successful books which provide a comprehensive introduction to French politics and which are written primarily for those whose first language is English. In these books, the author invariably outlines the main institutional and political characteristics of contemporary France and proposes a number of generalisations about the key features of the political system. This book, however, is very different from these standard texts. It does present some basic information about the functioning of certain aspects of the French political system. This information is included in the introductory section to each of the chapters which follow (see below). However, this book does not claim to provide a fully exhaustive account of the many, various and fascinating aspects of French political life, nor does it put forward a general thesis about the nature of the French political system. Instead, the aim of this book is to introduce students to a number of the most important debates and controversies in the study of contemporary French politics. It takes as its starting point the notion that there are disagreements amongst those who write about French politics and that these disagreements are often based on radically conflicting and often, although not always, mutually exclusive interpretations of the French political process. The purpose of the book, therefore, is to highlight the opposing viewpoints held by these writers and to identify the differences between them. In this way, it acts not as a competitor to the standard introductory texts on French politics but as a companion to them. In short, we hope that this book will complement existing textbooks and broaden the range of learning materials available to both students and teachers of French politics alike. In so doing, we also hope that it will stimulate further discussion of French politics and generate yet more debates in the future.

The structure of the book

The standard text on French politics tends to focus on the institutions of government and the politics of representation. Thus, following a brief outline of French political and constitutional history, such a text customarily includes chapters on the presidency and the government, parliament, local government and the civil service. More often than not, the standard text then goes on to examine elections and voting behaviour, political parties, the party system and interest groups. Finally, there is usually a concluding chapter which places France in a European context and/or which examines the extent of change in the contemporary political system. In order to act as a companion to the standard text on French politics, we have structured this book in a somewhat similar way.

The book begins with a chapter on the state. This is an overarching chapter which addresses one of the most long-standing preoccupations of French politics, namely what role does and should the state play in the organisation of political life. It also establishes the main themes which appear throughout the book as a whole, such as internationalisation, Europeanisation, the disaggregation of the policy-making process and the role of the public sector in contemporary democracies. In this way, it sets the scene for many of the debates that are examined in subsequent chapters.

Having identified these themes, the book then goes on to consider three more particular aspects of institutional politics: the distribution of responsibilities within the executive branch of government (or core executive), the role of elite civil servants in the policy-making process and the power of local authorities to shape political outcomes. These topics are considered not simply because they constitute three of the most fundamental elements of the political process, but also because they have been and continue to be the subject of some of the liveliest debates about French politics. Thus, there is great scope for the various and opposing points of view to be presented.

Having considered some of the most salient institutional debates in French politics, the book then turns to the examination of popular representation and political behaviour. Here, the first chapter deals with the influence of political parties. In one sense, this chapter also has an institutional focus in that it considers the extent to which political parties can shape the decision-making process. However, as will be seen, this issue is closely linked to the debate about the nature, role and organisation of political parties in the Fifth French Republic and so, in this sense, it is also inextricably concerned with the issue of party political representation. The next chapter concerns elections and electoral behaviour. It examines the issue of why people vote the way they do. Thus, it shifts the focus of attention away from institutions and parties and towards individual citizens and social classes. The following chapter then explores the role of interest groups. Again, it centres around the extent to which such groups are able to influence the policy-making process, but, as with the chapter on political parties, it is also fundamentally concerned with the ways in which collective social interests are expressed and represented.

The penultimate chapter presents an overview of many of the topics that have been considered in the book. It does so by focusing on the concept of the impact of Europe on the French policy-making style. What areas of French politics have been affected by the process of European integration and what has been the extent of change in these areas? More particularly, it examines the issue of whether there is something unique about French politics in a comparative context or whether politics in France is now conducted in a similar manner to politics in other European countries and, indeed, elsewhere. As with Chapter 1, this is an overarching chapter. As such, it rounds up many of the themes that have been addressed in the book as a whole.

We end with a very brief conclusion. This short chapter serves as the opportunity for us to provide some final thoughts about French politics and, more pertinently, about the ways in which French politics has been, and is currently being, studied. Here, we do not aim to outline our 'theory' of French politics or to outline our 'position' on the debates that have been covered in the preceding chapters. Instead, as throughout the rest of the book, we are interested in the study of French politics. In the conclusion, therefore, we confine ourselves to reflecting on developments in the discipline and future directions that intellectual inquiry may take.

In these ways, then, the basic aim of this book is to analyse many of the most important debates and controversies in the study of contemporary French politics. It is clear, though, that not every potentially fruitful line of inquiry will be examined. For the most part, we have deliberately confined ourselves to topics which are part and parcel of the usual focus of French politics textbooks. This is because, as noted above, we intend this book to be used as a companion to more introductory texts. As a result, however, we were obliged to concentrate on the areas which are most regularly covered by such texts and, hence, we focus primarily on political institutions and political behaviour. So, much as it would have been compelling to explore the ongoing and vigorous debates about, for example, foreign policy, immigration policy and women and politics, we set these topics aside. That said, the selection of topics was also determined by a number of more specific reasons. For example, little reference is made to the French legislature in the pages which follow. This is because there has been very little debate about its role under the Fifth Republic. It is certainly the case that in recent years there has been an attempt to rehabilitate parliament and increase its influence. However, the vast majority of those writing on this topic tend to agree that its capacity to shape the policy process is still very limited. Thus, reluctantly, we decided not to devote a special chapter to the legislature because it would have produced a very lopsided debate. In addition, with the exception of the key points identified in the first section of Chapters 5 and 6, little mention is made of the ideology of individual political parties. This is not because there is no debate about the contemporary values of, for example, the Gaullist Party (is it still Gaullist?), the Socialist Party (is it now social democratic?), or the National Front (is it a neo-fascist party?). On the contrary, there is plenty of writing on these and similar topics. Instead, these debates were omitted because the book is designed to examine more broad-ranging topics. Therefore, rather than incorporating separate chapters about each of the parties in the system or even individual chapters on the parties of the left and the parties of the right, we decided to include a more rounded chapter on the general question of the extent to which parties can influence the political process (see above). Finally, it should also be noted that there is one set of debates which we deliberately decided not to cover. We took the decision not to report explicitly party political, or at least ideologically inspired, views of French politics. So, we do not systematically include, for example, Marxist, New-Right or Green accounts of the policy process in the chapters which follow. Needless to say, these and other interpretations clearly have their supporters in the academic community. Indeed, they underpin certain accounts of French political institutions and political representation. However, when writing this book we sought to avoid becoming involved in partisan-inspired or normative accounts of how French politics 'should' function or how it 'ought' to be. Thus, we have excluded accounts of this sort from the debates which follow unless we consider them to be part of the mainstream set of intellectual controversies which we are endeavouring to analyse (see, for example, the chapter on local government).

Thus, what follows is, no doubt, an account of only a few of the debates and controversies in contemporary French politics. However, it is an account that covers many of the most important general topics with which crrent textbooks are concerned and, therefore, it is also one that, we hope, addresses the needs of most students of French political life.

The organisation of the chapters

One of our main preoccupations when writing this book was to arrange the material in an even and consistent way. To this end, each of the chapters is organised uniformly on the basis of two separate sections and a conclusion.

The first section of each chapter furnishes the reader with a basic introduction to the topic in question. This section is designed to provide sufficient background material with which to grasp the debate that is then examined. In this section, we do not pretend to include an exhaustive set of facts and figures, names and places, or information and material. This is the task of the more standard textbook. Instead, the first section of each chapter merely sets the scene and places the subsequent debate in context. Here, every effort has been made to present the information in an impartial and even-handed way. We have taken great care not to bias the debate which follows by making assumptions which are themselves essentially contestable. To the best of our ability, therefore, the information presented in this section is value free.

The second section of each chapter is quite different. This section analyses the scholarly debate itself. The key elements of this section are the various 'models' around which the debate is constructed. We took care to structure this section of the chapter in this way for a specific reason. As noted above, our key concern when writing the book was to identify the conflicting assumptions that are made by the various people who write about French politics. The models that we identify represent, we believe, the best way of capturing these fundamental differences. Each model corresponds to a particular viewpoint that a certain set of scholars has adopted on the topic in question. For each chapter, the set of models captures the range of different viewpoints that has been proposed. All told, therefore, we use these models simply as a tool to enable us to analyse the various debates with which we are concerned in the clearest way possible.

The identification of these models of politics represents the main innovation of this text. It may, therefore, be useful to elaborate briefly on their status and nature. In this context, three particular points should be noted.

First, it should be stressed that our use of the term 'model' is benign. Indeed, the term is employed in the same sense as Jacques Lesourne who notes that it 'can designate a schema, a simplified representation, a mental map' (Lesourne, 1998, p. 90). In other words, we use the concept of a 'model' in an heuristic sense, meaning that we employ it simply to draw attention to the conflicting arguments which different writers adopt and the different assumptions that they make. It is merely an analytical tool which helps to elucidate certain points. We do not use it to say that this is the only way of interpreting a particular debate and that all discussion has been or must be conducted in this way.

Second, with regard to some debates there is no doubt that writers state their opposition to each other very clearly. On these occasions there is public disagreement and the conflicting models, or schools of thought, are easily identifiable. In the chapters which follow, this is particularly noticeable in the debates about voting behaviour and interest-group politics. With regard to other debates, though, writers do not take issue with their colleagues quite so explicitly. They simply make an argument whose assumptions on close inspection can be deemed to differ from those who are writing on the same theme. On these occasions, the models we identify had to be constructed from scratch. In these cases, it was necessary to 'read between the lines' and tease out the sometimes hidden assumptions of certain writers. This was the case most notably in the debates about the core executive and party politics. Needless to say, in all cases, but in the latter ones particularly, we trust that we have not quoted people out of context and that we have represented the various arguments fairly and without prejudice.

Third, even though writers disagree with each other and make contrasting assumptions (either explicitly or implicitly), there is often a degree of overlap between their work as well. The result is that the boundaries between particular arguments may become somewhat 'fuzzy' and blurred. In this context, analysing a debate in terms of separate and competing models can sometimes exaggerate the differences between writers and mask the similarities that they undoubtedly share. For this reason, we have taken great care in each chapter both to identify the assumptions that the various models have in common and to signal the points of overlap between them. Thus, while we are primarily concerned with emphasising the differences between the various arguments to be considered, we also try to establish the similarities between them as well.

It is clear, then, that the models we identify constitute not only the main innovation of this book, but also the bulk of the text which follows. That said we can, of course, only outline the range of scholarly work that has been undertaken in any one area over time. We can only give a flavour of what are in many cases long-standing, highly detailed and quite complex arguments. As a result, we would encourage students to explore the biblio-graphical references for themselves so as to enrich their understanding of the nuances and subtleties of the French political system.

Finally, it should also be noted that we end each chapter with a brief conclusion. There were two main considerations here. First, we use the conclusion as a way of recapping the competing assumptions that have just been presented. In so doing, we remind readers of the intellectual consequences that go with choosing one model over another. Second, we indicate the current state of the academic debate. Which models are scholars now choosing to support? Is there a dominant paradigm, or a more open debate? If there is a dominant paradigm, will it retain this posi-tion for the foreseeable future? What are the likely directions for future scholarship? These questions are addressed in the conclusions to each of the substantive chapters. They are also addressed in somewhat more detail in the final chapter of the book as a whole.

The presentation of the models

Just as we were keen to arrange each of the chapters in a uniform way, so we were also at pains to present the material in each of the models in a consistent fashion. There are, thus, four distinct elements to all of the models presented in the book.

The first element comprises an overview of the model's basic assump-tions. Needless to say, any such overview is bound to gloss over the particular points that individual writers may wish to make. However, the aim of beginning the examination of each model in this way is to show most succinctly how the model in question differs from its rivals and why, therefore, it merits special attention.

The second element identifies the main proponents of the model in question. In some cases, writers have changed their attitude towards a particular topic over a period of time. Thus, in any given chapter an indi-vidual writer may be cited as supporting more than one model. However, in the vast majority of cases, each model is proposed by a completely different set of people. That said, we do not claim that the list of those who put forward the model in question is always an exhaustive one. This book does not attempt to classify the complete work of everyone who has ever written anything about French politics. This would be an impossible task. Instead, as a general rule, the original, the most well-known and the most recent proponents of the various models are prioritised. We should, therefore, apologise in advance if we have omitted the work of certain colleagues. Any such omissions should not be taken as a sign that the work is not worthy of consideration, but simply as a consequence of the fact that the word limit prevents us from examining every possible argument.

It should also be noted that, in the knowledge that this book is aimed primarily at an English-speaking audience, we do pay particular attention to English-language sources. It goes without saying, of course, that most of the work on French politics is carried out by scholars writing in French and, as will be seen, this work forms the core of the material considered here. However, one of our primary goals is to encourage students whose first language is English to follow up the various debates under considera-tion and to explore the various references for themselves. Thus, while we ensure that the most important French-language references are always included, we also take care to cite, where possible, English-language trans-lations of French texts rather than the French original and to ensure that equivalent material written in English is included alongside its French-language counterpart. (All translations from the French are by the authors.)

The third element of each model consists of the basic arguments which are made in its defence and the evidence which is marshalled to back them up. As noted above, for any given chapter there is sometimes a degree of overlap between the different models. Moreover, those who promote essentially the same model often do so in slightly different ways. However, we try to capture the fundamental differences (and similarities) between the various points of view by presenting a representative sample of the work associated with the model in question rather than by drawing up a complete list of all the studies which are potentially available.

The final element of each model comprises a small number of funda-mental criticisms. We are aware that the arguments against one model are often the arguments in favour of another model. Thus, rather than repeating information in two or more places, we simply outline the basic criticisms of the model in question and then invite the reader to consult the other models for an alternative and conflicting point of view. Thus, we signal the weaknesses of the various models, but we do not explore them in depth unless they are not covered elsewhere in the chapter.

Overall, it should be stressed that we do not aim to be judgmental about the various models that are being examined. We do outline certain problems with particular arguments and various shortcomings of more general debates. As far as possible, though, we try to present each debate in a neutral way so as to allow the reader to make an independent judgement about the validity or otherwise of the various viewpoints under consideration. More than that, we would encourage the reader to construct alternative models that capture the delightful complexity of French political life with an even greater degree of accuracy.

Debates in French politics

This book was born out of both passion and frustration. On the one hand, we have been schooled in French politics for all our academic careers and we have developed a fascination for the topic. We have had the privilege of having been taught by a number of the most influential writers in this field and we have been influenced by many others. We wish to share our thoughts with both our students and our colleagues and we hope that we can add to the long-standing tradition of successful English-language studies about this most compelling of countries. On the other hand, though, we have been repeatedly frustrated in our attempts to comprehend the French political system. Most notably, we have been dismayed to find that people writing on the same topic sometimes 'talk past each other', that they fail to engage their intellectual opponents in a clear and open debate and that on occasions they even seem to ignore, wilfully or otherwise, alternative points of view. In writing this book, we hope to stimulate discussion about French politics, we wish to encourage people to engage with each other and we want to broaden the frame of academic reference of the discipline. In short, we aim not just to examine but also to stimulate debates in French politics.

Acknowledgements

A large number of debts have been accrued while writing this book. In particular, the authors would like to thank David Hanley, Seán Loughlin and Michael Marsh for their comments on the first drafts of individual chapters. In particular, we would also like to single out David Hanley for particular thanks. Dave was a great source of encouragement and support throughout the whole course of the book. We would also like to thank the two anonymous reviewers, who took the time to read the first draft of the manuscript and who provided such helpful comments, for their reports. It goes without saying, of course, that the responsibility for the final draft lies solely with ourselves.

In addition, we would like to thank our contacts at Routledge, most notably Patrick Proctor, Vicky Smith and Craig Fowlie. Only academics can get away with being so late when a deadline is set. We would like to thank Patrick, Vicky and Craig for their flexibility and great forbearance.

Finally, we would like to thank our families, Madeline, Martha and Ruth, and Etain and Matthew, for their support throughout the whole of this project.

1   The state

The French policy-making process is traditionally said to be state-centred. Arguably, the state does not just react to the demands of civil society, parties, interest groups, social movements and so on. It is not considered to be a 'weathervane' state which simply registers the way in which the prevailing social wind is blowing. Instead, the French state has traditionally been viewed as a directive state. Societal forces are themselves said to be shaped and controlled by state institutions at both the central and local level. Recently, though, the role of the state has been called into question. The size of the state has been criticised. One popular catch phrase in the 1980s was 'too much state kills the state'. In other words, it was argued that the state was a positive force, but that its scope needed to be reduced in order for the state sector to operate more efficiently. In this context, people have argued that the role of the state has now changed and that its power has been reduced. For over a decade now, the state has been downsized. The principles of managerialism and consumerism have been accentuated and the state has, so it is argued, become more modest.

This chapter examines competing models of the French state. It considers the state's capacity to act autonomously in the policy process and its potential to structure, if not impose, patterns of political behaviour on groups and individuals. The competing conceptions of the strength of the French state lie behind contemporary debates on many of the topics to be dealt with in later chapters. For example, fundamental assumptions about the organisation and limits of the French state inform models of interest group politics (see Chapter 7) and party politics (see Chapter 5), debates over the influence of the bureaucracy in policy making (see Chapter 3), conceptions of the resources at the disposal of the core executive (see Chapter 2), interpretations of centre–periphery relations (see Chapter 4) and claims of the exceptionalism of French politics (see Chapter 8). However, the specific focus of this chapter is an examination of the tradition of *étatisme*, or the extent to which the state is a political actor in its own right, with its own preferences and with the capacity to influence the political process to its own ends.

The chapter begins by analysing the changing parameters of the French state in recent years. It then goes on to identify three separate models of the French state: the strong state model, the weak state model and the disoriented state model.

The organisation of the French state

The origins of state intervention lie in the absolutist politics of the pre-1789 Ancien Régime. Indeed, it was Louis XIV who declared: 'L'État, c'est moi.' Since this time, the role of the state has expanded both administratively, particularly during the late eighteenth and early nineteenth centuries, and economically and socially, notably during the twentieth century. Recently, though, the role of the state has been revised. New forms of state activity have emerged and old forms of state intervention have all but disappeared. In Chapters 3 and 4 respectively, the organisation of the central bureaucracy and local government will be analysed. In the first part of this chapter, though, the contemporary role of the French state will be outlined by focusing on three other key aspects of the state system: the number of public-sector employees, the range of state-sector institutions and the regulatory power of state representatives.

The number of public-sector employees

There are a large number of state employees in France. In 1996 a total of 5,316,800 people were in public-sector employment. In other words, nearly 25 per cent of the total workforce is employed by the state (official figures reported in *L'Express*, 30 October, 1997, pp. 44–5). In comparative terms, this is a large figure but not an exceptional one. It compares to only 15.7 per cent in Germany but as much as 32.7 per cent in both Denmark and Sweden. In France, not all of these state-employed civil servants work in government departments. Of all French public-sector employees, 846,900 people are employed as hospital workers, 1,442,700 people are employed by local authorities (see Chapter 4), 480,300 people work for France Télécom, 387,100 people are in the defence forces and 'only' 1,827,300 people work for government departments in the strict sense of the word. Moreover, in this latter category, over half are employed by the Education Ministry, as all school teachers are officially classified as civil servants. So, the number of departmental bureaucrats is actually much smaller than the brute figures might suggest. Still, though, the figure is not inconsiderable and the total number of people employed by the state in the widest sense of the term is larger still. Moreover, in the 1980s, at a time when governments in many other countries were cutting back on the number of public employees, in France the number of people employed by the state actually rose by 386,000 from 1980 to 1985 and by a further 112,000 from 1985 to 1990 (Ibid., p. 42). Furthermore, in 1997, the newly-elected left-wing government led by Lionel Jospin launched an ambitious plan to create 350,000 new state-sector jobs mainly for young unemployed people. For the most part, these people carry out only basic functions, such as security guards in schools, but they do still have a job and they are still paid by the state. All of this suggests, therefore, that there continues to be a very strong emphasis in France on the idea that the public sector performs a social as well as a purely administrative function, and that in this sense, it has a role to play in the fight against unemployment.

State-sector institutions

State-sector employees in France are employed in wide variety of organisations. One characteristic of the French state is the plethora of commissions, committees, companies and the like which have been established over the years to direct and manage the policy process. In recent years, the state has privatised some of its most well-known enterprises. However, the range of state-sector institutions still comprises a host of organisations.

State-sector institutions include central administrative organisations such as the Planning Commission, which was responsible for the post-war state-directed economic modernisation process, and the Regional Development and Action Authority (DATAR), which was established in 1963 to oversee the process of regional regeneration. In addition, there is a strong public-sector presence at the local level (see Chapter 4). For the most part, these officials are employed by local authorities, but there are also large numbers of state employees working in the field services of central government departments. Indeed, around 92 per cent of departmental civil servants work outside Paris.

In addition, the range of state organisations also includes a large number of public-sector companies. Indeed, such is the variety of these bodies that an official report by the Council of State concluded that they exhibit an 'immense variety of objectives, size, statutes and importance which defy any comprehensive categorisation'. In general, though, there are three categories of public companies.

The first may be called public enterprises of an administrative nature. These include organisations such as the state publishing house. They also include schools. Equally, they include organisations like the Chambers of Commerce, and bodies that charge for their services, such as museums. However, they are not, strictly speaking, commercial enterprises. One characteristic of these types of public enterprises is that all their employees have the status of civil servants.

The second may be called public enterprises of an industrial or commercial nature. These organisations have two points in common. First, the state is the sole shareholder. Second, they are subject to the terms of private law. They include nationalised industries, such as the state-owned electricity and gas companies (EDF and GDF, respectively). However, they also include mixed-economy enterprises, such as the ports authorities, the airports authorities and the National Forestry Commission. They are subject to strict supervision by the ministry to which they report. Their accounts are also checked by the state Court of Accounts (*Cour des Comptes*). One characteristic of these types of public enterprise is that, generally speaking, only the director and the accountant of the company have the official status of civil servants. The others are still public employees but they operate under a separate set of statutes.

The third may be called mixed-economy companies. These are a more recent form of state intervention. They consist of companies which have private shareholders but in which the state also has a stake. They are often new organisations which have been set up to meet the changing requirements of the state. However, they also take the form of older state-owned public companies into which private capital has been introduced and whose status, thus, has changed. Examples of these types of company include those which have been created to build large infrastructure projects, part of which are state financed and part of which are financed by private investors. They represent a way in which state intervention can be managed alongside private capital. In this sense, they are a more flexible form of state intervention and a less costly one to the taxpayer.

The increasing recourse to mixed-economy companies is a sign that the role of the state is changing. Indeed, a similar sign can be found in the recent process of privatisation. Since the mid-1980s, the state has sold off a number of companies to the private sector. To date, there have been two waves of privatisations.

The first wave occurred in 1986 when Jacques Chirac's right-wing coalition government won power and proposed a five-year privatisation programme consisting of a total of 66 companies, 1,454 subsidiaries and over 900,000 employees. In fact, the programme was cut short, first, by the October 1987 stock market crash, second, by Chirac's defeat at the 1988 presidential election and, third, because of criticisms of the programme – the price at which the shares were sold off was considered to be too low and the government picked a so-called '*noyau dur*', or stable core, of investors, many of whom had close links with the government. Nevertheless, by the time the privatisation programme had ended in 1988 a total of fourteen industries, including banking, advertising and glass-making companies, had been partly or completely privatised. This wave of privatisations brought in a total of 85 billion francs. Indeed, the privatisations were also very popular with the public. Many were oversubscribed and the number of private shareholders rose from 1.2 million in 1986 to over 7 million in 1988.

The second wave of privatisation began in 1993 under the right-wing coalition government headed by the gaullist, Édouard Balladur. The government indicated that twenty-one state-owned companies would be

sold off. Indeed, over the course of the next two years some very important companies were privatised. These companies were significant not just
in terms of their overall industrial strength, but also in terms of their political symbolism. They included 'historic' nationalised industries which had
been taken under state control in the gaullist-led Liberation government in
the immediate post-Second World War period. So, for example, the first
tranche of Renault shares was sold off in November 1994, yielding 8
billion francs. The second wave of privatisation then continued under the
next right-wing government from 1995 to 1997 headed by another
gaullist, Alain Juppé. During this period a further tranche of Renault
shares was sold off raising a further 2 billion francs. Equally, there was a
large-scale privatisation of the insurance company AGF, which yielded 9
billion francs.

As might be expected, the left has been more opposed to the privatisation
process but, in office, it has still gone ahead with a number of initiatives.
When President Mitterrand was re-elected in 1988, the privatisation
programme appeared to have been stopped. The president's manifesto
contained a commitment to the so-called 'ni-ni' strategy, meaning that there
would be neither nationalisation nor privatisation. In fact, though, the
socialist government from 1988–93 did renege somewhat on this commitment. It did so not by outright privatisation, but by blurring the distinction
between the public and private sectors. For example, in 1990 Renault signed
a deal with Volvo which allowed some private capital to be invested in the
company. Then, in 1991 it was announced that partial privatisations were
acceptable. The government would retain a majority stake, but a percentage
of the stock of nationalised companies could be sold off to the private sector.
Four companies were affected from November 1991 to March 1993 and, in
fact, in one case, the government failed to retain its majority stake-holding.
So, for example, in November 1991 the first tranche of Crédit Local de
France was sold off which yielded 1.5 billion francs. Similarly, a percentage
of the shares of the state-owned computer company, Bull, were sold to
American and Japanese investors. Since the election in 1997 of the left-wing
'plural' coalition, the process of privatisation has continued. Indeed, in the
space of less than two years in office the government had authorised the sale
of shares in companies such as France Télécom, Aerospatiale, Air France,
Crédit Lyonnais and Thomson to name but a few. In most cases, but not
Aerospatiale, the state retained more than a 50 per cent stake of the share-
holding. In the case of the bank Crédit Lyonnais, privatisation was forced on
the government by the European Commission. However, that a government
which included communist representation should even contemplate, never
mind approve, such a policy, and in such a wide variety of cases, is worthy
of note. Indeed, the contrast with the policy of the 1981 administration could
hardly be more striking.

All told, privatisation is likely to continue even under left-wing governments. There is now a sense right across the political spectrum that the

state does not have an obligation to control the commanding heights of the economy even for purely symbolic reasons.

The regulatory power of state representatives

The Constitution of the Fifth Republic severely curtailed the power of the French legislature. One of the many ways in which it did so was by specifying the 'domain of the law', or the policy areas in which the legislature is able to legislate (Article 34). Outside these areas, the prime minister has the power to issue regulations, or decrees, which have the force of law (*le pouvoir réglementaire*). In many cases, the precise wording of the decree will be prepared by individual ministers and will be subject simply to the prime minister's formal approval and signature. However, the prime minister does have the right to issue his/her own more general decrees (*le pouvoir réglementaire autonome*). In this sense, the prime ministership has come to resemble a substitute parliamentary chamber. For example, one writer has argued that the prime minister signs on average 1,500 decrees (*décrets*) and 7,000–8,000 ministerial orders (*arrêtés*) per year (Ardant, 1991). Moreover, in a range of areas the president also has the right to make appointments and issue similar decrees. One consequence of this general situation is that the state's representatives are in a position to control fundamental areas of policy making and implementation in a very direct and immediate way.

In recent years, though, the government's capacity to shape the policy process in this way has been curtailed somewhat. In particular, there has been an increasing recourse to independent administrative agencies. These are statutory organisations which have the responsibility for regulating particular policy domains. So, for example, prior to 1981 the broadcasting system was run by a government-controlled agency, the government appointed the senior figures in the industry and the Minister of Information intervened regularly to shape the broadcasting system even to the extent of altering programme scheduling. However, at that time the government established the first independent administrative authority, now known as the Conseil Supérieur de l'Audiovisuel (CSA), or Higher Council of Broadcasting, to police the functioning of the broadcasting sector. The CSA issues guidelines and has the power to impose sanctions if the industry fails to carry out its statutory responsibilities. Across all sectors, a considerable number of such agencies, and their equivalents, has been set up and a similar number of existing agencies has been reformed and given greater powers. There are now independent administrative authorities which regulate, amongst other examples, the insurance industry, competition policy and the stock market. In these areas and others, therefore, representatives of the state are no longer able simply to shape the policy process in such an immediate and personal way as before. As a result, the state's role in the policy process has become more circumscribed.

Against this general background, the different formulations of state power in France will now be considered in detail.

Models of the state in French politics

There are three main interpretations, or models, of the role played by the state in the organisation of French politics and policy making. These models are distinguished by their competing assumptions as to the degree of fragmentation of the state, its level of insulation from the demands of social actors, its capacity to ensure the implementation of policies and, finally, the extent of legitimacy or political authority attributed to the state (Hall, 1986, pp. 164–6). The first model, the statist account, might be considered to be the 'traditional' model in that its intellectual roots can be traced as far back as the French Revolution and before. The second model, that of the weak state, might be interpreted as the first of the more contemporary models of the French state to the extent that it emerged following a reappraisal of the influence of the state in the modernisation of the post-war economy. The third model, that of the disoriented state, might be seen as the attempt to provide a contemporary synthesis of the first two models, accepting both the strengths and weaknesses of the French state. There are two versions of this model. The first is the established variant which suggests that the strength of the state varies across policy sectors and from one stage of the policy process to another. The second is a more recent variant which stresses that the role of the state has changed over the last twenty-five years, creating the situation where it is now seeking new tools and modes of regulation.

The strong state model

Étatiste, or statist, accounts of French policy making perceive the state to be a strong and autonomous actor which pursues its own interests within the policy process. Indeed, rather than a passive set of institutions at the mercy of dominant societal interests, representatives of the strong state exploit the policy levers at their disposal so as to impose the implementation of policies across a wide range of sectors. The strength of the state is characterised, at the sectoral level, by the concentration of decision making in a single dominant agency and, at a wider level, by a cross-agency approach to policy making (Atkinson and Coleman, 1989, pp. 51–4). The state's autonomy from societal actors is determined by well-established definitions of the role of state agencies that are reinforced by coherent value systems and political support. Indeed, state agencies have a different professional ethos from those outside the state sector and both the state's responsibilities and those of societal interests are defined in a body of law and regulations. In addition, state agencies are able to generate in-house information which they can exploit to accomplish their tasks. Finally, the state is at its strongest in the situation where there are low levels of interest group mobilisation in civil society.

Historically, the state has been central to explanations of French politics 'even before Louis XIV claimed to be it' (Schmidt, 1996, p. 15). So, the foundations of the strong state model were laid under the Ancien Régime and were merely strengthened by the events of the post-revolutionary period. Writers such as Rousseau and de Tocqueville both recognised the centralisation of the French state. In particular, Rousseau raised the flag of the benevolent state acting as the guardian of the common good over and above the fractious interests of civil society. Indeed, it was Rousseau's recognition of the French state as the sole embodiment of the public interest that made the traditional conception of a strong state intellectually attractive. Equally prescriptively, the ideology of the Jacobin/Napoleonic state praised the technical competence, hierarchy and rules of the centralised interventionist state. Indeed, the potential strength and autonomy of the state was recognised by even Marx himself (Birnbaum, 1982a, pp. 4–7). More recently, in the period following the Second World War the gaullists lauded the role of the state, seeing it as an essential element of the Republican model and as something which was intrinsically French and which should be protected and promoted as such. So, for the main founders of the Fifth Republic, such as Michel Debré and General de Gaulle, the restoration of state power was one of the principal aims of the 1958 constitutional settlement. Overall, then, it is difficult to disagree with Rohr when he asserts that: 'an examination of French political discourse reveals the centrality of the state as the normative foundation for civil life in France' (Rohr, 1996, p. 121).

Over and above these normative views of state power, the strong state thesis is also derived from a detached description of the contemporary role, functions and ethos of state agencies. For example, the pervasive claims of the French state to expertise, coupled with its alleged superiority over the market, legitimised *dirigiste* industrial policies and indicative planning through which, it is argued, the state administrative elite pursued the post-war modernisation of the French economy. So, while the Fourth Republic (1946–58) stumbled from one political crisis to another, the French bureaucracy, it is said, provided continuity, stability and, indeed, forward momentum (see the technocracy model in Chapter 3). Similarly, the advent of the Fifth Republic seemed to bolster the legitimacy of the state and its capacity for independent action. For example, in a classic 1959 article Burdeau argued quite presciently that the Fifth Republic re-established the state (or 'State') as one of the motive forces of political life (Burdeau, 1959, p. 88; see also Burdeau, 1977, pp. 466–7). Indeed, for Burdeau, the 1958 Constitution installed the president as the incarnation of the new-found state power. (For an overview of the 'state power' approach to presidentialism, see Elgie, 1996a.) All told, the strong state model should be seen as the traditional model of state power in France and has been particularly associated with writers such as Badie and Birnbaum (1983), Birnbaum (1982a; 1982b), Chodak (1989), Crozier (1967; 1987), Rohr (1996) and Zysman (1983).

The backbone of the strong state model is the assumption that the French state has progressively augmented its power over civil society to the extent that it has become 'an immense and hermetic administrative machine capable of dominating all peripheral power centres' (Badie and Birnbaum, 1983, p. 105). The strength of the state is the result of a long-term process of institutionalisation resulting from, for example, the rise of executive power in the Fifth Republic, the growth of military and civilian bureaucracies, the creation of state-dominated industries and the use of elite civil service *corps* to spread state control throughout society (Badie and Birnbaum, 1983; Birnbaum, 1982b). In fact, the growth of the state from the Ancien Régime through to post-1958 gaullism is said to have provided France with the most institutionalised state in the world. It is, according to one set of writers, the 'natural result of a long historical tendency towards centralisation, which has succeeded in producing a state that is at last capable of setting itself the goal of "policing" the whole of society' (Badie and Birnbaum, 1983, p. 115). So, for example, in his study of the Fifth Republic, Rohr argues that the strong French state is underpinned by a powerful civil service, the importance of administrative law, a highly centralised system of centre–periphery relations, the absence of private-sector involvement in decision making, a state-directed programme of privatisation in the mid-1980s and a highly regulatory system of civil rights (Rohr, 1996). All told, there are links between the strong state model and the model of monocratic executive government (see Chapter 2), the agent model of weak local government (see Chapter 4), the state pluralist model of interest group relations (see Chapter 7) and the model of French exceptionalism (see Chapter 8).

A feature common to many of the strong state studies is the emphasis on the role played by the state's bureaucratic elite. Indeed, the strong state model is closely (although not exclusively) associated with members of the bureaucratic power elite school (see Chapter 3), such as Birnbaum (1982a). Here, the French state is identified as having a highly institutionalised political centre that dominates civil society and which attempts to 'run the social system through a powerful bureaucracy' (Badie and Birnbaum, 1983, p. 103). Likewise, Crozier (1967) identifies in France the predominance of a 'bureaucratic style' of policy making based upon administrative centralisation and an overriding state. His characterisation of France as a 'stalled society' attributes the dominance of the state to cultural actors, namely the fear in French society of face-to-face relations and the persistence of a hierarchical conception of authority (Crozier, 1994) In short, the French are said to eschew personal contacts which may cause either conflict between the various parties concerned or the dependence of one party on another. Instead, they seek out impersonal rules which are embodied in state institutions and which can be applied equally across society. These underlying cultural forces, encouraging the use of informal and uniform rules rather than interpersonal and flexible negotiation, are said to enable the survival of bureaucratised policy making. In this way, Crozier attributes the state with a primary responsibility for the immobilism of French society. Indeed, for Crozier, such is the autonomy and strength of this bureaucratised system of state power that change arrives primarily through crisis after long periods of routine policy making rather than through incremental reform.

That said, the strong state model is not simply premised on the existence of bureaucratic power. In fact, in his later work Crozier goes on to argue more generally that the French state is highly centralised and has 'attained in its unity and internal integration a higher degree of perfection than that of its neighbours' (Crozier, 1987, p. 74). Indeed, he raises the spectre of an overbearing state which monopolises conceptions of the general interest and takes 'priority' over both local and regional interests and private interests alike (Ibid., p. 67): the state 'is everywhere, intervenes in everything, invades society in all its aspects' (Ibid., p. 76). This overbearing state is supported not just organisationally, but also culturally by the mode of societal regulation and a 'philosophy of action and legitimation of state intervention which are deeply internalised by the best of the civil servants and which influence indirectly all the French, notably in the ruling circles' (Ibid., p. 95). However, Crozier does recognise the fragility of the French state and the problems it faces when trying to adapt to the challenges of a world experiencing accelerated change (Ibid., p. 175). As such, he leads into, if not straddles, the assumptions of the other schools of the French state (see below), although he remains wedded primarily to the concept of the strong French state, from which all its difficulties emanate. Indeed, the same is true of Chodak's study of state development in France which explicitly adopts Crozier's thesis (Chodak, 1989).

A somewhat contrasting account of state power can be found in Zysman's study of financial policy making in France, Germany and Japan (Zysman, 1983). This study adopts a comparative institutionalist approach and argues that institutional factors, such as the structure of the party system, the relations among various branches of government and the structure of economic actors, shape the policy-making process. The relative importance of these factors from one country to another is said to explain the presence or absence of statist patterns of policy making. In the case of France, Zysman recognises the importance of the institutional organisation of the financial system. He accepts that the 1958 Constitution of the Fifth Republic assured both the dominance of the executive over parliament and its insulation from interest group pressures. However, he concludes that the key variable in understanding state-led development in France is the structure of its centralised financial system which 'amplifies the power of a relatively small group of bureaucrats and political leaders' (Ibid., p. 104).

Indeed, he argues that the credit-based, price-administered financial system maximised the influence of the executive in this policy domain while minimising the access of other actors to the decision-making process (Ibid., p. 168). As such, Zysman asserts that the French state might be strong, but that studies of the state need to examine the configuration of institutions and not simply the lead given by bureaucrats across sectors and across countries.

It is apparent, then, that there is a considerable body of work which supports the strong state thesis and, moreover, that the need for a purposive state has been part of popular political discourse for many years. However, there are three general objections to the strong state thesis. The first objection suggests that the strong state model applies at too general a level to be convincing. The French state is no doubt strong in many respects, but the reality is more complex. In certain areas the state may be much weaker. If this is the case, then the first variant of the disoriented state model may be more appropriate. The second objection contends that the strong state model provides an outdated conception of the French state (see below). Some would argue that, even if in the past the state was virtually omnipresent, it has recently been subject to change and restructuring. These developments have rendered the state less powerful than before. Hence, the strong state model no longer applies and, instead, the second variant of the disoriented state model may be more germane. The final objection asserts that the strong state thesis consistently presented an inaccurate picture of the power and role of the French state. Some have argued that the state may simply have appeared strong but that its capacity to shape civil society was always limited. Thus, the strong state model was misconceived from the outset. According to this line of argument, the weak state model is more pertinent. It is to this model that we shall now turn.

The weak state model

The weak state model is, in many ways, no more than a mirror image of the strong state paradigm described above. A weak state is characterised by its inability to impose the implementation of policies and by its lack of autonomy from societal interests. As such, at the sectoral level, a weak state is marked by the absence of a lead agency, the dispersion of authority and bureaucratic competition and fragmentation (Atkinson and Coleman, 1989, p. 51–4). Indeed, the absence of autonomy from societal actors emanates from multiple failures: the failure to construct clear definitions of the role of state agencies, the failure to install a different professional ethos in state agencies from those outside the agency and the failure to define the responsibilities of bureaux in a body of law and regulations. Finally, the agencies of a weak state lack in-house expertise and information. Indeed, unlike a strong state, a weak state doubtless faces high levels of interest-group, or civil society, mobilisation.

In the French case, the weak state model is somewhat unusual. Few people argue that France has a 'weathervane' state (see above), such as might be found in pluralist-type systems, most notably the United States. Indeed, such is the *étatiste*, or statist, legacy in models of French politics that few accounts of policy making truly ignore the resilience of the discourse of the state, even if they only recognise its strength as a 'rhetorical mobilising device and as a pervasive myth' (Wright, 1997, p. 151). Instead, most proponents of the weak state thesis actually acknowledge that, in a comparative perspective, the French state is unusually vigorous (see, for example, Feigenbaum below). That said, the proponents of the weak state model stand in opposition to their strong state counterparts by virtue of the emphasis they place on the limitations to state power and the suggestion that the traditional view of the strong state is somewhat exaggerated. In this context, those who are associated with the weak state model include Cohen and Bauer (1985), Dupuy and Thoenig (1983; 1985), Feigenbaum (1985), Machin and Wright (1985) and Suleiman (1987a; 1987b).

Those who propose the weak state model tend to concentrate on three criticisms of the strong state school. First, they accentuate the fragmentation of the French state, undermining the conception of the French state as a unified actor co-ordinated by a homogeneous bureaucracy. Second, they emphasise the possibility of the state services being 'captured' by societal interests. Third, they attack the capacity of the French state to ensure the implementation of public policies. As such, the weak state model undermines arguments about the alleged strength and autonomy of the French state. Indeed, the supposed strength and autonomy of the state is questioned on the basis of its own internal fragmentation and the extent to which it possesses its own distinct set of policy preferences.

Typical of the works which accentuate the fragmentation of the state are Dupuy and Thoenig (1983) and Machin and Wright (1985). As noted in Chapter 3, Dupuy and Thoenig view the French state not as a homogeneous actor with a strong bureaucratic apparatus, but as a fragmented 'administration in pieces' (Dupuy and Thoenig, 1985). Internal administrative divisions and rivalries between elite civil service *corps* mean that state actors persistently engage in territorial battles over contested policy domains. Indeed, the most senior civil servants in the *grands corps* monopolise the management of certain sectors and are hostile to any policy developments which might lead others to encroach upon their 'territory'. On a more general level, Machin and Wright highlight the complexity of policy making in France (Machin and Wright, 1985, p. 9). In particular, they emphasise the fact that 'economic policy-making is characterized by the extraordinary proliferation of the actors involved' (Ibid.) both public and private and at the national and local level. As a result, they assert: 'With the State machine so extensive, so fragmented, so compartmentalized and so divided, policy is inevitably *éclatée* (splintered)' (Ibid., p. 11).

Thus, the state is not a homogeneous actor with a clear policy direction that it wishes to follow. Instead, the state is riven with internal tensions and competition which weaken its capacity to engage in strategic decision making.

An alternative approach to the study of the state is provided by Ezra N. Suleiman. In his most recent work, Suleiman has pointed to the transformation of the French state (Suleiman, 1995). In this sense, as with Crozier above, there is a temptation to consider his work as an example of the second variant of the disoriented state model. However, even in this later work Suleiman points out that the state 'never had the considerable power that was often attributed to it' (Ibid., p. 71). Thus, it is more appropriate to outline his approach under the heading of the weak state model here. In this context, Suleiman casts particular doubt on the widely held view of the strong French state in his study of the legal profession, or *notaires*. He does so by dismissing the assumption that highly centralised state institutions, as in France, necessarily result in the concentration of state power (Suleiman, 1987a; 1987b). Instead, he argues that the centralisation of power does not impede, but actually facilitates the take-over of the state by private groups (Suleiman, 1987a, p. 17). This is because groups need only to direct their lobbying at one centralised branch of the administration and, having successfully established a relationship with it, can then 'capture' that piece of the state machine for their own ends. Indeed, Suleiman views the 'capturing' of the state as inherent to the functioning of state agencies. Agencies designed to 'protect' certain sectors naturally foster clientelistic relationships with the groups in those sectors. This then weakens the capacity of the state to pursue its own preferences and implement policies which might undermine the privileges of the established client group (Ibid., p.18).

Concretely, Suleiman argues that the French state sponsored the development of the *notaires* to the extent that it compromised its own capacity to reorganise the working practices of the profession. He asserts that: 'the relationship between the notarial profession and the state typifies the cyclical historical process through which the state's strength ultimately leads to symbiosis with and possibly dependence upon private groups' (Ibid., p. 330). This process of 'capture', it is argued, is further facilitated by the administrative pluralism and fragmentation of the French state which allows private groups to play competing branches of the state off against each other. So, the failure of the Socialist Party to reform the practices of the *notaires* in the 1980s stemmed from the weak regulation of private groups by the French state, the capture of the French state by the group in question and the clientelistic relationships that had been established with the group. Indeed, in this case Suleiman argues that it is no longer possible to describe French society as 'weak and unorganised' (Ibid., p. 306). As such, he questions the notion that the French state possesses its own policy preferences when the definition of its interests is the product of a dialectical interaction with private groups (Ibid., p. 328).

The capacity of the French state to fall prey to clientelism and the notion that the boundaries between public and private sectors are blurred is further developed in studies of French indicative planning, industrial and economic policy (Feigenbaum, 1985; and Suleiman, 1978). For example, in opposition to the classic conception of the so-called *État développeur* in which the state directed economic growth and industrial policy, Feigenbaum's study of the relations between the French state and the major oil companies demonstrates the weak autonomy of the French state to the extent that the state pursued an industrial policy which was no more than the policy preferences of the major industrial groups (Feigenbaum, 1985). He asserts that: 'The French state is strong but it is not autonomous' (Ibid., p. 173). Indeed, he argues that: 'One can only understand the failures of French policy by viewing the state as intimately linked to society, and it is this link ... that limits the power of the state' (Ibid., p. 158). Indeed, this point is confirmed in Suleiman's early work where he argues that the relationship between the state and large firms was one of co-operation and partnership (Suleiman, 1978, p. 261) because the two sets of institutions had complementary interests, namely the desire to promote industrial growth (Ibid., p. 271). Further evidence in support of this line of argument is found in the study of industrial policy by Cohen and Bauer (1985). They argue that, despite politicians' conception of the French state as an *État développeur*, the state, in practice often stricken by internal quarrels, works more as an *État régulateur* unable or unprepared to dictate industrial strategies (Cohen and Bauer, 1985, pp. 278–86). As such, the French state can, they allege, consolidate the power of large industrial groups, such as Thomson and CGE, but cannot influence their economic strategies (Ibid., p. 282). If, indeed, the state is successful in resurrecting declining industries, it only succeeds in building up 'national champions' that then challenge the authority of the state (Cohen and Bauer, p. 286).

Finally, the weak state model argues that the traditional conception of the strong French state tends to overestimate its capacity to impose the implementation of its preferred policies. Evidence for such arguments is to be found in the refusal of hospital doctors to reorganise public hospitals at the request of the Mauroy government in the 1980s and strikes against health and social welfare reforms. Equally typical of this line of argument is Hollifield's study of immigration policy in France which accentuates the weakness or limitations of the French state in policy implementation (Hollifield, 1990). Hollifield argues that the 'real test' of the strength of the state is its capacity to effect changes in the behaviour of groups or individuals (Ibid., p. 57). When faced with such challenges of policy implementation, he concludes that even the 'strong' French state can be weak in terms of the gap between policy outputs and policy outcomes (Ibid., p. 74). Indeed, his study of immigration policy reveals that the French state was no more efficient than other states in the implementation of anti-immigration policies. Like Suleiman, he concludes that centralised authority is not necessarily the tactical advantage that it is assumed to be (see below) and that the French state is less powerful than the Jacobin ideological tradition suggests. Moreover, Hollifield argues that in immigration it is not the 'actions' of the state that are the key determinants in shaping policy, but social and economic conditions and, in particular, labour market conditions (Ibid., pp. 74–5).

In these ways, the weak state model provides a clear counterpoint to traditional models of the overbearing French state. There are, though, two basic problems with this point of view. The first problem is simply the reverse of the one which was voiced with regard to the strong state model, namely that the weak state model underestimates the strength of the state. It may be true that the influence of social groups, such as the *notaires*, cannot be dismissed, but this is not to say, so it might be argued, that the state is really captured by social forces. On the contrary, the state may be able to secure better implementation by working with social groups. It may also be able to shape their preferences to suit its own ends by so doing. In this case, then, the strong state model may be more appropriate. The second problem, linked to the next model to be discussed, is that the weak state model, like its strong state counterpart, paints too simplistic a picture of the role of the state. Even if, so the argument goes, certain groups, such as the *notaires*, really have captured the state in particular domains, this does not mean that the state has been captured by equivalent groups in every policy area. Instead, reality is untidy and the degree of state capture varies from one policy arena to another. Thus, according to this line of argument the state is neither strong nor weak, it is merely disoriented.

The disoriented state model

The model of the disoriented state assumes that the degree of state autonomy depends upon the nature of the policy area at stake and the particular stage of the policy process (whether policy initiation, formulation or implementation) in question. The essence of this model is the rejection of macro-level judgements, or systemic characterisations, of the balance between state and society, be they of the strong or weak state variety. So, one set of writers asserted that: 'we should view with intense suspicion any assumption that sectoral or micro-relationships can be read off from prescriptive formulations such as "*étatisme*" or the "social market economy"' (Cawson *et al.* 1987, p. 29). Instead, those who support this model opt for a disaggregated approach which asserts that the state has established a variety of relationships with private groups. As Sadran notes, it is not a matter 'of order *or* chaos, but order *and* chaos' (Sadran, 1997, p. 14 – emphasis in the original). As such, the model of the disoriented state might be classed as a composite model comprising a synthesis of both the strong and weak state approaches.

There are two variants of the disoriented state model, even if the difference between the two is largely a matter of emphasis. The first variant stresses the limited nature of state power *per se*. As such, it establishes a paradigm model of the disoriented French state. Thus, Kuhn argues that in the broadcasting sector 'the state in the Fifth Republic has never been as monolithic' (Kuhn, 1998, p. 296) as some would have us believe but that, at the same time, the 'result was less an impotent than a confused state' (Ibid., p. 292). In particular, though, this variant of the disoriented state model is primarily associated with the work of Hayward (1982; 1983), Wilsford (1988; 1991a; 1991b) and, less so, with Schmidt (1996). The second variant underlines the changing nature of state power in France. It accepts that the French state was strong, particularly during the period of post-war expansion, but argues that recent changes in the nature of the state and its economic and social environment have weakened traditional patterns of state-led policy making. This variant is particularly prevalent in the writing of Muller (1992a), Hall (1986), Rosanvallon (1990), Sadran (1997) and Cohen-Tanugi (1993). It might also be noted that there are clear links between this second variant and the model of the fragmented French bureaucracy (see Chapter 3), the local governance model of centre–periphery relations (Chapter 4) and the bounded singularity model of the French policy-making style (Chapter 8).

The disoriented state model: the paradigm

The basic assumption of the first variant of the disoriented state model is that strong states are not omnipotent and weak states are not powerless (Wilsford, 1988, p. 134). Thus, as Wilsford notes, it aims to reconcile the strong and weak state approaches so that 'sufficient importance is accorded to the fact that strong states can do things that weak states cannot, but that equally there are important limits to strong state power' (Ibid., p. 132). The main innovation in Wilsford's work is the argument that the French state enjoys various so-called 'tactical advantages' which enable it to pursue the preferences which it exhibits. This is broadly consistent with the strong state model of the policy process. However, in line with the limited state model, Wilsford argues that the possession of these tactical advantages does not mean that the state will necessarily be able to impose its policy outcomes upon interest groups or that it will be able to overcome its fragmentation on a particular issue. Thus, the state's role in policy making is considerable but also varied, resulting in the situation where the state is essentially vulnerable.

Wilsford identifies six tactical advantages that are available to the French state (see the list below). These advantages are endorsed by the ideological fragmentation of interests in France, the symbolism of consultation and a statist ideology which has for so long protected the bureaucracy and centralisation of the French state. Indeed, for Wilsford, the tradition of state authority engendered by the elite civil service training schools (see Chapter 3) is the state's most significant tactical advantage because it ensures that bureaucrats possess 'a common idea of the state [which] shapes administrators' judgements of where interests lie, which of these are compatible with the state's interest, and what types of conduct by decision-makers and the public are appropriate in this administrative–political universe' (Wilsford, 1988, p. 150). In this way, the strong state tradition provides a force which binds together the fissiparous fractions of French society to the extent that, while the interests of the state are sometimes perceived to mirror those of elite civil servants or economic groups, they are perceived 'just as often' as an 'amalgam or distillation of the interests of all, the community, the whole which is France' (Ibid., p. 159). The state, thus, can claim to act in the name of, and for the good of, the people as a whole.

The tactical advantages of the French state

- The government's proposal and decree powers in the Constitution of the Fifth Republic;
- The relegation of parliament in the Fifth Republic from a transformative to an arena legislature with few powers to write legislation;
- The existence of an executive which is strong in its own right;
- The tradition of influential ministerial *cabinets* which provide ministers with an instrument of control over bureaucrats;
- The existence of an homogeneously trained bureaucratic elite;
- The advantage of a limited judiciary and little tradition of judicial review.

Wilsford, 1988

Although Wilsford is at pains to emphasise the state's tactical advantages, he also argues that the autonomy and strength of the state leave it vulnerable to direct action and exit from normal politics. Borrowing from Crozier (see above), he argues that the state's capacity to resist the demands of interest groups forces these groups to undertake direct action through strikes, demonstrations and boycotts. This direct action can 'stall the state's plans', leading to intermittent crises which pressurise the state into compromises and even policy reversals (Wilsford, 1988, pp. 155–6). During crisis periods, such as the student demonstrations in 1986 or the train strikes in the winter of 1987, Wilsford argues that 'paradoxically the strong French state is sometimes weak indeed' (Ibid., p. 156). By freezing groups out of the policy-making process, the state simply encourages these groups to exit traditional channels of political representation in order to voice their concerns (Ibid., p. 160). Thus, there are clear links between

Crozier's model of the stalled French society and Wilsford's model of the state's tactical advantages. The two approaches differ, however, in the emphasis that they place on the causes of the change. Crozier underlines the importance of cultural norms which impede face-to-face contact and, in the face of an intransigent state, bring about conflict, whereas Wilsford argues that it is the very nature of the state itself which results in periodic upheaval.

Another writer whose work is consistent with this variant of the disoriented state model is Jack Hayward. He argues that it is simplistic to argue that one actor is dominant in the false dichotomy between state and society (Hayward, 1986, p. 20). Although it is certainly the case that in a comparative perspective the image of the *volontariste* and *dirigiste* French state 'is not excessively misleading' (Hayward, 1988, p. 91) and that, in some areas, the boldness of state-directed policy change 'stands out as distinctly assertive' (Hayward, 1983, p. 279), Hayward also notes that the traditional picture of a monolithic and all-powerful state sector is exaggerated. Instead, the state is fragmented (Hayward, 1982, p. 117), he argues, and senior public sector officials and political actors are obliged to seek out representatives of peak interest groups in order to maximise the chances of policy success. As a result, whereas in some cases the state can impose its will, for the most part there is a 'collusive interdependence' (Hayward, 1986, p. 20) between groups and the state. Indeed, Hayward emphasises the 'paradox of [the French] state with immense potential power' (p. 34) which 'usually ends up underwriting what the major industrial groups decide among themselves and consolidating their power' (Ibid.). In this way, he argues, 'the mobilisation of private interests in the service of public ambitions is ... the salient element of the French policy style' (Hayward, 1982, p. 137). It might be noted, though, that in later work Hayward has argued that there is now 'a less state-centred approach to problem-solving and a new relationship between government and other actors which involves mutual accommodation, consultation and compromise rather than an imposed *fait accompli*' (Hayward, 1990, p. 295). In this sense, Hayward's later work straddles both the first and second variants of the disoriented state model (see below).

A similar line of argument is taken by Vivien Schmidt. She attempts to reconcile the strong and weak state approaches by distinguishing between the distinct capacities of the state at different stages of the policy process. She characterises the policy-making process in France as 'statist' only in the sense that the state is both strong, in particular at the formulation stage of policy making, and weak, primarily at the implementation stage of policy. In the case of policy implementation, she argues that societal constraints oblige the state to engage in the politics of accommodation and co-option (Schmidt, 1996, p. 47). Thus, she employs the term 'statist' to 'define a polity in which the so-called strength of governmental decision makers intent on putting through heroic policies is often offset by their apparent weakness when engaging in everyday policies or faced with organised opposition or disorganised protest' (Ibid., p. 49). As such, the French government may unilaterally formulate 'heroic' policies with little or no consultation only to find itself obliged to consult with private interests at the implementation stage where the construction of compromises with societal actors is primarily undertaken through the politics of confrontation, accommodation and co-optation. Indeed, where policies are more 'everyday', the consultation and accommodation procedures may even begin during the policy formulation stage and private interests can actually capture the direction of policy making from the outset. Thus, the success of policies is often guaranteed because they are in the interests of those affected (Schmidt, 1996, pp. 48, 57).

In this way, Schmidt accepts the limitations of the strong state and explicitly recognises the autonomy of the state in certain sectors. However, even in 'everyday' policies where the extent of consultation can blur the boundaries of implementation and formulation, Schmidt continues to label the policy process as 'statist' in that 'the government retains the upper hand, to invite outside interests in, or to freeze them out' (Ibid., p. 57). Indeed, Schmidt argues that these heroic policies do mark out the capacities of the French state from other states: France was able to undertake the industrial restructuring of the 1980s, she argues, because of 'the heroism of its statist policy making combined with its cultural openness to nationalisation and its institutional strengths, in particular its elite civil service' (Ibid., p. 53). She concludes that the 'heroic' state-led approach to policy making in France has not disappeared, it has just become less abundant and less successful with the increased independence of business and the reduced power of government (Ibid., p. 65). This reference to the changing nature of state/society relations orientates her analysis in the direction of the second variant of this model. Indeed, this orientation has been confirmed in a more recent article (Schmidt, 1997). However, Schmidt's concern with the long-standing implications of the state's organisation and the corresponding difference between the state's role in the formulation and implementation of policy means that she is best considered alongside Wilsford as a proponent of the first variant of the disoriented state model. All told, she argues that 'the state, both as a concept and concrete representation, remains embedded in French culture and embodied in its institutions, with change able to come only through the state and not against it' (Ibid., p. 442).

The disoriented state as a recent development

This variant of the disorientated state model invariably accepts that the French state was strong particularly during the period of post-war expansion, but argues that recent changes in the nature of the state and the economic and social environment in which it operates have weakened traditional patterns of state-led policy making in France. Indeed, both economic internationalisation and the globalisation of capital have eroded the *dirigiste* policies of the early governments of the Fifth Republic. Equally, with the inability of successive governments to resolve permanently the post-1973 economic recession, the legitimacy and cultural authority of the French state has declined. As such, this model assumes that the relationship between the state and civil society is not set in stone, but is dynamic and open to progressive change. Thus, the evolution of the political and economic system has not simply resulted in a weak French state, but new and sometimes contradictory patterns of state regulation. Again, therefore, this variant takes the form of a combination of the strong and weak state models. As Sadran notes, 'nothing indicates that a single paradigm can take account of all the ways in which such a vast and differentiated organism as the administrative system has reacted [to recent changes]' (Sadran, 1997, p. 143).

Typical of this school is the work of Muller (1992a). He argues that the standard or traditional pattern of policy making in France attributed a central role to the state. The state dominated the political agenda and exercised a monopoly over the framing of public policy. The supremacy of the state was reinforced by both the recourse to sectoral corporatism (see Chapter 7), which furnished the state with a privileged role in the representation of interests, and the predominance of the central state over local actors (see Chapter 4). The high point of the state-led policy making was the so-called '*trente glorieuses*', or thirty years of post-war economic growth, when the state worked behind the policy discourse, or *référentiel*, of modernisation with its *grands projets* and the predominance of the elite civil service (Muller, 1992a, p. 280). However, Muller also argues that this state-led process has entered into crisis and, with it, the centrality of the state and its senior civil servants has been lost. Indeed, he argues that the sectoral corporatism which marked French policy making has become increasingly unstable as the demobilisation of traditional actors and the emergence of new actors has undermined the state's influence. In fact, this disorientation of the French state emanates, for Muller, from several changes in the social and political environment. First, the new policy discourse of the market and global interdependence has weakened both traditional administrative practices and the modernisation *référentiel* in which the state was attributed a primary responsibility for economic growth and social change. Second, the crisis of the external services of the central state and the moves towards decentralisation have fostered the development of 'local' public policies. (Ibid., pp. 275–6) (see Chapter 4, this volume). Finally, European integration has undermined traditional patterns of policy making through both the modification of national decision-making circuits, as, for example, interest groups transfer their lobbying activities to Brussels, and the introduction of new norms and codes of conduct in standard administrative practices (Ibid., pp. 282–95). Thus, Muller concludes the 'strong' French state is losing its autonomy and central place in the French political system with Europe increasingly providing a new arena for the production of policy frames and the articulation of interests (Ibid.).

A similar argument is proposed by Peter Hall (1986). Hall's study of macroeconomic and industrial policy making in Britain and France concludes that the institutional strength of the Finance ministry and the important role played by the higher civil service and officials in the Planning Commission endowed the French state with a capacity and willingness to intervene in the economy that was not present in Britain and Germany. However, Hall also argues, somewhat paradoxically, that the post-war interventionism of the French state undermined *étatiste* policy making as it persistently eroded the state's legitimacy to act as a neutral referee. Through its indicative planning, the state entered into alliances with leading sectors of capital thereby reducing its independence from social groups. In addition, the work of the Planning Commission exploited exceptions to regulations and undermined traditional channels of administrative influence, thereby weakening the alleged unity of the French state. Indeed, while the French state sought to re-establish its claims to legitimacy by peddling its claims to expertise, it ultimately came to base its legitimacy upon its capacity to achieve results, particularly in terms of economic management. (Hall, 1986, p. 179). As such, the intervention of the French state became exceptionally vulnerable to economic recession as witnessed in the 1970s and 1980s. In this context, the state itself was reshaped and the relationship between the state and civil society was reformulated throughout the 1980s. Thus, there is still pressure on the state to engage in *dirigiste* economic policies, but the state's capacity to do so is now more restricted than it used to be (Hall, 1990b, pp. 186–7).

An alternative interpretation of the disoriented state model is provided by Cohen-Tanugi (1993). He argues that the disoriented French state is not so much in crisis as conforming with the rule of law. He identifies the weakening, since the end of the 1960s, of the predominance of the French state over civil society. The state has progressively given ground to the rule of law based upon the protection of fundamental human rights and the acceptance of 'law as an alternative mode of regulation of the economy and society and as the framework for a more autonomous civil society in relation to the state sphere' (Cohen-Tanugi, 1993, p. 58). Whereas before democracy stopped 'where the interests of the state began' (Ibid., p. 65), now the a priori belief in the state has been replaced by wary concern (Ibid.). Indeed, the legal system increasingly serves as the guardian of the administration, signalling an increased role for national and international judges (Ibid., p. 59). This evolution of state/society relations has emerged on the back of a number of factors: anti-authoritarianism and the social changes of post-1968, the birth of constitutionalism, *cohabitation* and minority government, Europeanisation and the emergence of regulatory authorities. The 1958 Constitution enshrined the primacy of fundamental constitutional rights and freedoms over parliamentary law and the French state. This constitutionalism was subsequently reinforced by the consensus surrounding the Fifth Republic and by the judgements and work of the Constitutional Council, particularly following the widening in 1974 of those able to seek recourse to the Constitutional Council. In the 1980s and 1990s, the fragmentation of the executive under *cohabitation* and the rejection of the absolutist conception of the state epitomised by the Rocard minority government (1988–91) demonstrated that the state could limit itself, so introducing an imperfect separation of powers. More importantly, Europeanisation liberalised the French national economy, calling into question state intervention and subsidies, whilst introducing a partial system of regulation by the European Commission and the primacy of law (Ibid., p. 48). Indeed, it introduced new legal channels and freedoms, enabling individuals to appeal to the European Court of Justice. Finally, the emergence of independent administrative authorities has, unlike traditional administrative practices, set state action within legal frameworks. The emergence of independent administrative authorities responds to the desire to keep political actors out of certain sectors and leads to an increasing role for social and economic actors in policy making. Indeed, the return to the market and economic internationalisation itself leads economic leaders to look towards different modes of regulation (p. 59).

Support for Cohen-Tanugi's thesis comes from Slama (1995) who argues that 'French law is thus becoming less and less sovereign, and the State is less and less the primary source of law' (Slama, 1995, p. 57). He explains the emergence of judges and experts in the policy process as the quest for a new basis of legitimacy, the resolution of ethical problems born of technological progress, the desire to rationalise individuals' behaviour and, finally, the product of the increasing social regulation required to deal with the return of old fears such as unemployment and crime (Ibid., pp. 61–2). However, unlike Cohen-Tangui, Slama views these developments as producing a significant crisis for the state. The state, he argues, 'is now in a serious quandary' (Ibid., p. 60) Alternative conceptions of law and citizenship have undermined the legitimacy of the state and produced a set of social problems that it cannot resolve through its traditional practices. These dilemmas are common across post-industrial societies, but, he concludes, 'the problem is particularly pronounced in France given the sharpness of the break with traditional concepts of the state' (Ibid., p. 60). As before, the result is not the absence of state power, but the presence of contradictory forces to which the state is subject.

At first sight, the great merit of the disoriented state model is that it eschews overgeneralisations. It rejects macro-level theories of the role of the state. It differentiates between the power of the state both at particular stages in the policy process and from one policy sector to another. In this way, it avoids the objection that it either overestimates or underestimates the role of the state. On further reflection, though, this merit is also a potential source of criticism. A number of the most influential people who propose the disoriented state model base their conclusions on sector-specific studies of the policy process. That is to say, they focus on one issue area and draw general conclusions about the dominant pattern of state/society relations on the basis of evidence drawn from this one area. However, from a methodological point of view, such studies are bound to skew the analysis towards sectorally based explanations of the policy process. Thus, the methodology, it might be argued, drives the conclusion, which is unsatisfactory. In fact, there is nothing necessarily meritorious about micro-oriented, 'untidy reality' models, such as this one. True, macro-level interpretations, such as the strong and weak state approaches, may fail to capture the dynamics of policy making in certain areas. However, there is no reason why, if properly formulated, they cannot provide cogent explanations of the overarching nature of the state's role in the policy process. Thus, there may be much to commend the disoriented state model, but we should be wary of adopting it simply because it seems to present a supposedly 'realistic' picture of the policy process. The other models that have been considered may, in their own way, provide just as coherent an account of the relationship between state and civil society.

Conclusion

There is, thus, considerable debate about the role of the French state (see Table 1.1) and those studying the state face a number of intellectual choices. The most fundamental choice concerns the nature of the French state itself and whether or not it is best characterised as a homogeneous actor in pursuit of its own interests. If so, can we then make macro-level judgements about the autonomy of the state, its patterns of decision making across agencies, and its possession of either in-house resources or a coherent value system? If we can, then we can conclude, according to which argument is preferred, that the state is either strong or weak. If not, and the state is best considered as a disaggregated collection of agencies, can we expect to find a disoriented model of state activity with a variety of state–society relations with different degrees of state autonomy across policy sectors? Those who study the French state have increasingly tended to follow the latter line of reasoning, stressing both disaggregated accounts of decision making and, indeed, emphasising the gradual transformation of the French state over the course of the last twenty years (see, in particular, Chapter Three). So, while traditional models of French political life, relating to the core executive, bureaucracy, local government, political parties and the French policy-making style, have often been underpinned by assumptions about a relatively strong French state, support for the disoriented state model has begun to flourish.

Table 1.1 Models of the French state

	Strong state	Weak state	Disoriented state
Definition/key assumptions	1 State is a strong, autonomous actor pursuing its own interests 2 Concentration of decision making in a single dominant agency and cross-agency approach to policy making 3 Well-established definitions of the role of state agencies reinforced by coherent value systems and political support	1 State's inability to impose the implementation of policies and lack of autonomy from societal interests 2 Absence of a lead agency, the dispersion of authority and bureaucratic competition and fragmentation 3 State lacks in-house expertise and information	1 Degree of state autonomy depends upon policy area and stage of the policy process 2 Macro-level judgements are not appropriate 3 State establishes a variety of relationships with private groups
Proponents	Badie and Birnbaum (1983), Birnbaum (1982a, b), Chodak (1989), Crozier (1967, 1987), Rohr (1996), Zysman (1983)	Cohen and Bauer (1985), Dupuy and Thoenig (1983), Feigenbaum (1985), Suleiman (1987a, b)	Wilsford (1988, 1991a, b), Schmidt (1996), Muller (1992a), Hall (1986), Sadran (1997), Cohen-Tanugi (1993)
Argument/evidence	1 Historical development, growth of state institutions 2 Emphasis on power of bureaucratic elite 3 Centralisation of the state, e.g., financial policy	1 Fragmentation of the state, lack of bureaucratic homogeneity 2 Capture of the state by special interests 3 Entrenched veto-groups, vulnerability to protest politics and implementation deficits	*Variant one: paradigm* 1 State neither strong nor weak 2 State enjoys tactical advantages *Variant two: recent changes* 1 Economic internationalisation and the globalisation of capital have eroded *dirigiste* policies 2 Economic crises have changed state–society relations 3 New and contradictory patterns of regulation have emerged
Criticisms	1 Too general. There are areas where the state is weak 2 Outdated 3 Overestimates power of the state	1 Underestimates power of the state 2 Paints too simplistic a picture of the state	1 Methodology skews analysis towards sectorally based explanations 2 If properly formulated, macro-level explanations can be persuasive

Arguably, the emergence of the disorientated state model is evidence of the exhaustion of the strong/weak state paradigm in studies of French politics. That said, to a large degree this model is itself still underpinned by the traditional terms of the strong/weak state debate. This is because, for many people, the French state is considered to be 'disoriented' only in the sense that it no longer fits neatly into a place somewhere on the strong/weak state continuum. Instead, it is simply strong in some areas and weak in others. Might it not be better, though, to argue that the French polity has become, like other advanced liberal democracies, a 'differentiated polity' characterised by functional and institutional specialisation and the fragmentation of policies and politics (Rhodes, 1997, p. 7)? If so, rather than simply accepting the agenda set by the long-standing strong/weak state debate, might it not also be better to change the terms of the debate and focus attention on, for example, the networks of organisations that deliver services and manage decision making, the interdependencies that structure society, and the multiple centres of power that provide for plenty of governments within the French polity? This lead has already been taken in studies of local government and interest groups in France and new models of political life have emerged (see Chapters 4 and 6). The likelihood is that studies of the state will follow down the same intellectual path in the years to come.

Against this background, it is extremely tempting to agree with one writer who has argued that the study of the state 'has if anything occupied too much space' amongst the academic preoccupations of political scientists studying French political life (Hayward, 1990, p. 282). So, whereas in Anglo-American political science there has been a growing trend towards 'bringing the state back in' to the study of politics and a move back to institutional perspectives of the policy process, in France the state-centred, institutionalist approach has never been out of vogue. The state has always featured large in the study of French politics and, as has been seen, in a comparative perspective the role of the state is still considered by virtually all commentators to be relatively well developed even by those who promote the weak state model of the political system. As has been argued, the nature of the debate about the state may be transformed in the years to come if the various elements of the differentiated polity model are examined. However, in the context of the present book, the long-standing state-centred institutionalist approach to French politics is particularly significant because the organisation of the French state informs many of the debates to be outlined in the chapters that follow. Thus, the state (be it strong, weak or disoriented) has long been central not only to virtually all aspects of French political life, but also, as we shall see, to virtually all aspects of French political studies. This is a point to which we shall return in future chapters.

2 Executive politics

In France the study of executive politics has tended to take one of two forms. The first consists of sensationalist kiss-and-tell accounts of particular governments or leaders. These tend to be written either by the protagonists themselves or by journalists with an interest in 'court' politics. Both can provide extremely useful information about behind-the-scenes intrigues. The former, though, tend to be self-congratulatory, self-justifying and self-promoting, whereas the latter can sometimes be somewhat superficial and are always anti-theoretical. The second comprises textbooks on constitutional law and political science. In France, these two terms are sometimes synonymous and almost always complementary. The aim of these studies is usually to give both a comprehensive account of the juridico-constitutional powers of the various institutional actors in France and to compare the nature of the French regime with those in other countries. These books provide an indispensable source of reference without which any account of the French executive would be incomplete. The reading matter, however, usually tends to be somewhat 'dry' and the effect of a few is unequivocally soporific.

This chapter examines the nature of executive politics in France. In so doing it refers to the work of political leaders, journalists, constitutional lawyers and political scientists. In addition, it also draws heavily upon some of the other more systematic studies of executive politics that have been conducted in both the comparative and the French literature in recent years. In this context, the first section sketches the basic framework of the French executive. It examines the position of the executive in relation to the legislature and the respective powers of the president and the prime minister within the executive itself. It also provides a brief overview of political leadership since 1958. The second section identifies four separate and distinct models of executive politics in France, each of which corresponds to a particular interpretation of how executive power is usually exercised under the Fifth Republic. These are: monocratic government, shared government, segmented government and ministerial government. In the conclusion, the current state of the debate about French executive politics will be addressed.

The French executive

In France executive politics takes place in the context of a strong executive branch of government in which the presidency and the prime ministership are the two principle actors. As such, two key elements can be singled out for attention: the constitutional position of the executive and the relationship between the president and prime minister.

The constitutional position of the executive

There are three key elements to the constitutional position of the executive under the Fifth Republic. These are: first, executive control of the legislature; second, the shared powers of both the president and the prime minister; and, third, the direct election of the president.

The Fourth Republic was established in 1946. It suffered from persistent governmental instability and it collapsed in 1958 when the crisis in Algeria threatened to spill over onto mainland France. In the light of this experience, the 1958 Constitution aimed to reinstate the authority of the executive. To this end, the executive was provided with the means by which to dominate the legislative process. For example, as noted in the previous chapter, Article 34 restricts parliament's ability to legislate in certain areas by setting out the so-called 'domain of the law'. In addition, Article 38 states that the government can ask parliament to allow it to legislate by ordinance (or enabling legislation) for a limited time, so speeding up the legislative process and giving great discretion to the prime minister and government ministers. Article 40 forbids deputies from proposing amendments which have the effect of increasing government spending or decreasing government revenue. Article 42 obliges parliament to begin the legislative debate by examining the text of the government's bill rather than a revised version that may have been proposed in a parliamentary committee. Article 43 restricts the number of committees to just six. Article 44 allows the government to refuse to consider any amendment that has not previously been considered by a committee and gives it the right to call for a package vote (*vote bloqué*) on a bill containing only the amendments that the government itself selects. Article 45–2 permits the government to declare a bill to be urgent, so truncating the normal parliamentary process, and Article 45–4 allows the National Assembly to rule definitively on legislation if there is a difference of opinion with the Senate. Finally, Article 49–3 allows the government to pass a text without a vote, unless an absolute majority of deputies in parliament pass a motion of no-confidence in the government.

This constitutional situation has accurately reflected the actual state of executive/legislative relations since 1958. The legislature has clearly been subordinate to the executive. Keeler has demonstrated the extent of this subordination during the first three decades of the Fifth Republic (Keeler,

1993). For example, governments declared a bill to be urgent 571 times from 1959–91. The government also requested the right to legislate by ordinance twenty-four times in this period. In addition, the package vote was invoked in the National Assembly on 266 occasions and in the Senate 273 times during the same period. What is more, Article 49–3 was used seventy-three times to pass thirty-eight pieces of legislation between these dates. Finally, although Article 45–4 was rarely employed before the socialists came to power in 1981, it was then used to pass nearly 25 per cent of all bills from 1981 to 1985, thus allowing the government to circumvent the right-wing dominated and, hence, potentially obstructive upper house. These figures are all illustrative of the fact that under the Fifth Republic, as Philip Williams noted, 'the Parliament of France, once among the most powerful in the world, became one of the weakest' (Williams, 1968, p. 21).

If the 1958 Constitution unequivocally skews power towards the executive, within this branch of government there is a more subtle (some would say confused) distribution of power. In essence, the constitution gives considerable powers to both the president and the prime minister. For example, Article 20 states that the government decides and directs the policy of the nation, that it has the administration and the armed forces at its disposal and that it is accountable to the National Assembly. Article 21 then states that the prime minister is in general charge of the government's work and is personally responsible for national defence and the implementation of laws. Furthermore, Article 8 states that the prime minister has the right to propose the names of government ministers to the president for approval. So, in theory at least the constitution seems to place the prime minister at the head of a government, the members of which he or she has chosen and which is collectively responsible for the day-to-day realisation and implementation of public policy. At the same time, the president, who serves for seven years and who may not be dismissed from office except for the crime of high treason (Article 68), is also directly involved in the policy-making process. Most fundamentally, Article 9 gives the president the power to appoint (but not dismiss) the prime minister. In addition, Article 8 indicates that the president chairs the weekly meetings of the Council of Ministers; Article 16 states that in times of national emergency the president may issue decrees which have the force of law; Article 52 makes the president responsible for negotiating and ratifying international treaties; and, finally, Article 5 provides the president with a wide-ranging responsibility for seeing that the constitution is respected, for ensuring, by his arbitration, the regular functioning of public authorities and the continuity of the state and for guaranteeing national independence and territorial integrity.

Over and above these responsibilities, the 1958 Constitution gives further powers to both the president and the prime minister. On the one hand, the president is the head of the armed forces (Article 15) and is responsible for accrediting French ambassadors abroad (Article 14) and for naming three of the nine members (including the president) of the Constitutional Council (Article 56). In addition, the president has the right of pardon (Article 17) and the power to dissolve the National Assembly, although not more than once a year (Article 12). On the other hand, the prime minister has the right to issue decrees in the areas in which parliament is not permitted to legislate (Article 21) and is generally responsible for the government's powers in relation to the legislature. Finally, both the president and the prime minister have the right to make certain civil and military appointments (Articles 13 and 21); to submit a bill to the Constitutional Council for approval (Article 61) while the president has the right to propose constitutional amendments at the prime minister's request (Article 89). In short, for one observer at least, the overall result of this rather complicated distribution of executive power was that: 'The central question of any constitution – who rules? – is fudged' (Wright, 1989, p. 12).

This fudge was further complicated by the 1962 constitutional amendment. In 1958 the constitution established an indirectly elected presidency. The president was elected by a wide-ranging electoral college comprising nearly 80,000 people, consisting mainly of parliamentarians and representatives of local government. In October 1962, though, the constitution was amended. Henceforth, the president would be directly elected by universal suffrage. This meant that there were now two separate sources of popular authority in the system: presidential elections and parliamentary elections. It also meant, as Vincent Wright nicely put it, that if the 1962 constitutional amendment granted the president no new powers then 'it did afford him an important new *power*' (Wright, 1989, p. 13). The president could now claim – and with some justification – to represent the will of the French people. All told, then, the effect of the 1962 constitutional amendment was twofold: first, it established the presidential election as the focal point of the political process and, second, it institutionalised the potentially conflictual duality at the heart of the French executive.

Against this constitutional background, the process of political leadership in the Fifth Republic has revolved around the president, the prime minister and the relationship between them.

Presidents and prime ministers in the Fifth Republic

(For a list of presidents and prime ministers since 1959, see Table 2.1). The first president of the Fifth Republic was Charles de Gaulle. The General, a wartime hero and consistent opponent of the Fourth Republic, was a towering figure who inspired great loyalty and devotion amongst his supporters. He was overwhelmingly elected as president by the electoral college in December 1958 and he was easily re-elected by direct election in 1965. Overall, he served in office for over ten years until his resignation in April 1969 following the defeat in a referendum of his proposals to reform the Senate and local government.

Table 2.1   Presidents and prime ministers in France, 1959–98

President	Prime minister
Charles de Gaulle (1959–69)	Michel Debré (1959–62)
	Georges Pompidou (1962–8)
	Maurice Couve de Murville (68–9)
Georges Pompidou (1969–74)	Jacques Chaban–Delmas (1969–72)
	Pierre Messmer (1972–4)
Valéry Giscard d'Estaing (1974–81)	Jacques Chirac (1974–6)
	Raymond Barre (1976–81)
François Mitterrand (1981–95)	Pierre Mauroy (1981–4)
	Laurent Fabius (1984–6)
	Jacques Chirac (1986–8)
	Michel Rocard (1988–91)
	Edith Cresson (1991–2)
	Pierre Bérégovoy (1992–3)
	Edouard Balladur (1993–5)
Jacques Chirac (1995–)	Alain Juppé (1995–7)
	Lionel Jospin (1997–)

During de Gaulle's presidency there were three prime ministers. All three were initially appointed because they were long-time trusted companions of the General. All three lacked a strong party base. All three were essentially technicians rather than career politicians. The first prime minister, Michel Debré, was in office from 1959 to 1962. He was opposed to de Gaulle's Algerian policy but his loyalty to the General was such that he only resigned when the Algerian question and, hence, the threat of civil war was resolved. The second prime minister, Georges Pompidou, was a political unknown at the time of his appointment. However, he quickly went on to establish a large degree of support inside the Gaullist Party and came to see himself and to be seen as the presidential *dauphin* at which time he was promptly sidelined by the General. The third prime minister, Maurice Couve de Murville, was a diplomat by training and a largely ineffectual political figure. The precise relationship between de Gaulle and his prime ministers is a matter of interpretation (see below). However, it is uncontroversial to say that none of the prime ministers had the personal authority of the General and none could match his political charisma.

The second president was Georges Pompidou. The former prime minister easily won the 1969 presidential election which was provoked by the General's abrupt resignation. Pompidou had a sound knowledge of the most important political issues of the day by virtue of his time as prime minister. He also shared a similar conception of the role of the presidency as de Gaulle. This is at least part of the reason why the relationship with his first prime minister, Jacques Chaban-Delmas, was so conflictual. Chaban-Delmas, himself a gaullist, was a reformist prime minister but the tenor of his proposed reforms did not necessarily match that of the president. As a result, soon after the prime minister's political authority was strengthened by a supportive parliamentary vote, the president dismissed the prime minister (something for which there is no constitutional provision). By contrast, the relationship between Pompidou and his second prime minister, Pierre Messmer, was less strained. This is partly because of Messmer's loyalty, partly because he was a weak political figure and partly because the president was in increasingly poor health. In April 1974 Pompidou died, so provoking an early presidential election.

The 1974 presidential election was won by Valéry Giscard d'Estaing. Giscard's victory seemed to signal a new beginning for the Fifth Republic. Giscard belonged to a different political generation to his two predecessors and he was the first non-gaullist president, belonging, instead, to the right-wing liberal-leaning Independent Republican Party. He appointed a gaullist, Jacques Chirac, as his first prime minister. The appointment was a reward for the fact that Chirac had supported Giscard at the 1974 election ahead of Chaban-Delmas, the gaullist candidate. Soon, though, the rivalry between the two became unbearable to the extent that in August 1976 Chirac resigned claiming that the president was thwarting his reform proposals. In his place, Giscard appointed Raymond Barre, a then unknown technocrat who did not belong to any party but who was politically close to the president. The personal relations between the two were cordial but the political relations between the president's supporters and the gaullists in parliament became increasingly tense, which weakened the government's authority. This tension was primarily caused by the fact that both Giscard and Chirac had their sights firmly set on the 1981 presidential election. In the end, though, neither was successful.

The fourth president of the Fifth Republic was the socialist, François Mitterrand. Mitterrand was a complicated figure. He was a consummate politician: he gained control of the Socialist Party in the early 1970s; he then brokered an alliance with the communists which worked to the advantage of the socialists; and he was consistently supported by a loyal group of followers from the political, economic and cultural worlds. He was, though, also a very private person: he did not have the charisma of the General; he was fond of 'court' politics; and he persistently engaged in behind-the-scenes politicking. Mitterrand was president for fourteen years. He presided over a reformist government from 1981 to 1982 before agreeing to an economic and social u-turn from 1983 to 1986. He was then re-elected in 1988 as the candidate of the status quo. Throughout his presidency he consistently promoted European issues and he played a key role in negotiating both the Single European Act and the Maastricht Treaty. His personal reputation, though, was tarnished towards the end of his second term in office, most notably as a result of allegations that his wartime record was not as honourable as he had made it out to be.

There were two distinct sets of presidential/prime ministerial relationships during the Mitterrand presidencies. The first corresponds to the periods when the president was able to appoint a socialist prime minister. The first prime minister, Pierre Mauroy, was an old-style party notable. In office he was loyal to the president. He led a government which included four communist ministers but which collapsed after three years in the face of increasing social unrest and popular disillusionment. The second prime minister, Laurent Fabius, was a young presidential protégé. He did distance himself from the president during his administration but the differences of opinion were more symbolic than substantive. The first prime minister of Mitterrand's second term in office was Michel Rocard. Rocard was a long-time rival of Mitterrand who harboured his own presidential ambitions, which Mitterrand opposed. Rocard's time in office was marked by a period of barely disguised trench warfare before the prime minister was eventually dismissed. The other two socialist prime ministers during Mitterrand's second term were notable for their failure. The first, Edith Cresson, was an unmitigated disaster whose main claim to fame was that she became the most unpopular prime minister in the Fifth Republic up to that time. The second, Pierre Bérégovoy, was in office during a period when the president, the Socialist Party and he himself were all tainted by allegation of scandals. There was a distinct whiff of *fin de règne* politics in the air. Bérégovoy fatally blamed himself for the disastrous socialist defeat at the 1993 legislative election but he was guilty of nothing more than being in the wrong position at the wrong time.

The second set of presidential/prime ministerial relationships during the Mitterrand presidencies corresponds to the periods when the president was obliged to work with a right-wing prime minister. By virtue of Article 20 (above) the president has to appoint a prime minister who is acceptable to the National Assembly. This means, though, that when the parliamentary majority is opposed to the president, then the president must appoint a prime minister who is also opposed. This is known as *cohabitation*. It occurred for the first time under the Fifth Republic during the Mitterrand presidency and it occurred on two occasions, at the end of both his first and his second terms in office. The prime minister during the first period of *cohabitation* was Jacques Chirac. In the run-up to the 1988 presidential election Chirac and Mitterrand were rivals. Both tried to maximise their authority over the political process and relations were distinctly competitive. The prime minister during the second period was another gaullist, Édouard Balladur. This time Mitterrand's position was weaker than before. This was mainly because the right's victory in 1993 was much greater than in 1986 and because the president was weakened by illness and age (he was 76 in 1993). Overall, Mitterrand was less interventionist than before and popular attention focused on the battle between Balladur and Chirac as both massed their troops with a view to being the best-placed right-wing candidate at the 1995 presidential election.

The victor at this election was Jacques Chirac. A man of few convictions,

Chirac has had a number of seemingly contradictory political discourses during his career and he is notoriously reliant on the advice of those around him. He won the 1995 election by building a wide-ranging coalition of support based on an uneasy mixture of promises. In office his reforming ambitions were abandoned and the first two years of his presidency were marked by a growing level of civil disruption and general disillusionment. During this period, Chirac's relationship with the fellow gaullist prime minister, Alain Juppé, was excellent. The prime minister had been the president's most loyal supporter during the election campaign and the two formed a harmonious couple at the head of the executive. Their policies, though, were unpopular. In an attempt to create a political shock and restore the government's authority, the president dissolved the National Assembly in April 1997. The tactic backfired disastrously. The right was thrown out of office and was replaced by a so-called 'plural majority' coalition, which was dominated by the socialists but which also included the communists, the Greens and representatives of two small left-wing parties. The president, therefore, was forced to 'cohabit' with a left-wing prime minister, Lionel Jospin, whom he had beaten in the second round of the presidential election just two years previously.

These sketches of presidential/prime ministerial relations demonstrate the elasticity of executive politics during the Fifth Republic. Against this background, it should come as no surprise to know that there is no single and all-encompassing account of the politics of the French executive. Instead, the experience of the last forty years has been the subject of a number of contrasting interpretations. In the next section, these interpretations will be explored.

Models of French executive politics

In recent years, there has been an increasing number of systematic studies of executive politics. In this body of work, an article by Dunleavy and Rhodes about the British system of government has proved to be particularly influential (Dunleavy and Rhodes, 1990). In contrast to the long-standing and rather sterile debate about whether there was prime ministerial or cabinet government in Britain, Dunleavy and Rhodes identified five competing models of the British core executive. Each model assigned different roles to the principal political actors within the governmental system. Since their article was first published, this methodology has been applied to the study of executive politics in other contexts. As a result, equivalent models of core executive operations have been identified both comparatively (Elgie, 1997a) and in individual countries such as Austria (Müller, 1994), France (Elgie, 1993; 1998) and Ireland (O'Leary, 1991). In the French context, various models of executive politics can be identified. In the section which follows, four such models will be explored. These are: monocratic government, shared government, segmented government and ministerial government. (There is no model of cabinet government in France and the nature of bureaucratic politics will be explored in the next chapter.) Each of these models corresponds to a separate and mutually exclusive interpretation of how executive power is exercised under the Fifth Republic. Each proposes a particular configuration of the relationship between the president, prime minister and government ministers. In each case, the model will be defined, those who propose each of the models will be identified, the assumptions of their various arguments will be presented and the basic criticism of the positions will be outlined.

Monocratic government

Monocratic government may be defined as the exercise of personal leadership by a single individual. In the French case, it refers to individual leadership by either the president or the prime minister. According to those who put forward this model there is monocratic presidential government outside periods of *cohabitation* and monocratic prime ministerial government during these periods. In the former it is the president who initiates policy, decides the content of policy and is responsible for the success or failure of policy, whereas the prime minister is a wholly subordinate figure who simply acquiesces to the president's demands. By contrast, in the latter it is the prime minister who is the principal policy maker, whereas the president is a secondary actor who is not powerless but who is able to influence the policy process in only a very restricted number of areas. In both cases ministers are largely insignificant figures who have few if any opportunities to challenge the authority of their political superiors.

Monocratic government is undoubtedly the most common model of French executive politics. Its origins date back to the very early years of the Fifth Republic and the practices established by General de Gaulle. Not surprisingly, therefore, it has been proposed by a large number of eminent writers. For the most part, these writers tend to focus on the exercise of monocratic presidential government because this is considered to be the 'normal' way in which the Fifth Republic operates or, at least, has operated until recently (Colliard, 1994, p. 16). So, for example, Frears provides a classic statement of this model when he argues that the 'general aura of the presidency ... with its disdain for political parties and electioneering, its self-consciously regal style, the absence of direct public accountability, and the increasingly wide range of policies and decisions which come within the personal ambit of the President, gives some validity to the phrase 'president–king'' (Frears, 1981, p. 30). In a similar vein, Duverger has classified the president as a 'republican monarch' (Duverger, 1974), a phrase which is echoed by Alain Duhamel who has written that 'France is governed by an elected sovereign, a republican monarch, almost an enlightened despot' (Duhamel, 1980, p. 23). At times, though, monocratic presidential government is replaced by monocratic prime ministerial government.

On these occasions, the language used to describe the prime minister's role is generally somewhat less florid. Nevertheless, it is still commonplace to read that on these occasions the 'presidentialist regime faded away' (Gicquel, 1995, p. 517) and that the prime minister became the 'de facto as well as de jure head of government' (Gaffney, 1989, p. 7).

Those who promote the model of monocratic government make one key assumption: that the executive is dominated by a single person. However, precisely who dominates the executive depends on the particular circumstances of the period in question. So, during periods of monocratic presidential government, the president is said to control the system, whereas the prime minister, government and parliament play merely a subordinate role. For example, during these periods Goguel talks of the 'decisive preeminence of the president of the republic over both the government and parliament' (Goguel, 1983, p. 49). Similarly, Bernard Chantebout argues that 'the head of state confiscated the constitutional powers of the government which was reduced to simply implementing the president's policies' (Chantebout, 1989). Likewise, Chabal and Fraisseix refer to the phenomenon of 'presidential predominance relegating the government and the prime minister to the level of stooges executing "presidential ukases"' (Chabal and Fraisseix, 1996, p. 46). Equally, Carcassonne suggests that outside *cohabitation,* 'it is the President of the Republic who is the real ruler of France, that it is he and not the government, despite the text of Article 20, who "determines and conducts the policy of the nation"' (Carcassonne, 1988, p. 245). Indeed, so great is said to be the extent of monocratic presidential government that some people argue it has transformed the very nature of the Fifth Republic itself. For example, Jean Gicquel states that 'the [1958] constitution put in place a renovated parliamentary regime. However ... it has since been replaced by a presidentialist regime under the authority of the head of state' (Gicquel, 1995, pp. 508–9). Similarly, Dominique Turpin notes that the Fifth Republic 'has evolved into a presidentialist-type regime with the head of state dominating all other public powers (Turpin, 1992, p. 338).

There is, it would appear, plenty of evidence to support the monocratic presidential interpretation of executive politics. It is noted that various presidents have gone beyond the bounds of their constitutional powers. Most notably, de Gaulle called a referendum in 1962 in rather dubious constitutional circumstances and, like Pompidou's removal of Chaban-Delmas, Mitterrand dismissed Rocard as prime minister when strictly speaking he had no right to do so. In addition, presidents have involved themselves in the policy-making process. For example, de Gaulle personally took the decision not to devalue the franc in 1967 and he insisted on holding the politically fatal referendum on local government reform in 1969 against advice to the contrary. In a similar vein, Pompidou oversaw the government's reform of the broadcasting system. More generally, Giscard used to map out the government's policy agenda six months in advance. Indeed, it was his desire to control policy making directly that resulted in Chirac's decision to resign as prime minister in 1976. Mitterrand was personally responsible for introducing the government's austerity package in 1983 and he was the driving force behind the Europeanisation of French politics throughout the 1980s. Finally, it was Chirac who announced in October 1995 that France was committed to meeting the Maastricht convergence criteria, which marked a clear redefinition of the then government's priorities. All of these examples suggest that France has regularly experienced periods of monocratic presidential government.

At the same time, those who support this model usually argue that France has also experienced periods of monocratic prime ministerial government during *cohabitation*. On these occasions, the executive is still dominated by one person. However, it is argued that power shifts from the president to the prime minister. There is still a form of personal leadership, therefore, but this time it is exercised by the head of government and not the head of state. So, Suleiman notes that from 1986 to 1988 'the policy process came to be dominated by the government' and that 'the fact remains that the president did not govern' (Suleiman, 1994, p. 150). Moreover, as Chabal and Fraisseix state: 'The new distribution of powers signified the consecration of governmental leadership characterised by the recognition of independence and the real exercise of prime ministerial powers' (Chabal and Fraisseix, 1996, p. 50). During *cohabitation*, though, the president is still said to maintain some very important prerogatives. For the most part, however, these 'come under the heading of control and arbitration rather than government in the strict sense of the word' (Duverger, 1996, p. 547). This is confirmed by Gicquel who, speaking of the first period of *cohabitation*, suggests that Mitterrand 'although remaining present and vigilant ... fell back and took refuge in his role as arbitrator' (Gicquel, 1995, p. 517).

Once again, those who promote this model suggest that there are many examples which confirm the presence of monocratic prime ministerial government during *cohabitation*. For example, during the first period of *cohabitation* it was Chirac who decided which of the state-controlled television channels should be privatised and he also oversaw the most important arbitrations in the budgetary policy-making process. In addition, he also established a 'diplomatic unit' at Matignon which challenged the president's pre-eminence in the field of foreign and defence policy. During the second period Balladur played a similar role. For example, he was instrumental in determining France's position during the GATT world trade negotiations and he also decided the manner in which the July 1993 constitutional amendment, limiting the right of political asylum, was adopted. Finally, during the third period Jospin has once again emerged, so it might be argued, as the executive's leading decision maker. For example, he was the one who insisted on the reform which attempted to limit the working week to thirty-five hours.

It is apparent, then, that there are plenty of people who put forward the model of monocratic government and that there is plenty of evidence to suggest that this model provides the most appropriate interpretation of executive politics in the Fifth Republic. And yet, it is also open to a number of criticisms.

First, it might be argued that many of those who put forward this model exaggerate the extent of presidential power. For example, one observer has argued that: 'If the term "imperial presidency" can be applied with any degree of validity, one might choose to apply it to the President of France rather than to his counterpart in the United States' (Suleiman, 1980, pp. 103–4). Equally, another has identified France as the only West European example of a system in which there is a 'hegemonic presidency' (Duverger, 1996, p. 506). Arguably, though, this sort of language over-states the personalisation of the decision-making process. Even if it is certainly the case that outside *cohabitation* the president is an important political figure, is it really the case that the presidency should be described as 'imperial', 'hegemonic', 'despotic' or other such adjectives? Surely, it might be argued, political reality is such that the president operates in a system in which there are other senior political figures whose influence cannot simply be ignored. In this way, it might be argued that the model of monocratic presidential government provides little more than a caricatural interpretation of executive politics.

Second, it might equally be argued that a similar number of those who put forward this model exaggerate the extent of prime ministerial power during *cohabitation*. As noted above, those who support this approach usually stress that during *cohabitation* the president still maintains a degree of power. So, the president is said to be a 'controlling power' during these periods, or an 'arbitrator'. As such, though, it might be argued that this situation does not correspond to a period of monocratic government at all. Instead, it might be more appropriate to class such as situation as one of shared government, or segmented government (see below). In these cases, then, the evidence suggests that *cohabitation* is not characterised by monocratic prime ministerial government, but by a different form of government altogether.

Third, it might also be argued that this model is outdated. In particular, one general characteristic of this model is that it fails to place presidential/prime ministerial relations in the context of the wider political system. It is true that the study of executive politics is primarily concerned with the study of politics within the executive and not the study of the position of the executive within the political system more generally. However, presidential and prime ministerial power is at least partly dependent upon external political forces. Arguably, the configuration of these forces has changed over time. For example, the role of the state has been reduced and the political system has become more fragmented (see Chapters 1, 3 and 8). As a result, it might be argued that individual ministers are more important and that the president and prime minister have less opportunity to assert their authority over the political process. In this way, it is conceivable that the model of monocratic government might have provided an accurate picture of executive politics in the early years of the Fifth Republic but that it now runs counter to developments in other areas of the political system. In this sense, if at one time it was accurate, it has now lost its salience.

Shared government, or executive co-operation

In a comparative context, shared government, or executive co-operation, may be defined as the situation where a highly restricted number of people within the executive 'share formally, effectively, and in a continuous manner in the general affairs of the government' (Blondel, 1984, p. 75). It is the situation where two or three individuals (and rarely more) have joint decision-making responsibilities within the executive. According to this interpretation, responsibility for all aspects of policy making is shared among these people who collectively oversee the governmental decision-making process. In a French context, though, the model of shared government has a particular slant. Here, as Blondel notes, ' "shared" leadership may not mean "equal" leadership' (Blondel, 1980, p. 65). Instead, executive co-operation may be defined as the situation where the president and prime minister share decision-making responsibilities on an ongoing basis, but where the division of executive power is nevertheless skewed towards the president, except during *cohabitation* when it is skewed towards the prime minister. In this way, then, the model of shared government is a close cousin of the model of monocratic government. The essential difference between the two lies in the tone of the two models. In the monocratic-government model the emphasis is on the unequivocal pre-eminence of either the president or the prime minister. By contrast, in the shared-government model the emphasis is always on the closeness of the relationship between the president and the prime minister. It is argued that the one cannot govern without the other either in 'normal' periods of executive politics or during *cohabitation*. The president and prime minister, then, are treated as partners in the decision-making process even if it is conceded that one of the partners is invariably more senior than the other.

Fewer people put forward the model of shared government than propose the model of monocratic government. However, one variation of the shared government thesis is provided by Massot. He writes that:

> there is an extraordinary complexity in the relations between the head of state and the head of government. If the normal situation is indeed that there is a certain hierarchy which guarantees presidential pre-eminence, it is also the case that ... the President cannot do without a

Prime Minister. ... [T]he sharing of roles, in other words a dyarchy, is also a necessity.

(Massot, 1993, p. 174)

Another, slightly different but essentially similar, variation of the shared government model has been put forward by Burin des Roziers, who, speaking of the Debré prime ministership, argues that '[t]here was no dyarchy at the head of the state. In other words, there was no division of responsibilities between the President and the Prime Minister, each one in charge of his own area, but the common exercise of power' (Burin des Roziers, 1990, p. 87). Other variations of this model variously characterise the Fifth Republic as a system of dual leadership (Blondel, 1977, p. 37), as a dualist presidential regime (Chagnollaud and Quermonne, 1996, p. 782), or as a twin-headed executive (Elgie, 1997b). Whatever variation is preferred, the key assumption of this model is that 'it is by the common action of the head of state and the head of government that the executive discharges its responsibilities' (de Baecque, 1986, p. 283), or, as Avril puts it, 'if the President of the Republic is the keystone of the regime ... the prime minister is the kingpin' (Avril, 1986, pp. 241–2).

The argument that there is shared government rests on a particular perception of the Fifth Republic's political process. Those who put forward this model do not deny that the president is a powerful political figure. So, for example, de Baecque acknowledges that 'the head of state exercises a direct influence on the government of the country' (de Baecque, 1976, p. 166). Indeed, it is undoubtedly the case that for much of the Fifth Republic 'the president has been the dominant force within the executive' (Elgie, 1997b, p. 2292). At the same time, though, those who put forward this model also stress that the nature of the governmental process is such that the president cannot govern alone. In this way, as Massot notes, 'the originality of the Fifth Republic is not that it created a republican monarchy, but that it reconciled the previously contradictory terms, dyarchy and hierarchy' (Massot, 1993, p. 174). In this sense, those who propose the model of executive co-operation argue that the Fifth Republic should not be classed as a system of monocratic government, but as a system in which power is shared between the president and prime minister both during 'normal' periods of government and during *cohabitation*.

Perhaps the fullest and most eloquent presentation of this argument has been proposed by de Baecque who, in his study of the first two presidents of the Fifth Republic, makes the following argument:

Governing, at the end of the day, is the process of drawing up and implementing policy. These two aspects are inseparable. If this definition is accepted, it must be admitted that the President of the Republic and the Prime Minister govern France together.

(de Baecque, 1976, p. 165)

In a similar vein, Chagnollaud and Quermonne state that:

> governmental functions in the broad sense of the term are shared
> between a head of state, popularly elected and given real powers, and
> an apparently collegial government, led by a prime minister who is
> politically responsible to the lower house of parliament.
>
> (Chagnollaud and Quermonne, 1996, p. 782)

Equally, when comparing France with the US, Debbasch argues that 'one is
naturally led to the conclusion that the bicephalism at the head of the
executive is expressed by way of a sharing of decision making power
which has no equivalent in the US' (Debbasch, 1986, p. 202). These state-
ments all suggest, then, that in 'normal' times the Fifth Republic is
something other than just a presidentialised regime. The same point
applies to *cohabitation* with regard to the prime minister. On these occasions, there is a 'forced cooperation' (Chagnollaud and Quermonne, 1996,
p. 38) between the president and prime minister which is reminiscent of
'the balance of power which, for several decades, guaranteed at the international level the peaceful coexistence of the two superpowers'
(Chagnollaud and Quermonne, 1996, p. 38). At all times, therefore, the
president and the prime minister both have an indispensable role to play in
the policy-making process. As one study puts it, 'in all cases, the dualism
of executive power dominates political contingencies' (Chagnollaud and
Quermonne, 1996, p. 783). In this sense, there is shared government.

There is plenty of evidence to support the model of executive co-
operation. For example, the final details of the 1997 budget were decided
at a weekend meeting between Chirac and Juppé at Brégançon on 24–25
August 1996. Similarly, during the third period of *cohabitation* in 1997
Chirac and Jospin jointly launched an (ultimately unsuccessful) initiative
to ensure that the first president of the European Central Bank would be a
Frenchman. Over and above these particular examples, the structure of the
policy-making process means that the president and prime minister are
both involved either directly or indirectly in the minutiae of decision
making. For example, both see each other prior to the weekly meeting of
the Council of Ministers to discuss policy and, if need be, to present a
united front at the meeting. Equally, presidential and prime ministerial
advisers both attend the final stages of the policy elaboration process. This
ensures that the views of their political superiors are represented and that
the conclusions of the meetings are reported back. In these ways, neither
actor is simply excluded from the process. Both are in a position to shape
it. In this sense, there is shared government.

As with the previous model, the model of shared government is open to
criticism. The basic objection to this model lies in the very conceptualisa-
tion of presidential/prime ministerial relations that it proposes. At the
outset, it was noted that the main difference between the model of shared

government and the model of monocratic government was primarily one of emphasis. Those who put forward the model of shared government do not deny that outside *cohabitation* the president is the most senior political actor. They simply emphasise the fact that the prime minister is also an integral part of the decision-making process. However, critics might argue that the opportunity to participate in a particular process is far removed from the ability to influence that process in a systematic and coherent way. For example, the prime minister has formal responsibilities with regard to French defence policy. After all, the head of government is constitutionally responsible for national defence (see above) and is a member of the committee which co-ordinates defence policy. However, it would take a brave and perhaps foolhardy person to argue that the country's defence strategy has ever been decided by anyone other than the president personally. If this is the case, then it might better to argue that there is either a concentration of decision-making responsibilities, as suggested by the model of monocratic government, or a division of such responsibilities, as indicated in the next model to be considered.

Segmented government

The model of segmented government may be defined as the situation where there is a sectoral division of labour within the executive in which responsibility for one set of matters is incumbent upon one person and responsibility for another set of matters is incumbent upon another person. According to this interpretation, different actors within the executive have their own mutually exclusive spheres of influence. In the French context, the model of segmented government corresponds to a particular distribution of responsibilities between the president and prime minister. In particular, the president is said to be responsible for decision making in the area of 'high' politics, such as foreign and European affairs, defence, statecraft and crisis decision making, whereas the prime minister is responsible for decision making in the area of 'low' politics, such as domestic policy, budgetary policy and routine decision making. It should be noted, though, that none of the people who proposes the French variant of the segmented government model suggests that the president is always powerless in the domain of 'low' politics. In this way, there is, once again, a certain overlap between this model and the two previous models. As before, the difference between the various models is one of emphasis. What distinguishes this model from either of the previous two is the stress that is placed on the president's overwhelming preoccupation with 'high' politics and the prime minister's primary concern for 'low' politics. It should also be noted that, as with the two previous models, in this model ministers play little or no substantive role in the decision-making process.

The model of segmented government was first proposed by a politician, Jacques Chaban-Delmas, who at the time was the leader of the gaullist parliamentary party and who later went on to be prime minister. In a speech to the 1959 Gaullist Party Conference, he stated that 'the presidential sector consists of Algeria, without forgetting the Sahara, the French–African Community, foreign affairs and national defence. Everything else is open. In the first sector the government implements presidential decisions, in the second it decides for itself' (quoted in Maus, 1985a, p. 81). In this way, Chaban-Delmas argued that there was a strict division of labour within the executive. The president was responsible for a so-called 'reserved domain' of policies, decisions concerning which he and only he could take. By contrast, the prime minister was responsible for all other policy matters and could take decisions free from presidential interference. There is no doubt that Chaban-Delmas's formula struck a chord. For example, the notion that there is a reserved presidential domain has persisted in the journalistic psyche ever since. There is also no doubt, though, that this formula was at least in part politically motivated. Chaban-Delmas was implicitly defending de Gaulle against those who were already criticising what they considered to be his increasingly solitary exercise of power. Thus, he was not simply engaging in an academic exercise.

Leaving aside the original motivation for this model, it is apparent that the concept of segmented decision making still has a limited but nevertheless influential number of proponents. These include Samy Cohen (1986), Raphaël Hadas-Lebel (1992) and Jolyon Howorth (1993). For example, Howorth states that 'the accumulated tradition of the *domaine réservé* continues to confer on the tenant of the Elysée powers in the field of foreign and particularly defence policy which go far beyond those enjoyed by any other world leader' (Howorth, 1993, p. 189). Similarly, Cohen portrays the president as a 'nuclear monarch' who is the 'sole and real head of French diplomacy' (Cohen, 1986, p. 15). Equally, although Hadas-Lebel is keen to stress the overall strength of the president, he also points out that the head of state is 'the man of the long-term' whereas the prime minister looks after 'the immediate action' (Hadas-Lebel, 1992, p. 211) or, put another way, that the Fifth Republic has a 'president who is responsible for that which is permanent and essential' and a 'prime minister who deals with contingent problems' (Hadas-Lebel, 1992, p. 213). What is common to these views is the emphasis that is placed on the division of labour within the executive.

In the segmented government model the president's powers are skewed towards a particular area. For example, according to Cohen, only the president 'can decide to declare war or make peace. Only he can decide to send the Foreign Legion to Kolwezi. ... Only he can order the disengagement and withdrawal of French forces. Only he, above all, can launch a strategic nuclear strike' (Cohen, 1986, p. 15). A similar point is made by Howorth who argues that the president's ' "special role" in foreign and defence policy is widely perceived as amounting to virtual *carte blanche* where diplomacy and security policy are concerned' (Howorth, 1993, p. 150). By contrast, the prime minister's powers in this area are weak. As Cohen notes, in this area 'the prime minister "determines" and "directs" nothing whatsoever' (Cohen, 1985, p. 94). More particularly, Howorth points out that on occasions the prime minister 'hardly seemed to exist' in this area, something which 'has further contributed to the shoring-up of the *domaine réservé*' (Howorth, 1993, p. 167). At the same time, though, the prime minister's influence in other areas is not insignificant. For example, Cohen points out that, whereas the prime minister only 'plays a small role in the formulation of foreign and defence, he is at the forefront of economic and social policy making' (Cohen, 1986, p. 20). Similarly, speaking of the de Gaulle presidency, Cohen states that 'in sectors other than diplomacy, defence and Algeria, the prime minister maintained important preroga- tives' (Cohen, 1985, p. 97). Speaking of the same period, Maus asserts that 'From 1959 onwards, de Gaulle left it up to Debré to give the necessary orders in all areas which did not impinge on Algerian, State, or foreign affairs' (Maus, 1985b, p. 24).

The evidence for segmented government is seemingly considerable. Indeed, political mythology has it that presidents make the real decisions and that prime ministers set the price of milk. More concretely, though, the tradition of segmented government clearly began with de Gaulle. For example, successive decrees in 1962 and 1964 centralised the operational responsibility for the conduct of hostile operations and the power to launch a nuclear strike solely in the hands of the president. At the same time, prime ministers were left to wrestle with matters such as a reform of the education system (Debré in 1961) and problems of social unrest (Pompidou in 1968). Equally, as noted earlier, Mitterrand was overwhelm- ingly preoccupied with European matters during his second term of office and he was certainly the main player in determining France's involvement in the Gulf War. This meant that prime ministers were free to address issues like the political situation in France's overseas departments (as Rocard successfully managed to do in 1988) and immigration policy (as Cresson disastrously attempted in 1991). What is more, it might be argued that at no time is the division of presidential/prime ministerial responsibili- ties more clear than during periods of *cohabitation*. Here, the president's influence is strictly confined to the realm of foreign and defence policy, whereas the prime minister has free rein elsewhere. So, for example, in 1986 Mitterrand was able to insist that France's short-range nuclear arms were 'tactical' and not 'strategic', but he was only able to delay the govern- ment's privatisation programme and employment policy reforms for a matter of a few weeks.

Despite the apparent evidence for this model, it, like its counterparts, is subject to criticism. The main criticism concerns the division of responsi- bilities that it puts forward. More specifically, it might be argued that presidential influence is not simply confined to foreign and defence policy. So, for example, Wright has argued that there were five components to the president's reserved domain: foreign and defence policy; economic, financial and industrial policy; social and environmental policy; crisis decision making; and policies which attracted the president's interest for purely personal reasons (Wright, 1989, p. 55). Similarly, Massot has noted that under Pompidou 'the head of state's "reserved domain" went beyond matters of defence and foreign affairs and included industrial development, educational reform, urban growth and, above all, the broadcasting system' (Massot, 1988, p. 33). If the division of presidential and prime ministerial responsibilities is in fact not strictly delineated, then the basic rationale for this model disappears. In this case, it might be better to argue that there is monocratic government, which acknowledges that presidential influence extends far beyond any supposed 'reserved domain'. Indeed, it might also be better to argue that there is shared government, which can concede that the president is to all intents and purposes supreme in the 'reserved domain' but which also suggests that in all other areas the president and prime minister govern together.

Ministerial government

The model of ministerial government may be defined as the situation where individual ministers are able to have a significant impact on policy in the area which falls under their jurisdiction. The implication of this model is that there is no predominant individual within the decision-making process. Instead, ministers are the key political actors. They take decisions individually and the role of the most senior political figure(s) within the executive is simply to oversee and co-ordinate the policy process. In the French context, the model of ministerial government suggests that ministers are solely responsible for the initiation of policy and for decisions about the content of policy. By contrast, the president and the prime minister merely co-ordinate the policy-making process and ensure that it functions smoothly. Their role is more symbolic than substantive. It is apparent, therefore, that the model of ministerial government is quite distinct from the three previous models of government.

The model of ministerial government remains largely unexplored in the literature on the French executive. One writer has argued that the first fifteen years of the Fifth Republic marked the 'golden age' of ministers in the Fifth Republic (Rigaud, 1986, p. 13). Another has stated that the political weakness of both president Mitterrand and prime minister Cresson from 1991 to 1992 meant this period 'approximated more than any other to a ministerial mode of executive relations' (Cole, 1994, p. 89). However, it should be stressed that neither of these writers was explicitly arguing in favour of this model of executive politics; both were simply commenting on the nature of governmental decision making at a particular period of time. For the most part, therefore, the model of ministerial government is, at present, merely notional. Nevertheless, it is examined here because it provides a good counterpoint to the three previous models which were examined and because a reasonable case can, in theory at least, be made for it.

Ministers, it might be argued, are not necessarily the inconsequential figures that they are sometimes portrayed as being. For example, they have considerable legal and administrative powers at their disposal. They have the power to appoint top officials in their department as well as the power to issue delegated legislation in policy areas under their jurisdiction (usually subject to presidential, prime ministerial or Council of Ministers approval). In addition, there is little doubt that ministers jealously guard their own policy patch. They resent any encroachment on their own polit-ical responsibilities and they promote and defend their departmental interests. Furthermore, the most senior ministers will also have a consider-able personal standing and political bargaining power which means that their views have to be taken into account for fear of creating a political crisis. At the same time, it is also the case that the president and prime minister undoubtedly carry out co-ordination functions. Their intervention comes towards the end of the policy-making process. Their primary role, it might be argued, is to arbitrate between the conflicting demands of the various ministers. And yet, this means that they intervene when many of the principles and details of legislation have already been decided. It means that they have to balance the conflicting demands of the different ministers and broker political deals rather than necessarily imposing their own vision of affairs upon disinterested political actors.

In this way, it might be argued that the organisation of the policy process is one which at least accommodates, if not encourages, a tendency towards ministerial government. Indeed, one writer notes that 'political and adminis-trative reality offer the minister wider and more guaranteed perspectives' of political influence than those which are outlined in the constitution (Rigaud, 1986, p. 7). In this context, Rigaud suggests that under the de Gaulle and Pompidou presidencies the Foreign Minister, Maurice Couve de Murville, had sufficient personal and political authority to be able to influence policy and that the same applied to Valéry Giscard d'Estaing when he served as Finance Minister (Rigaud, 1986, p. 13). Similarly, Cole indicates that under the Mitterrand presidency during the prime ministership of Edith Cresson the Finance Minister, Pierre Bérégovoy, was in a position to take key policy decisions (Cole, 1994, p. 89).

These examples demonstrate that it may at least be possible to construct a coherent model of ministerial government. More generally, it might be argued that if writers exited the intellectual mindset of presidential/prime ministerial politics and actively went in search of evidence to support this model, then other, perhaps more convincing, examples might be found. At the present time, however, the basic problem with this model is that there is very little evidence to back it up. So, for example, one study of minis-terial government concluded that the 'notion of ministerial autonomy' is of limited applicability in the French Fifth Republic' (Thiébault, 1994, p. 148). Indeed, even those writers, such as Rigaud and Cole, who are at least willing to entertain the idea of ministerial government, suggest that it has only been applicable in certain, quite restricted, circumstances. In this respect, the model of ministerial government remains almost completely unexplored in the French context.

Conclusion

This chapter has demonstrated that there are a number of models of core executive politics (see Table 2.2). It has also demonstrated that there is a degree of overlap between the various models of executive politics. In particular, there is an overlap between the first three models that were examined. In these cases, the models correspond more to a difference of emphasis about the nature of core executive politics rather than a fundamental disagreement about their respective roles. And yet, the fact that such differences of emphasis can be identified in the first place illustrates the point that different people do conceptualise presidential/prime ministerial/ministerial relations in different ways. In other words, different people make somewhat different assumptions, put forward slightly different arguments and can be associated with essentially different schools of thought. As such, there is an ongoing debate about the true functioning of the executive branch of government which can be captured in the different models of executive politics that were identified. In this context, students of the core executive have certain choices to make. Does the evidence suggest that the policy initiation and co-ordination process is dominated by one person? Alternatively, is the top-level management of this process a joint affair between the president and prime minister? If so, do the two actors work together across all policy areas or do they have their own separate spheres or responsibility? Finally, is it the case that the influence of the president and prime minister is exaggerated and that ministers are the key political players? In fact, most observers still support the monocratic government model of core executive relations. This is still the dominant frame of reference in the study of executive politics.

There is, though, an alternative approach (Elgie, 1993, pp. 184–5). The first section of this chapter illustrated what was called the 'essential elasticity' of executive politics during the Fifth Republic. In their different ways, most of the models considered accounted for this elasticity. However, they did so within the framework of the model itself. Most notably, the model of monocratic government stressed the fact that there is a shift from monocratic presidential government to monocratic prime ministerial government during periods of *cohabitation*. And yet, it might be better to conceive of the elasticity of executive politics not in terms of a shift of responsibilities within the framework of a single model but in terms of a general shift from one model to another (Elgie, 1993). For

Table 2.2 Models of the French core executive

	Monocratic government	Shared government	Segmented government	Ministerial government
Definition/key assumptions	1 The executive is dominated by a single person – normally the president, the PM during cohabitation 2 One person initiates policy, decides the content of policy and is responsible for the success or failure of policy 3 Ministers have few powers	1 President and PM have joint decision-making responsibilities 2 President and PM do not necessarily have equal power, but they share tasks 3 Ministers have few powers	1 Sectoral division of labour within the executive 2 President and PM have mutually exclusive spheres of influence 3 President is responsible for 'high' politics and the PM for 'low' politics 4 Ministers have few powers	1 Individual ministers are able to have a significant impact on policy in the area which falls under their jurisdiction 2 President and the prime minister merely coordinate the policy-making process
Proponents	Chabal and Fraisseix (1996), Colliard (1994), Duverger (1974), Frears (1981), Goguel (1983), Suleiman (1980), Turpin (1992)	Avril (1986), Blondel (1977), Burin des Roziers (1990), Chagnollaud and Quermonne (1996), de Baecque (1976), Elgie (1997b), Massot (1993)	Cohen (1986), Hadas-Lebel (1992), Howorth (1993)	Cole (1994), Rigaud (1986)
Argument/evidence	Presidents have taken key decisions, e.g., de Gaulle's decision not to devalue in 1967 Presidents go beyond their constitutional powers, e.g., they have dismissed PMs During cohabitation, PMs take key decisions, e.g., Balladur and GATT negotiations	Decision-making power is shared, e.g., final details of the 1997 budget decided by the president and PM together Many meetings between president and PM. President's and PM's advisers both attend the final stages of the policy process	President controls foreign and defence policy, e.g., Mitterrand and the Gulf War. PMs responsible for domestic policy, e.g., Debré and education Cohabitation does not change the basic division of responsibility	Ministers have considerable legal and administrative powers. Ministers jealously guard their own policy turfs Ministers influence the crucial early stages of the policy process Examples – the de Gaulle presidency and the Cresson premiership
Criticisms	1 Presidential power is exaggerated 2 During cohabitation the president still maintains power 3 Outdated – the executive is less powerful than before	1 There is little difference between this model and the model of monocratic government 2 Underestimates presidential power in general or at least it underestimates presidential power in certain policy areas	1 Underestimates prime ministerial power generally and in specific areas 2 Underestimates presidential power in certain policy areas	1 Underestimates presidential power generally 2 Underestimates presidential power generally and in specific areas

example, it might be better to argue that there is a general tendency towards monocratic presidential government in the Fifth Republic, but that during *cohabitation* there is a shift not to monocratic prime ministerial government but to, say, shared government. Indeed, it might be better still to conceive of the elasticity of executive politics in terms not just of a single shift from one model to another but in terms of a variety of shifts between different models according to the political conjuncture of the time. So, it might be better to argue not that there is a general tendency towards any particular model in the Fifth Republic but that there was a shift from, say, segmented government from 1959 to 1962 to monocratic presidential government from 1962 to 1976, then a further shift to shared government from 1976 to 1981, then a shift back to monocratic presidential government from 1981 to 1984, then a return to segmented government from 1984 to 1986 and then a shift to monocratic prime ministerial government from 1986 to 1988 and so on (see Elgie, 1993). This is a departure from the traditional approach to the study of executive politics in France. However, it may provide a more fruitful way of capturing the complexities of core executive politics since 1959.

3 The bureaucracy

According to Alain Madelin, former Finance Minister and leader of the right-wing Démocratie libérale party (see Chapter 5), 'Italy has the Mafia, Spain has ETA, Ireland has the IRA and France has ENA'. This view, which was expressed as recently as 1997, is both quite outrageous and totally repugnant. Undoubtedly, however, the existence of elite civil service training schools, such as ENA, and the consequences of them have long been a source of controversy and criticism in France. Indeed, more generally, the proper role and actual functioning of the French bureaucracy has also been a persistent subject of political, popular and academic debate. All told, such is the basic preoccupation with the perceived inadequacies of the administrative system that, in the last twenty years alone, there has been a seemingly endless series of government-sponsored laws, reports and circulars, all of which have attempted to reform the organisation of the officials who are engaged in one of the most fundamental functions of government.

This chapter examines the academic debate about the French bureaucracy. It begins with a brief overview of its general structure and outlines basic characteristics of the higher civil service. It then identifies four competing models of the French bureaucracy: the technocracy model, the power elite model, the administration and politics model and, finally, the fragmented bureaucracy model.

The civil service

The modern-day organisation of the French civil service dates back to 1946. Prior to this time, the system had undergone a century or more of piecemeal change. However, in 1946 the so-called General Statute of Public Service became law. This statute effectively unified the civil service, put it under the control of the prime minister and set out the legal status of civil servants. Since this time, the General Statute has been revised. Most notably, there were minor changes in 1959 at the beginning of the Fifth Republic and then major reforms in 1983 and 1984 in the early years of the Mitterrand presidency. In addition, further laws in 1984 and 1986 revised the status of local authority employees and public health sector officials respectively. In this context, two aspects concerning the basic organisation of the French civil service can be highlighted: first, the general structure of the bureaucracy and, second, the position of higher civil servants.

The general structure of the bureaucracy

The General Statute of Public Service created four categories of state civil servants: A, B, C and D. Within each of these categories there are different sub-categories known variously as grades, classes and echelons. The four basic categories are hierarchically organised. Category C and D civil servants are the least senior officials. They perform basic clerical work, provide secretarial support and carry out routine administration. It might be noted, though, that Category D civil servants have now all but disappeared. Category B civil servants are the next most senior level. They are largely responsible for the basic implementation of policy, although this category also formally includes primary school teachers. Finally, Category A civil servants are the most senior officials. They are involved in executive management and administrative decision making. So, for example, directors of government departments are usually Category A civil servants. This category is itself split into various sub-categories, the highest of which consists of the so-called *grands fonctionnaires*. So, directors of departments also usually have this title.

Appointment to the basic categories is by competitive entrance examination, of which there are two sorts: external examinations, for those not already in the civil service, and internal examinations, for those who are. In addition, Category B civil servants are also required to have a *baccalauréat* (the equivalent of English A Levels), and Category A civil servants must have a degree-level qualification. It might be noted, though, that a large percentage of Category C civil servants have a *baccalauréat* and that a similar percentage of Category B civil servants have a degree-level qualification.

All categories of civil servants have a basic security of tenure. They may be made redundant, but only if a special legal process is undertaken by the minister and compensation may be awarded. They may also be dismissed from their post, but this usually involves a lengthy formal process before independent administrative tribunals at which the person concerned can defend him/herself. In general, employment in the civil service is still seen as a job for life, especially at the lower levels. Indeed, since the 1970s and the end of the so-called 'thirty glorious years' of unparalleled economic growth, the number of people seeking to enter the civil service has greatly increased at least partly for this reason.

With few exceptions, civil servants have the right to join trade unions and political parties. Equally, with the exception of the police, the army and magistrates, they also have the right to strike. What is more, they can also stand for election and, if defeated, they can still return to their post. In this way, civil servants can engage in political activity and this is one reason why there are so many people with civil service backgrounds in parliament. Indeed, typically between 30 and 40 per cent of parliamentarians now have a civil service background. However, civil servants do have what is known as the 'obligation of reserve', which means that they must take care not to express their personal political opinions in the course of their official duties.

Pay structures are fixed according to the various categories and sub-categories of civil servants. These structures are based on the grid-payment system, which became law in 1948, and which fixed a series of pay differentials across the civil service. This means that every grade of the civil service has its corresponding pay level. Pay increases are no longer index-linked, but the grid system is extremely rigid. This is because any civil service salary increase applies to all levels on the basis of existing differentials. In recent years there have been attempts to change the grid system so as to increase flexibility, but with little success. More generally, there has been some concern that civil servants are too well paid and that the cost of the civil service pay budget is too great for the state to be able to maintain. So, for example, civil service pay takes up around 40 per cent of the state budget. The director of a department will earn over 32,000 francs per month and a basic Category C worker will earn around 7,500 francs per month. However, as with reform of the grid system, the attempt to reduce overall pay levels has been very difficult to achieve. There have been pay freezes but in budgetary terms their net impact has been negligible.

In most cases, promotion within the civil service is based on either seniority, meaning length-of service, or competitive examination. However, for some of the most senior civil servants, promotion is not simply a function of seniority or merit, but political patronage. A large number of posts are officially at the discretion of the government. As a result, newly elected governments have not been slow to place officials who are broadly sympathetic to their aims in these posts. For example, when the right won power in 1993, the socialist Director of the Budget, one of the top positions in the Ministry of Finance and a key figure in economic policy making, was replaced by a civil servant with broadly gaullist associations. In most cases, these changes take place gradually over a two- or three-year period. However, this means that if a party remains in power for a long period of time, it can appoint its sympathisers to most key posts in the highest levels of the administration. Thus, in recent years there have been right-wing claims that the socialists installed a Socialist Party (PS) state from 1981 to 1986 and then socialist claims that subsequent right-wing governments established a gaullist state (See Chapter 5). For some, this element of political patronage in the system seems to blur the apparently clear constitutional distinction between politicians and administrators and will be discussed below.

The higher civil service

The higher civil service in France is characterised by its specialised training procedure, the importance of the *grands corps* and the phenomenon of *pantouflage* – the practice whereby bureaucrats leave the civil service to take up posts in public or private sector organisations.

Most senior French civil servants have attended an administrative training school, or *grande école*. There are a number of *grandes écoles*, but most senior civil servants have studied at either the École Polytechnique or the École Nationale d'Administration (ENA). The École Polytechnique, otherwise known as the X, was founded in 1794. It specialises in technical training for scientists and engineers. The École Nationale d'Administration was set up in 1945. It provides a more general administrative training background in politics, constitutional and administrative law, public administration, budgeting and so on.

Each of these two schools only has an intake of around 80–100 people per year and entry to them is by way of a competitive public exam. The number of people wanting to enter the schools is large, so there is fierce competition. There are various types of candidates who take the entrance exam. The majority of successful applicants are external (i.e., non-civil service) candidates. Typically, having completed a first degree, these candidates prepare for the entrance exam by attending a year of special preparatory classes which are put on by certain institutions, most notably the Institut d'Études Politiques (or Sciences Po) in Paris. Indeed, entrance to these classes at Sciences Po is itself determined by a public exam. The other main category of applicants comprises internal candidates, or those who have already been employed in the civil service for at least five years. Again, these applicants often attend special interministerial preparatory classes, entrance to which is also usually determined by a competitive exam. Here, the classes last either for a year, if the person in question has a degree-level qualification, or two years if not. The civil servant is officially on secondment from his or her department during this period. Finally, there is another mode of entry which, when it was introduced by the socialists in the early 1980s, attempted to open up the recruitment procedure to a wider range of people, such as trade unionists. To date, though, the number of people who enter the schools via this route remains relatively small.

Once at the schools, the training period usually lasts for just over two years. The first year is usually spent on an external placement, often in a public sector organisation, and allows students, who, incidentally, already have the status of civil servants, to learn about the practicalities of administration. The students are then graded on the basis of their performance and this assessment counts towards their final mark. The second year is spent in Paris (and now Strasbourg as well) where the student takes classes on various topics. In the case of ENA, these include budgeting, local administration, EU affairs and the like. At the end of the second year, the students take a series of written tests, produce a number of group reports and face a set of oral examinations.

On the basis of the marks they receive in all of these assessments (and others, including physical education classes), the students are ranked in order of merit. Needless to say, the aim of students is to be ranked as highly as possible. However, this ambition is not simply a matter of personal pride. It is also motivated by the fact that students have the right to choose which administrative post to take up on the basis of this rank order. In other words, the person who is ranked first has the opportunity to land the most prestigious of the very limited number of administrative positions that the minister has placed on offer that year. In fact, the top 20 per cent of students each year usually choose to enter one of the prestigious *grands corps*. The rest will usually enter a government department. All told, therefore, the specialised training procedures for higher civil servants creates not just an elite, but an elite within an elite – the *grands corps*.

In the context of the civil service, the term '*corps*' refers to a group of officials who enjoy the same conditions of service and who carry out the same tasks within the administration. Consequently, every civil servant is a member of a *corps* and there are over 1,300 different *corps* within the French administration. For example, there is a *corps* for civil administrators in Category A of the civil service, as well as for primary school teachers in Category B. At the most senior levels of the administration there are a number of extremely prestigious *corps*. These include the diplomatic *corps* and the prefectoral *corps*. However, the most renowned *corps* are the members of the five *grands corps*: the Inspection des Finances (Finance Inspectorate) for public sector tax inspectors; the Cour des Comptes (Court of Accounts) for public sector auditors; the Conseil d'État (Council of State) for constitutional and administrative lawyers; and both the Mines and the Ponts et Chausées (Bridges and Highways) for technical engineers.

The prestige of the *grands corps* is a result of three main factors. First, they are relatively small institutions. For example, in 1996 there were just fewer than 300 *conseillers d'État* and just over 200 *inspecteurs des Finances*. As a consequence, entry to the *grands corps* is highly sought after. This is one reason why the most successful students at ENA invariably choose one of the three non-technical *corps* ahead of all the other administrative positions that are on offer. Second, many of the members of the *grands corps* are not simply engaged in the execution of government policy, they also have the task of overseeing the work of the other civil servants in the system. So, for example, the Inspection des Finances checks the regularity of public sector expenditure and the Conseil d'État is the highest court of appeal in the system of administrative law. Thus, they occupy a privileged position of responsibility within the administrative system itself. Third, members of these *corps* are regularly to be found not simply in their own specialised institutions, such as the *Conseil d'État*, but right across the highest posts of the administration in general. This is because there is ample opportunity for members to be seconded to ministerial advisory units (or *cabinets*), to government departments or to other key decision-making bodies and also because it is possible for officials to rejoin their *corps* of origin whenever they so wish. This point applies to members of both the technical and non-technical *grands corps* alike.

In fact, the transfer of senior civil servants away from their original posts into new positions is part of a much wider phenomenon known as *pantouflage*. As a result of their demonstrated talents, members of the higher civil service are much sought after. Indeed, many officials take advantage of the contacts they have made to leave the administration altogether and enter the economic and political sphere. With their contacts within the administration and knowledge of how the system works, these officials are extremely attractive to businesses. Indeed, it has been calculated that two-thirds of the hundred largest public and private sector firms in France are headed by graduates of the *grandes écoles*. Equally, as noted above, senior officials often choose to enter politics (see Chapter 5). In this way, the influence of highly trained civil servants is felt not just within the administration, but in many other sectors of civil and public life as well.

Models of the French bureaucracy

There are four main interpretations, or models, of the French bureaucracy. The traditional model, the technocracy model, considers the French civil service to be part of a highly trained, modernising elite. The second model, the power elite model, views the higher civil service as being a part of a powerful and socially unrepresentative ruling class. The third model, the administration and politics model, indicates the interpenetration of the political and administrative classes, underlining both the politicisation of the bureaucracy and the bureaucratisation of politics. The final model, the fragmented bureaucracy model, notes the tensions which exist within the senior civil service and which prevent the emergence of a homogeneous class of decision makers. These four models neatly capture the fundamentally conflicting viewpoints of those who have written about the French bureaucracy. In addition, two general points should be noted about these models. The first is that, as with the analysis in previous chapters, there is a certain degree of overlap among them. Indeed, the differences between the various models are often ones of emphasis and implication rather than conviction and assertion. Second, there are commonalities between models of the French bureaucracy and models of the French state. In particular, there are close links between the first three models presented here and the model of the strong state that was outlined in Chapter 1. Most writers, although not all, assume that the bureaucracy is a constituent part of the French *étatiste* tradition. In addition, there are also close links between the fourth model considered in this chapter and the model of the disoriented state. Here, the fragmentation of the bureaucracy is deemed to be a key element of the heterogeneous nature of the state more generally.

The technocracy model

There are many possible definitions of technocracy. At its most simple, a technocracy may be defined as government by technicians. More broadly, a technocracy occurs where 'an autonomous ruling group [legitimises] its actions by calling upon a coherent "scientific" doctrine of administration' (Stevens, 1996, p. 152). In France, the contemporary analysis of technocracy relies on evidence of the rational and managerial way in which policy problems are approached. All told, three key assumptions are associated with this model. First, senior bureaucrats are considered to be part of an homogeneous set of elite decision makers. Second, the common feature of the members of this elite is that they have undergone a specialised training process. By virtue of this process they are motivated not by ideology or self-interest, but, it is said, by efficiency, modernity, cost/benefit analysis and conceptions of the general interest. Third, those who have undergone this process occupy not just senior positions in the administration, but equivalent positions in both the public sector more generally and, indeed, the private sector as well. Thus, technocrats in the bureaucracy form just one part of a block of actors who put faith in their own capacity to provide technical solutions to social dilemmas.

The origins of the technocracy model go back a long way. Indeed, the desire to install such a system can be traced as far back as the creation of the École Polytechnique in 1794. Somewhat more recently, the basic assumptions of this model are inherent in many studies of the Third and Fourth Republics (1870–1940 and 1946–58, respectively). These regimes were characterised by political and governmental instability and it is often suggested that elite civil servants filled the resulting decision-making gap in order to ensure the continuation and coherence of public policies. Indeed, such was their influence at this time that technocrats were often praised for both their disinterestedness and their foresightedness. It was only with the onset of the Fifth Republic, however, that the technocracy model truly came into intellectual fashion, even if at this time the reputation of technocrats also began to decline. For the most part, those who have proposed the technocracy model since 1958 were writing either in the early years of the regime or about the policy-making process during this period. In this sense, the technocracy model might be seen as the traditional approach to the study of the French bureaucracy under the Fifth Republic. Nevertheless, these studies, it might be argued, maintain a contemporary resonance. Indeed, the accusation that France operates as a technocracy is still levelled against senior bureaucrats by members of the political class, even if it is somewhat ironic that many of those who make this claim have themselves benefited from the specialised training procedures which they are denouncing. Against this background, those who are associated with the technocracy model in the academic context include Meynaud (1968), Powell (1997), Stoffaës (1986), Thoenig (1973) and Williams and Harrison (1971).

The notion that the Fifth Republic might be characterised as a 'technocrat's paradise' (Williams and Harrison, 1971, p. 236) was based on two key arguments. The first argument emphasised the specialised training procedures which these officials had previously undertaken. More often than not those who were recruited to high administrative office had been to either ENA or the X. In this way, senior officials were said to be united by common educational bonds. More specifically, those who passed through these schools were believed to approach problem-solving in the same way. They were trained to think not in terms of ideology but in terms of the most efficient way to pursue policies (Powell, 1997, p. 204). In addition, these bonds were reinforced by the fact that the most successful students at these schools went on to enter the *grands corps*. Here, they received further training which reinforced the basic set of technocratic beliefs which had already been instilled in them. What emerged from this process was a set of highly trained and extremely able officials who were linked by a strong public sector ethos, by a commitment to modernisation and by a grounding in rational decision-making procedures.

The second argument suggested that the newly formed regime provided bureaucrat-technicians with the means by which to exert policy influence. The Fifth Republic increased the role of the state. Thus, technocrats were well placed to be appointed to the most senior levels of the state-centred policy process by virtue of their demonstrated abilities and policy expertise. Moreover, by virtue of the phenomenon of *pantouflage*, *énarques* and *polytechniciens* (graduates of ENA and the X, respectively) developed a privileged set of networks throughout the public and private sectors. Technocrats were to be found not just in the administration but in government, parliament, local government, nationalised industries and the private sector as well. Indeed, the unbiquitousness of technocrats was the key element of Thoenig's classic analysis of policy making under the Fifth Republic. He noted the fact that the most successful graduates of ENA and the X entered the *grands corps*. He then underlined the extent to which members of the *grands corps* were to be found in all areas of policy-making responsibility. As such, he emphasised the 'network of friendships and affinities' which unites members of the *grands corps* and which means that they share 'an intellectual and emotional past, a way of reasoning and common memories' (Thoenig, 1973, p. 274). He also stressed that the *grands corps*, 'enjoying the legitimacy of the State' and 'exploiting their exceptional abilities' (Ibid., p. 278), had no difficulty in occupying key posts from which to exercise influence. In this way, Thoenig was one of those who linked the technocracy model with the strong state model of policy making (see Chapter 1).

On the basis of these arguments the technocratic bias in French policy making was identified in a number of areas. These included studies of French economic planning, industrial policy and rail transport policy. For example, Stoffaës, who identifies the influence of technocrats in his study of high technology policy, argues that the interpenetration of administrative and industrial technocracies 'has no equivalent in the western world, not even in Japan' (Stoffaës, 1986, p. 43). He alludes to the common views of members of the elites who are trained in the same schools and in the same technical subjects. In fact, he argues that it is the level of interpenetration between technocrats in the administrative and industrial sectors which explains 'the close coordination and mutual trust that exist between policymakers in government and planners in large corporations' (Ibid.). He argues that leading bureaucrats, such as Pierre Guillaumat, who founded Elf-Aquitaine, or André Giraud, who worked at the head of the Commission for Atomic Energy in the 1970s, played important roles in the promotion of industrial and technological projects. Indeed, the French policy of national economic champions and the propensity towards high-tech *grands projets* was a consequence, so it might be argued, of the pervasive influence of a state-trained technical elite.

More recently, the role of technocrats in the French policy-making process has been emphasised by Powell (1997). She has indicated the significant role of the 'technostructure', or a 'closely integrated technico-administrative community with a common culture' (Powell, 1997, p. 203), in the formulation of railway policy, particularly in the development of the French high-speed train, the TGV. Powell argues that members of this technostructure, who are trained primarily in the *grandes écoles*, shared similar educational backgrounds and a non-partisan public-service ethos and that the technostructure was endowed with a culture of technical progress, modernity and the objectivity of reason (Ibid., p. 205). The members of this technostructure, she argues, spoke 'the same language' (Ibid., p. 206); and the numerous informal lines of communication and the ease of co-operation between its members meant that officials pursuing the TGV project 'possessed sufficient authority to win over the support of other ministerial divisions and ultimately political backing' (Ibid.). This elite also put long-term interests before short-term political gain and, acting as a policy broker, the 'technico-administrative elite formulated and implemented a railway policy in which engineering concerns ranked high' (Ibid., p. 204). For Powell, therefore, the development of the TGV is best described as an example of ' "technico-economic *dirigisme*" which is to say that direction was imparted not by politicians but by State engineers' (Ibid., p. 208). This is an unequivocal statement of the technocracy model. It might also be noted, though, that Powell argues that the influence of technocrats in the private sector has allowed the policy process to be captured by non-state interests (Powell, 1997). In this sense, she departs from the norm by supporting both the technocracy model and the weak state model (see Chapter 1).

All told, the technocracy model has entered the political mythology of the Fifth Republic. However, it is perhaps significant that many of those associated with this model are careful to temper their analysis of both the extent to which technocrats can shape the policy-making process and the ways in which they do so. So, for example, Williams and Harrison underlined the considerable influence of bureaucrat-technicians, but stated that the Fifth Republic cannot be 'labelled neatly' (1971, p. 243) as a technocracy. Similarly, Thoenig argued that by the 1970s France had entered the era of technocrats, but played down the importance of the training procedures that such officials had undergone. Instead, he argued that their power was a function not so much of their supposed expertise, but the network of contacts which are gained through studying at the *grandes écoles* and by membership of the *grands corps* (Thoenig, 1973, p. 277). Also in this vein, Meynaud (1968) acknowledged the divisions that exist between public and private sector technocrats. He also argued that technocratic power can be constrained by internal rivalries, reactions of pressure groups and the resistance of public opinion (Ibid., pp. 109–10). Furthermore, he argued that it is open to control by determined politicians who 'can intervene and take control of any of these sectors at any time as we have seen from recent developments in economic matters' (Ibid., p. 143). In short, he argued that by the late 1960s government by technocrats had still to be realised (Ibid., p. 73). And yet, unlike those who propose the fragmented bureaucracy model, he did not deny the validity of the technocratic thesis at this time, arguing that technocrats occupied key positions of influence in numerous sectors. He also refused to accept the arguments that played down their influence (Ibid., p. 128). In this way, Meynaud, despite his somewhat circumspect approach to the topic, can still be associated with the technocracy model.

In addition to these auto-qualifications to the technocratic thesis, there are a number of more important critiques of the model by other writers. One common concern is with the definition of technocracy. For example, Suleiman argues that the term is defined in so many ways that it undermines the very validity of the concept. In fact, he asserts its meaning is sometimes stretched so far that it is 'possible to find instances where it means nothing at all' (Suleiman, 1978, p. 162). More specifically, some writers attack the basic assumptions of this model. So, the assumption that studying at a *grande école* provides the basis for technical expertise is often questioned. In particular, it is argued that the training process produces not so much specialist technicians, but generalists. Thus, the administration comprises 'an elite that has made something of a cult out of amateurship' (Suleiman, 1978, p. 166). In addition, the notion that elite civil servants form a homogeneous elite or coherent group is also undermined. The supposedly monolithic technocracy is said in practice to be criss-crossed by multiple cleavages which are not overcome by reference to a common 'language' or shared educational backgrounds. In this case, the fragmented bureaucracy is to be preferred. Finally, even if it is acknowledged that there is a homogeneous bureaucratic elite, the nature of this elite is analysed differently. Thus, for some writers, the French system produces not simply a highly trained elite, but one that is socially unrepresentative. Indeed, this is the key difference between the technocracy model and the next model to be examined.

The power elite model

Like the technocracy model, the power elite model is founded on three basic assumptions. Indeed, the first assumption is the same in the case of both models, namely that senior bureaucrats form part of a homogeneous block of policy actors. The second assumption, however, is where the main difference between this model and the previous one can be found. Here, it is assumed that this block of actors does not constitute a new managerial class, but a socially unrepresentative elite. The power elite, it is argued, works not in the interests of rational or professional objectives, but in defence of the interests of those who share this common social background. Thus, the power elite model dismisses the importance of the alleged expertise and specialised knowledge of senior bureaucrats. Rather, it views the emergence of a power elite as the result of an entrenched system of social reproduction, stressing the shared class, family and educational origins of senior civil servants and the common geographical background from which they are drawn. Finally, and like the technocracy model, the power elite model also assumes that the members of this socially unrepresentative elite have colonised key posts in the economic and political spheres. Thus, it argues that senior bureaucrats form merely one part of a more widespread ruling class that dominates the French decision-making process.

The supposedly meritocratic foundations of the French educational system were questioned as early as the mid-1960s (Bourdieu and Passeron, 1964). That said, the power elite model emerged somewhat later than the technocracy model. Indeed, the main set of studies which can be associated with this model appeared only in the mid-1970s. However, whereas in recent times the technocracy model has gone somewhat out of favour at least among the academic class, the power elite model remains intellectually popular, particularly as a left-wing, neo-Marxist critique of political life. Amongst others, this model has been proposed in the work of some of France's leading sociologists. All told, those who can be identified with the bureaucratic power elite school include Birnbaum (1982a), Birnbaum *et al.* (1978), Denni (1993), Dorandeu (1994) and Marceau (1981).

There are clear links between the technocracy model and the power elite model. For example, Birnbaum, characterising the Fifth Republic as the Republic of functionaries (1982a, p. 45), states that the 'technocratic professionalism of the senior bureaucrats who define the general interest as they understand it has taken precedence over the political professionalism of the traditional politician' (Ibid., p. 65). Moreover, like proponents of the technocracy model, he stresses the process by which elite civil servants have managed to colonise party politics, parliament, ministerial *cabinets* and a significant majority of government posts, arguing that elite civil servants have replaced traditional professional politicians in key areas of decision making. Indeed, he also places particular emphasis on the consequences of *pantouflage* and the presence of elite administrators in the leading managerial posts of nationalised companies and private firms, particularly in the media and banking sectors (Ibid., pp. 102–9). The widespread presence of civil servants in strategic policy-making positions, it is argued, produces a unity of action within the summits of the Fifth Republic, with members of the *grands corps*, who are united by informal networks and common backgrounds, dominating social and economic decision making. As Marceau puts it: 'Powerful persons may be linked together through the overlapping of personnel, through their social contacts (reinforced through marriage in particular), and through the symbolic (cultural) factors encouraging the cohesion of the group. The separation is an artificial one – in reality all are aspects of the same phenomenon. Whether in politics, administration or business, personal linkages tend towards the closure of the ruling groups' (Marceau, 1981, p. 66).

The main difference between the power elite model and the technocracy model concerns the emphasis which is placed on the social background of this 'ruling class' (Birnbaum *et al.*, 1978): 'recruited from the same social space, from amongst the same social class, the French ruling class appears as a social group which is closed upon itself' (Ibid., p. 187). So, in a study of senior officials Birnbaum found that an overwhelming percentage (103 of 253) of those who had graduated from ENA between 1953 and 1963 and who had then gone into one of the *grands corps* were also the children of higher civil servants (Birnbaum, 1982a, p. 69). It was also discovered that a large percentage of higher civil servants lived not just in the Paris region, as one might expect given that they work there, but predominantly in the more fashionable areas of the capital and its closest suburbs (Birnbaum *et al.*, 1978, pp. 151–3). Indeed, one writer quotes a subsequent study which showed that 40 per cent of all *inspecteurs des Finances* lived in one of the two of the most exclusive districts in Paris, namely the 7th or the 16th *arrondissements* (Dorandeu, 1994, p. 118). Perhaps most importantly, an extremely high percentage of senior officials came from a privileged social background. So, 50 per cent of *énarques* who were members of a *grands corps* were from a bourgeois family background (Denni, 1993, p. 420). Furthermore, as noted in the first section of this chapter, there is also a considerable educational homogeneity to the senior civil service. Not only did most senior bureaucrats study at ENA or the X, but many also took preparatory classes at the Institut d'Études Politiques in Paris and, moreover, a considerable number went to school at one or other of the most prestigious *lycées* in the Paris region.

Overall, it is argued, the system is characterised not so much by the functional homogeneity of the bureaucratic elite as they carry out many different tasks, but more by a collective social identity (Dorandeu, 1994, p. 119). Moreover, this identity is shared not just by the members of the senior civil service, but by members of the wider public and private sector elites as well – the ruling class. Finally, the links between the members of this class continue, so it is argued, 'to act to limit severely the possibilities of access to powerful positions by members born into any groups but those already in dominant positions' (Marceau, 1981, p. 75).

Despite the compelling survey evidence in favour of the bureaucratic power elite model, this thesis appears to suffer from the same basic problems as the technocracy model. First, some writers prefer to place the emphasis not so much on an all-encompassing ruling class but on the development of a politico-administrative set of decision makers. Here, the social background of the senior members of the bureaucracy is less important than both the politicisation of the higher levels of the administration and the extent to which bureaucrats have moved into political life. Second, other writers stress developments such as the creation of independent administrative authorities (see Chapter 1), Europeanisation and the 'hollowing out' of the French state. These developments, it might be argued, undermine the foundations of bureaucratic power and so render unimportant any evidence about the common social origins of senior officials. This line of thought can be discerned in the fragmented bureaucracy model. Third, and perhaps most importantly, some writers argue that the notion of an all-pervasive elite ruling class is flawed, because it simply does not exist. For example, in his study of graduates from ENA Kesler not only disputes the existence of an '*énarchie*' (1997, p. 23), but argues that the high-profile nature of *énarques* in politics has led to an over-emphasis of bureaucratic power in France (Ibid., p. 24). Instead, his research suggests that many of those who occupy important positions within the administration are actually drawn from quite modest social backgrounds. In this context, the reforms which attempted to open up the process of recruitment to the *grandes écoles* in the early 1980s appear to have borne some fruit.

The administration and politics model

The administration and politics model makes two key assumptions. As before, the first of these assumptions is that senior bureaucrats form part of a homogeneous block of policy actors who share certain common characteristics. Moreover, many of the most influential writers associated with this model acknowledge the importance of the elite administrative training schools and stress the socially unrepresentative nature of this set of decision makers. However, the main difference between this model and the two previous models concerns the second assumption which is made. Here, overwhelming emphasis is placed, first, on the party political nature of the bureaucracy and, second, on the extent to which bureaucrats have entered the political sphere. There has been, so it is argued, an interpenetration of the higher echelons of the bureaucracy and party politics. There has been a politicisation of the bureaucracy and a bureaucratisation of politics. In short, the Fifth Republic has witnessed the emergence of a politico-administrative class of senior decision makers, or, more accurately, it has witnessed the emergence of two opposing politico-administrative classes, one associated with the left and another with the right.

The administration and politics model emerged during the Fifth Republic. In particular, it appeared in response to developments under the gaullist presidencies and the evidence which suggested both that the Gaullist Party was colonising senior posts in the administration and that more and more leading bureaucrats were entering political life (see Chapter 5). That said, the main body of academic literature associated with this model appeared in the late 1970s. The presidency of Giscard d'Estaing supposedly accelerated the intertwining of the political and administrative spheres. Thus, it was argued that by this time the relationship between decision makers in the two domains had been fundamentally altered. In this context, the main body of work associated with this model constitutes the contributions to the de Baecque and Quermonne (1981) edited volume and also includes Quermonne (1991).

There is a certain degree of overlap between this model and both the previous model and the model which follows. So, for example, Quermonne acknowledges the privileged social backgrounds from which senior civil servants are drawn, stating that the higher civil service forms 'not only part of the administrative elite, but also the country's ruling class' (Quermonne, 1991, p. 193). Equally, Quermonne signals some of the factors which fragment the administration. In particular, he distinguishes between two types of senior civil servants: the managers and the leaders, the latter, in contrast to the former, being the ones who enter the *grands corps* and who can hope to hold top office (Ibid., p. 214). He also distinguishes between two types of *énarques*: the *grands fonctionnaires*, whose career lies solely within the public sector, and the *transfuges* who leave the administration often to enter politics (Ibid., p. 217).

This overlap aside, the distinguishing feature of those associated with this model is that above all else they emphasise the links between the administrative and political classes. In this context, de Baecque provides ample evidence of the extent to which bureaucrats have moved into political life (de Baecque, 1981). For example, he shows that in the 1962 government 27 per cent of all government ministers were appointed directly from the senior civil service (Ibid., p. 25). Indeed, the number of ministers who had a civil service background, even if subsequently they had gone into politics, was even higher. So, 66 per cent of the total number of ministers in the 1973 Messmer government were drawn from this socio-professional category (Ibid., p. 28). In addition, de Baecque illustrates the bureaucratisation of the legislature. He shows that 13.2 per cent of all deputies in the 1978 legislature were members of the *grands corps* (Ibid., p. 34). What is more, if this figure is calculated to include not just senior civil servants but all state employees (including teachers and military personnel), then the figure increases to nearly 39 per cent (Ibid.). In a similar vein, he also demonstrates the extent to which civil servants are present in the highest institutions of political parties and in local government too (Ibid., pp. 44–5). All told, these figures lead him to assert that 'we are quite entitled to ask ourselves about the risks to the proper functioning of the regime and the very principles of democracy which is caused by the extensive interpenetration of political and administrative figures' (Ibid., p. 21).

In the same study, de Baecque questions the political colonisation of the administration, even though he does note that an increasing number of deputies were appointed by the government to head task forces that themselves had an administrative dimension (Ibid., p. 50). However, in a later work, Quermonne argues that there is now a very specific French type of spoils system whereby incoming governments have the opportunity to shape the party political complexion of the bureaucracy (Quermonne, 1991, p. 237). Thus, the arrival of a new government regularly brings with it a series of changes in the higher levels of many state structures. This is particularly true with regard to prefects, the central state's main representatives in local government (see Chapter 4); heads of departmental divisions, the most senior administrative figures within a ministry; ambassadors; directors of education (*recteurs*); even leading figures in the wider public sector, including nationalised industries. Indeed, in 1986 the General Secretary of the Government, the most senior civil servant in the governmental system and who had been appointed under the socialist administration, was replaced in his post when the gaullist-dominated right-wing coalition took power (see the party government model in Chapter 5).

With regard to the administrative colonisation of politics, three factors help to explain this phenomenon. First, the rules that govern the civil service encourage bureaucrats to enter political life because they know that, if unsuccessful, they can return to their administrative post at any time. Second, the general mistrust of political parties (see Chapter 5) encouraged political leaders, particularly in the early years of the Fifth Republic, to privilege the role of bureaucrats and bring them into the political domain. Third, the interpenetration of administration and politics is self-reinforcing. Bureaucrat-politicians use their administrative contacts when searching for party political appointments and their political contacts when looking for administrative appointments. In terms of the party colonisation of the administration, Quermonne also cites three factors which account for this practice (Quermonne, 1991, pp. 237–8). First, the government has a large number of senior administrative posts at its discretion. Indeed, the number of posts under this heading was increased in 1985. Second, the role of ministerial *cabinets*, or personal advisory staffs, has become more important. Members of these organisations, which consist of loyal appointees who share the minister's political preoccupations, will often intervene in the work of the permanent administration in order to pursue the minister's interests. Third, successive governments have used their powers to appoint party figures to the *grands corps*. However, rather than rendering the *corps* more socially representative as was initially envisaged, this practice has merely politicised entry to the *grands corps*.

There is now, therefore, a distinct politico-administrative class, or, more properly, two competing and politically opposed politico-administrative classes – one left wing and one right wing (Ibid., p. 237). The effect of this development has been to change the traditional relationship between the administration and politics. Previously, the two spheres were separate. The political class was charged with making decisions because it was accountable. The administrative class was responsible for the impartial implementation of those decisions. Now, though, the two spheres of activity are no longer so autonomous. On the one hand, the politicisation of the bureaucracy means that governments increasingly rely on their extensive powers of administrative appointment in order to facilitate the implementation of their programme. On the other hand, the bureaucratisation of politics means that the power of the state, or State power (*le pouvoir d'État*), has been reinforced (Quermonne, 1981). For Quermonne, these changes are closely bound up with the presidentialisation of the Fifth Republic under de Gaulle, Pompidou and Giscard (see Chapter 2), as well as the general re-establishment of political authority and the stability of the regime since 1958.

There are two basic criticisms of the administration and politics model. The first criticism concerns the emphasis of the model. Those who promote other schools of thought do not neglect the developments which have just been outlined. Indeed, an analysis of the interpenetration of the political and administrative classes was one of the key elements of Birnbaum's thesis (Birnbaum, 1982a). Instead, these writers simply prefer to play down the importance of this aspect of the political system and privilege other factors which are considered to be more salient, such as the socially unrepresentative nature of the French ruling class as a whole (like the power elite model) or the managerial bias of senior decision makers (like the technocracy model). The second criticism concerns the assumption that the politico-administrative elite, or at least both left- and right-wing manifestations of it, can be considered as a homogeneous set of people. For some writers, this assumption is false. Instead, the senior civil service comprises a host of separate and warring fiefdoms. In this case, the fragmented bureaucracy model, it might be argued, provides a better description of administrative reality.

The fragmented bureaucracy model

The fragmented bureaucracy model shares a number of common points with previous models. In particular, those who propose the fragmented bureaucracy model rarely attempt to deny that senior civil servants and members of the wider policy-making community are overwhelmingly drawn from a particular social background. Equally, most of the people associated with this model would also acknowledge the growing links between the administrative and political classes. Instead, what distinguishes this model from the previous ones is the emphasis that its proponents then place on the factors which divide the members of the higher civil service and which also divide these senior civil servants from members of the wider public- and private-sector elites. The analysis of the precise causes of these divisions, be they educational, functional or a mixture of both, varies from one writer to another. However, what is common to those who put forward this model is the argument that senior civil servants do not comprise a homogeneous group of decision makers. Instead, the bureaucracy is said to be racked with tensions, with bureaucrats being more concerned with intra-administrational turf wars than rational, directive policy making.

The fragmented bureaucracy model has a considerable pedigree and is supported by a number of very eminent writers. It first emerged in the late 1960s and 1970s as an explicit reaction to the technocracy model. At this time, it was particularly associated with the work of Ridley (1966), Ridley and Blondel (1964), Stevens (1978), Suleiman (1974; 1978) and Wright (1974; 1989). More recently, though, the fragmented bureaucracy model can be associated with a different set of work. This work focuses on the transformation of the French state in the 1980s and 1990s. In particular, so it is argued, the introduction of new public management reforms and the Europeanisation of the policy process has affected the organisation of the French bureaucracy, rendering it less cohesive and less exceptional in comparative terms (see Chapter 8). In this context, the fragmented bureaucracy model can be discerned in the work of Dupuy and Thoenig (1983; and 1985), Muller (1992a), Rouban (1990; 1998) and Thoenig (1987).

In the earliest studies associated with this model writers were concerned to address the issue of whether France had become a technocracy. In this context, Ridley (1966) and Ridley and Blondel (1964) concluded that the elite civil service 'has been one of the main driving forces, if not the driving force in French life – and it is likely to remain so' (Ridley and Blondel, 1964, p. 54). They even went as far as to claim that it is 'undeniable that much of the industrial process of France since the war has been due to the skill and initiative of these technicians–administrators' (Ibid., p. 212). At the same time, however, these writers explicitly attacked the presumed homogeneity of the elite civil service. For example, although Ridley acknowledged that civil servants share a broad outlook on what might be termed standard practices and general objectives, he also argued that they did not share a common policy on specific issues (Ridley, 1966, p. 42). In particular, Ridley identified five factors which served to divide the higher civil service: the distinction between technical and politico-legal services; conflicts based on functions, such as spending ministries versus the Finance Ministry; the different spheres of competence within a ministry itself; the rivalries between different *corps*; and the differences between the politicised elements of the civil service, notably members of ministerial *cabinets*, versus the non-politicised elements (Ridley, 1966). All told, Ridley concluded that the elite members of the civil service do not act as a class and that they are motivated not so much by concerns about modernisation but by other factors, such as the pursuit of personal goals (Ibid., p. 52).

In his work, Vincent Wright offers a somewhat similar argument but with a slightly different slant (Wright, 1974; 1989). Indeed, he provides an explicit critique of Ridley's thesis. In so doing, he focuses on the issue of what motivates civil servants. In particular, he casts doubt on Ridley's assertion that the common social origins and training of higher officials mean that bureaucrats necessarily share any common loyalties or outlook (Wright, 1974, pp. 52–3). Instead, he suggests that the beliefs of civil servants are affected by a multiplicity of factors. Indeed, in a memorable quotation he states that the 'attitudes of a one-legged Protestant transvestite bourgeois *Énarque* may be shaped as much by his physical deformity, his religion or his sexual abnormality as by his social origins or his professional training' (Wright, 1989, p. 121). In particular, Wright emphasises the functional differences between civil servants. It is in this respect that the arguments of both writers resemble each other. However, there is no doubt that Wright is quite unequivocal on this point. Indeed, he states that the 'importance of function in determining attitudes cannot be underestimated' (Wright, 1974, p. 54). Moreover, Wright also suggests that the divisions within the civil service weaken the capacity of the state to pursue the policies that it wishes. 'Certain officials in parts of the administration', he states, 'do enjoy considerable influence but they are by no means alone in the complex fabric of public decision-making, and the price of their power is dependence upon, and co-operation with, the other decision-makers' (Wright, 1989, p. 131). All in all, he argues, France has a 'politico-administrative system which appears to evoke more readily the surrealism of the Wonderland of Alice than the intellectual order of the Universe of Descartes' (Wright, 1974, p. 65).

A similar, but somewhat more comprehensive, argument is pursued in the work of Suleiman (1974; 1978). As with other writers, Suleiman repeatedly stresses that the French system is characterised by an elite, based around the *grands corps*, which shares certain common educational and social characteristics. At the same time, it is the diverse nature of this elite, he argues, which is the key characteristic of the system. He argues that, in order to maintain the interests of their members, the *grands corps* have been forced to adapt to changing economic and political conditions. The result, though, is that they 'are obliged, like Marx's capitalists, to search constantly for other markets. In doing so, they inevitably create a certain element of diversity within themselves' (Suleiman, 1978, p. 211). In short, the *corps* have developed as little more than 'placement bureaux' (Ibid., p. 176) for their members who use their experience of 'state educa-tion and state service as a base from which to launch themselves into other careers' (Ibid., p. 12). However, the inherent imperialism of the *grands corps*, and the concomitant imperative to extend their influence, attract the 'best' and legitimise their standing undermines any classification of their members as a homogeneous elite pursuing a coherent set of policies. Instead, even though there is inter-*corps* solidarity when the interests of the system as a whole are threatened, there is also inter-*corps* rivalry as well. For the most part, this rivalry is expressed through competition for posts, rather than issues of policy (Ibid., p. 184). As Suleiman states:

> The commitment of the elite is to the health and well-being of its corporate organisations, rather than to a set of policies. Policies are looked upon as a means of enlarging a *corps*' domain, of leaving it unchanged, or of reducing it. The reaction to particular policies depends on such criteria.
>
> (Ibid., p. 249)

At the same time, like Ridley and Wright, Suleiman also stresses that members of the elite civil servants carry out quite separate functions. In this case, their common social origins and training are unlikely to provide the opportunity for a homogeneous response to policy issues across sectors (Ibid., p. 245). Ultimately, he concludes that the demands of the office held by individuals dictate their behaviour. Indeed, Suleiman directly counters Meynaud's argument about technocracy in this respect. He argues that when:

> Meynaud discusses the homogeneity of technicians, he reverts to their social origins to prove his point. And it is this that indicates a basic flaw in his analysis: he makes no allowance for any degree of func-tional autonomy and thus misconstrues the nature of interests upon which men [sic] act.
>
> (Suleiman, 1974, p. 378)

Instead, Suleiman stresses the 'internecine' (Ibid., p. 379) conflicts which occur between civil servants which often shape policy making. The policy-making process, therefore, is by no means rational. Indeed, like Wright, he argues that the divisions within the bureaucracy weaken the overall capacity of the state to direct the course of policy making (see Chapter 1).

In addition to these early studies, more recent work has confirmed the fragmentation of the French bureaucracy. This work, though, tends to do so by emphasising the changes that the administration has undergone since the 1980s. These changes, it might be argued, have undermined the capacity of the bureaucracy to act as a homogeneous block. As such, in these studies the contemporary role of the bureaucracy cannot be dissociated from the crisis of traditional modes of state intervention in France (see the model of the disorientated French state in Chapter 1).

An example of these studies is provided by Dupuy and Thoenig (1983; 1985) and Thoenig (1987). In contrast to Thoenig's earlier work (see above), these studies underline the increasing fragmentation of the French bureaucracy by examining the changes that it has undergone since the 1970s. In particular, five points are emphasised. First, the portrayal of the bureaucracy as a monolithic organisation is now rejected in favour of the picture of a 'shattered and varied universe of multiple bureaux and institutions of all sorts' (Dupuy and Thoenig, 1983, p. 128) based on the *corps*, the importance of local administrative actors and the functional differences between state services (Thoenig, 1987, p. 531). Second, the bureaucracy is no longer governed by such rigid rules as before. There is now more latitude for civil servants to deal with issues on a more flexible basis (Ibid., p. 532). Third, the bureaucracy is no longer characterised by a top-down pyramid of authority. There are horizontal co-ordinating agencies as well as localised areas of responsibility which, again, reduce the level of cohesion within the administration (Ibid., pp. 533–4). Fourth, there is a much clearer distinction between policy making and policy implementation (Ibid., p. 534). Fifth, the very notion that the state and the bureaucracy should play such an important part in political life as before has been undermined (Ibid., pp. 535–6). The state is more of a regulator than a force for change. In sum, Thoenig states that 'there is no longer an Administration, but as many administrations as there are areas of public-sector intervention and collective problems' (Thoenig, 1987, p. 529).

More explicitly, Rouban (1990) argues that the traditional model of the French administration is in crisis and in three particular ways. First, there has been a general increase in the number of people who want the state and the public sector, including the bureaucracy, to play a more managerial role. In other words, there is a crisis of faith in what public administration can successfully achieve. As a result, governments have had increasing recourse to independent administrative authorities or regulatory agencies (see Chapter 1). These institutions have served to create a more 'polycentric model' (Rouban, 1990, p. 533) of decision making in which the leading role of the public sector is questioned. Second, and like the previous model, Rouban highlights the increased politicisation of the civil service which subordinates elite administrators to political actors and which undermines their claims to expertise and neutrality (Ibid., p. 534). In addition, this phenomenon also increases the vertical divisions between divisions within the same ministry and between ministries themselves. In this context, policy co-ordination is more difficult and policy making becomes more sectoral. Finally, decentralisation has reversed previous top-down information flows between the centre and the local and increased the range of actors, public and private, who are involved in the policy process (Ibid., p. 536).

Finally, in a more recent and wide-ranging book, Rouban provides an explicit counter-argument to the technocracy model. Consistent with his previous work and with other writers associated with this model, his thesis is based on the argument that the bureaucracy is fragmented and he attacks those who put forward the technocracy thesis for assuming the opposite. On the contrary, he states, the 'fact that one belongs to the higher levels of the public service is not a sufficient condition of homogeneity' (Rouban, 1998, p. 43). That France cannot be considered a technocracy is at least partly a func-tion of the rivalries between *corps*, the politicisation of the administration and the different functional loyalties that can be observed amongst the set of senior civil servants. However, Rouban also points to a number of specific developments which render the basic assumptions of the technocracy model redundant. First, he emphasises the increasing number of social actors in the policy process. Public sector actors are now faced with a bewildering variety of often contradictory demands. This renders the capacity for coherent and systematic action more difficult. Instead, the administrative system is more and more 'porous' (Ibid., p. 59) as new, hybrid and sometimes *ad hoc* methods of state–society interaction are sought. Second, Rouban examines the changing context of policy expertise. The political agenda is now concerned not just with traditional issues about the organisation of the economy and society, but with new issues, such as medical ethics, environ-mental issues and questions of personal morality (Ibid., p. 70). In these areas, bureaucrats cannot hope to claim a monopoly of expertise. Again, therefore, they are obliged to interact with social actors in new and differentiated ways. Third, Rouban also focuses on the growing importance of the EU in the policy-making process. In particular, he stresses the extent to which national administrations are now increasingly preoccupied with the implementation of European-inspired policies in many different domains, rather than the elaboration of strategic policy initiatives (Ibid., pp. 84–5). Finally, he pays particular attention to the reform of the public sector in France. The need for public services to respond more to the wishes of the citizen–consumer, the desire to provide a more collective approach to problem solving and the increasing importance of policy evaluation have all changed the traditional role of the bureaucracy (Ibid., pp. 98–9).

There are number of potential flaws in the thinking of those associated with the fragmented bureaucracy model. First, it might be argued that this model unfairly plays down the capacity of senior decision makers to co-ordinate the fragmented policy process. According to this line of thought, technocrats, or members of the ruling class, or the politico-administrative elite (depending on which model one supports) occupy a privileged position from which to provide some sort of coherence to policy making. So, it can be acknowledged that there are functional divisions, and, indeed, many other sorts of divisions, between members of the administration, but the French practice of elite training schools, *grands corps* and *pantouflage* creates a unifying, co-ordinating force at the apex of the system. Second, there is a further argument which is reminiscent of the criticism of some of the other more contemporary models in this book. The contempoary academic trend is to deconstruct the decision-making process, to examine politics sectorally and to avoid macro-level analysis. By its very nature, though, this type of approach is bound to result in the rejection of 'grand' theories based on the identification of apparently homogeneous blocks of actors. Instead, it promotes supposedly realistic, essentially pluralist, accounts of political life. What this means, though, is that the fragmented bureaucracy model is simply the function of a specific research approach. If this is the case, then other models which are simply the function of a different research approach, but one that is more amenable to macro-level generalisations, are, arguably, equally valid. In this case, the first three models to be considered in this chapter remain intellectually plausible.

Conclusion

There are strong links between the study of the state (see Chapter 1) and the study of the bureaucracy. This is hardly surprising. After all, bureaucrats (understood in the broadest possible sense) staff the many and varied organisations that comprise the state sector. At the same time, though, the debate about the bureaucracy has its own separate and competing assumptions (see Table 3.1). Students of the bureaucracy have to decide which of these assumptions is the most convincing on the basis of the best available evidence. In this context, the most fundamental choice currently concerns whether or not senior bureaucrats form part of a wider and homogeneous set of elite decision makers. If so, then further choices must be made. Is this elite defined by their rational approach to decision making, by their privileged social characteristics or by their party political affiliations? If not, is it the case that the bureaucracy consists of a fragmented body of organisations and, therefore, that bureaucrats comprise distinct and heterogeneous sets of competing individuals? Those who study the bureaucracy have increasingly tended to follow the latter line of enquiry. Over time, in this area as elsewhere, disaggregated accounts of the decision-making process have increasingly been promoted at the expense of broader generalisations. So, while it is certainly the case that the power elite model still has some very influential proponents, it is also the case that support for the fragmented bureaucracy model has flourished.

The continuing development of the fragmented bureaucracy model is particularly encouraging because for a long time the study of the French bureaucracy has been extremely narrow and unnecessarily restricted, at least from a comparative perspective. As has been seen, studies in this area were for the most part dominated by quasi-sociological research projects which were designed to identify the social and political background of the politico-administrative elite. Much of this work was concerned with identifying where senior civil servants live, which *lycées* they attended, what professions their fathers were engaged in, which administrative training schools they went to, the *grands corps* to which they belonged and so forth. The portrait of a typical senior bureaucrat could then be constructed on the basis of which a picture of the values, attitudes and motivations of the entire senior bureaucracy could be posited. There was, and there remains, a great deal to commend in research projects of this sort. They provide a large data base of information which would otherwise not be available. They also permit the development of sophisticated and competing sets of arguments. They do, however, represent only one way of approaching the issues surrounding the nature of a bureaucracy in a contemporary political system. There are, it must be appreciated, many alternative perspectives which could be adopted. This is why the continuing development of the fragmented bureaucracy model is so important. This approach adopts not just a different set of key assumptions from the technocracy, power elite and administration and politics models, it also generates a completely different type of research agenda. Here, what needs to be explored is the issue of how preferences are formed in the first place, how they are expressed in the workplace and how they are transformed over time. These types of questions necessitate qualitative rather than statistical studies. They privilege individual histories, rather than broad generalisations. They emphasise the need to contextualise the subject matter rather than abstract it. There is, clearly, a considerable degree of scope for this model to be expanded. It does, however, show that there is a methodological alternative to the quasi-sociological studies that have dominated the study of the French bureaucracy for so long. It also suggests that there may be considerable merit in applying other, equally different, methodologies to the study of this topic. There is, for example, scope for budget-maximising models to be explored in the context of the French bureaucracy, for the bureau-shaping model to be applied to the French administration and for the literature on network analysis to be adapted to suit the French case.

All told, the study of the French bureaucracy has a long and highly auspicious intellectual history. At the same time, it can only be hoped that the study of this topic will diversify in the years to come so as to generate a new and perhaps somewhat more invigorating research agenda.

Table 3.1 Models of the French bureaucracy

	Technocracy	Power elite	Administration and politics	Fragmented bureaucracy
Definition/key assumptions	1 Bureaucrats are part of a homogeneous elite 2 Members of this elite have undergone a special training process 3 Those with this training occupy other senior positions in the public and private sectors	1 Bureaucrats are part of a homogeneous elite 2 Members of this elite are from a socially unrepresentative class 3 Those from this class occupy other senior positions in the public and private sectors	1 Bureaucrats are part of an homogeneous elite 2 The members of this elite form a politico-administrative class	1 Bureaucrats do not comprise a group of homogeneous decision makers 2 Bureaucrats are more concerned with turf wars than rational policy making
Proponents	Meynaud (1968), Powell (1997), Stoffaës (1986), Thoenig (1973) and Williams and Harrison (1971)	Birnbaum (1982a), Birnbaum *et al.* (1978), Denni (1993) and Dorandeu (1994)	The contributions to de Baecque and Quermonne (eds.) (1981) and Quermonne (1991)	Dupuy and Thoenig (1983, 1985), Ridley (1966), Ridley and Blondel (1964), Rouban (1990, 1998), Suleiman (1974, 1978), Thoenig (1987) and Wright (1974, 1989)
Argument/evidence	Technocrats are united by common educational bonds (ENA and X) and approach problem solving in terms of the most efficient way to pursue policies Through *pantouflage*, technocrats develop networks throughout the public and private sectors	The members of the ruling class, including senior bureaucrats are drawn from a socially unrepresentative, middle-class, Paris-oriented background	Bureaucrats have moved into political life The bureaucracy has been politicised	Bureaucrats do not act as a class. They are motivated by self-interest and institutional loyalty Recently, the state has become more divided. There is less opportunity for common action. The policy process is more fragmented
Criticisms	1 The concept is defined in too many different ways 2 Civil servants are not experts but generalists 3 Bureaucrats do not form a homogeneous elite 4 Even if they are an elite, they are united by social origins not technocratic training	1 Bureaucrats do not form a homogeneous elite 2 Even if there is an elite, it is a politico-administrative elite 3 Evidence suggests a ruling class simply does not exist	1 This model is not inconsistent with the technocracy or power elite model: these models simply assert that party political concerns are not the main motivating force 2 The politico-administrative class does not form a homogeneous elite	1 Senior decision makers can co-ordinate the fragmented policy process either because of their technocratic, social or politico-administrative background 2 The methodology is antithetical to 'grand' theories. However, other methodologies are valid

4   Local government

France is a patchwork of local, regional and sub-national identities. There are long-standing micro-national aspirations in Corsica, the Basque area, Catalonia and Brittany. There are well established cultural and sociological differences between the south-west and the north (Todd, 1990). There are highly entrenched local rivalries between neighbouring communes, departments and regions. In this context, it was frequently argued that the only way to bring together the disparate elements of the French hexagon was to rule them from the centre – from Paris. The central state had to be strong and directive, so the argument went, because if the different sub-central areas were given the power to rule themselves then the country would collapse and break up into its constituent parts. Over time, though, the traditional organisation of central–local relations was challenged. Most notably, following his election in 1981 François Mitterrand promised to make decentralisation the '*grande affaire*' of his presidency. To this end, he appointed the long-serving mayor of Marseilles and socialist 'baron', Gaston Defferre, to the post of Minister of the Interior and Decentralisation. The first Defferre decentralisation law was passed on 2 March 1982 and over the course of the next four years a further 22 laws were passed and 170 ministerial decrees were issued in this domain. In terms of the quantity of legislation, if nothing else, decentralisation was indeed the main undertaking of Mitterrand's first term of office.

Arguably, however, local government was never as constrained as many of the traditional accounts of French centre–periphery relations have led us to believe. Moreover, for some, the Defferre reforms, and subsequent initiatives, merely reinforced rather than revolutionised the complex nature of centre–local relations that had previously been in place. In short, there is a long-standing debate as to the true nature of centre–periphery relations in the supposedly 'one and indivisible Republic'.

This chapter examines the competing models of centre–local relations in France. It considers the nature of local government, the key actors in the relationship between central and local government and the patterns of interaction between representatives at the two levels. The chapter begins by analysing the changes in French local government in recent years, particularly in the light of the Defferre reforms. It then goes on to identify three separate models of centre–local relations in France: the agent model, the model of cross-regulation, which has both an institutional and a sociological variant, and the model of local governance.

The organisation of French local government

The roots of the contemporary system of local government go back to the French Revolution and the immediate post-revolutionary period. During this time, centre–local relations were conceived in terms of two overriding concerns: national unity and equality before the law (Schmidt, 1990, p. 4). The fear that local democracy would weaken the very foundations of national unity meant that the centre was reluctant to concede autonomy to the localities because of the potential consequences of so doing. At the same time, the fear that liberty at the local level would create inequalities between different local areas meant that central government was unwilling to grant local representatives significant decision-making responsibilities. These concerns resulted in a jacobin-inspired system of unitary government. According to this system, actors at the local level could exercise only those few powers that had been granted to them by those at the central level. Indeed, this system, which was further underpinned during the Napoleonic regime, constituted the basis of the French form of local government for many years thereafter. Since this time there have been only two periods of major reform to the structure of centre–local relations. The first main reforming period was from 1871 to 1984 at the beginning of the Third Republic. The most notable change at this time was the increased powers of mayors and the general reorganisation of local government at the departmental and communal level. Although certain regionalisation reforms were introduced in the period from the 1950s to the 1970s, the second main reforming period was from 1981 to 1986 when the socialists won power for the first time in the Fifth Republic. The Defferre decentralisation reforms redefined the powers of local government, established a third tier of elected authorities at the regional level, but maintained a unitary system of government. Thus, the history of centre–periphery relations in France is marked by both strong elements of continuity and short periods of not insignificant organisational change. Against this background, it is useful to identify the organisation of the three main actors in the centre–local relationship: elected local authorities; state-appointed prefects; and ministerial field services.

Elected local authorities

There are three levels of elected local authorities: communal, departmental and regional.

The commune system was created in 1789. There are over 36,000 communes in the country. This figure means that most of the communes are very small. Indeed, over 60 per cent of communes have fewer than 500 inhabitants, 80 per cent have fewer than 1,000 inhabitants and 90 per cent have fewer than 2,000 inhabitants. At the same time, though, some communes are very large. Major cities, such as Paris, Bordeaux and Lille, are all communes in their own right. The elected authority in the commune is the municipal council which is made up of directly elected municipal councillors. Elections to municipal councils take place every six years on the basis of a mixed proportional representation/majority system. Since the Third Republic reforms, incoming municipal councillors have elected a mayor from amongst their number. Mayors are very much more than just ceremonial figureheads. The mayor is the chief executive of the commune. Mayors are responsible for a number of administrative duties, registering births and deaths, drawing up the electoral registers and conducting civil marriage ceremonies. More politically, they are formally responsible for the work of the municipal council and, hence, for the functions that the council carries out. In larger towns, this means that the mayor is an extremely important and respected local political figure. Communes have responsibility in their area for matters such as hygiene (refuse collection and water supply), primary schools (although they do not employ teachers nor do they set the curriculum), libraries and museums, certain town planning functions and the upkeep of local roads. In the exercise of these functions, municipal councils employ large numbers of people. Indeed, in the case of large city communes the municipality may employ thousands of workers. One consequence of this situation is that 60 per cent of all state transfer payments to local authorities go to municipal councils.

Departments were reorganised in 1790. There are currently 100 departments, including four overseas departments: Guadeloupe and Martinique in the West Indies, Réunion in the Indian Ocean and French Guyana in South America. The elected authority at the departmental level is the general council. General councillors are elected every six years by way of a two-ballot majority electoral system in constituencies known as cantons. Since they were reformed in the early years of the Third Republic, departmental councils, or general councils as they are called, have each been headed by a president. However, these people have traditionally been less important figures than mayors. This is because the key person in the department was always the centrally appointed prefect (see pp. 76–7). Indeed, until the socialist decentralisation reforms of 1982, the chief executive of the general council was the prefect and not the president of the elected council. Furthermore, until the Defferre reforms, the general council had no executive branch and so did not employ large numbers of council workers. The general council is responsible for the maintenance and upkeep of certain major roads. It also runs the council housing system, organises the school bus system, provides tourist facilities and is responsible for rural development. Moreover, since the Defferre reforms, the department has assumed a certain responsibility for sanitation, the running of *collèges* (or junior high schools) and the administration of social welfare functions. In total, 30 per cent of all state transfer payments to local authorities go to the departmental level.

Regional councils were first established in 1972. At this time they were created as administrative co-ordinating units rather than decision-making entities. This changed, though, with the 1982 decentralisation reforms. Since 1986, regional councils have been directly elected by way of a proportional representation system. This has given regions a legitimacy which they did not previously enjoy. Elections are now held every six years. In addition, the profile of regional government has also increased because of the EU's decision to administer structural funds at least partly through regional authorities. This has encouraged some politicians, who might otherwise have sought election to municipal or general councils, to stand for office at the regional level. So, arguably, regional councils are becoming increasingly important local actors. They have the power to draw up regional economic plans, to facilitate apprenticeship schemes and to promote local businesses. Since the Defferre reforms, they are also responsible for running secondary schools (or *lycées*). In total, 10 per cent of all state transfer payments to local authorities go to regional councils. In this way, despite their increased profile, they remain the least well-developed tier of local government.

The different levels of local government are not organised hierarchically. No tier of government is formally subordinate to another. Moreover, there is a degree of overlap between office-holders at the various levels of local government and, indeed, office-holders at these levels and those at the national level by virtue of the practice of multiple office-holding, or the *cumul des mandats*. This is the situation where individuals can hold elected office at more than one level of government simultaneously. The Defferre reforms limited to two the number of elected offices which could be held at any one time. However, most national political figures continue to hold elected office at the local level as well. Finally, it should be noted that in a historical context the practice of multiple office-holding helped to created local barons, or *notables*, whose influence in their local area was often extremely pronounced.

Prefects

The prefectoral system was established by Napoleon Bonaparte in 1800. The system was deliberately designed to facilitate the control of the periphery by the centre. The prefect is the official representative of the central government in each department. The prefect is a civil servant and is appointed by the Minister of the Interior in Paris. In this way, the prefect is, very often, a political appointment and, in this respect, prefectoral appointments form part of the spoils systems that governments enjoy when they take office (see Chapter 3). In 1981–2, for example, the newly elected socialist government replaced 103 of the 124 prefects in the mainland and overseas departments.

Prior to the decentralisation reforms of the early 1980s, the prefect was the chief executive of the general council and exercised control in the name of the council. Moreover, the prefect enjoyed the power of 'tutelage' (*la tutelle*) over the council's business, meaning that the prefect was responsible for ensuring that the council acted within the domain of the law. By extension, the power of tutelage meant that the prefect had the right to strike down decisions of the council if they went beyond the law. Indeed, the prefect had the *a priori* power to do so, meaning that decisions could be prevented from ever coming into effect in the first place. In addition, the prefect was responsible for drawing up the department's budget, for implementing the decisions of the general council and for maintaining public order. The prefect also had a role to play in implementing the directives of central government in the localities. All told, the prefect was the most visible symbol of central state power at the local level.

The Defferre reforms changed the role of the prefect (indeed, even the title of the office was changed for a short period until the right came back to power in 1986). The most significant reform was the abolition of the *a priori* right of prefectoral tutelage. As noted above, in 1982 the president of the general council became the head of the departmental administration and in this capacity is now responsible for implementing the general council's budget. By contrast, the prefect now merely has the right to exercise *a posteriori* control of the council's decisions, meaning that the prefect can only appeal to an administrative court for a departmental decision to be overturned and then only after the decision has been taken. All told, the prefect's powers are less extensive than before (although this is not to imply that they were necessarily used in an authoritarian way even prior to the 1982 reforms). However, the position of prefect is still much coveted. The prefectoral *corps* (see Chapter 3) maintains a reputation for excellence. And prefects have been encouraged to emphasise different aspects of their traditional role, notably playing a more active part in directing the policies of ministerial field services (see below) and adopting a higher profile in economic affairs as the arbitrators in disputes between unions and management.

Ministerial field services

French ministries are highly decentralised. Around 92 per cent of all civil servants work in field offices rather than in the central ministries in Paris. Officials at this level carry out three main tasks. First, they administer the policies of the ministry in the locality. This means that officials will be variously engaged in a wide range of manual, managerial and clerical activities relating to the ministry's business. Second, they work with the departmental prefect. As noted above, prefects have the task of co-ordinating the work of most of the different government ministries in an attempt to avoid policy overlap. Third, they interact with representatives of local authorities. The nature of this interaction can be accommodatory or hostile depending on the model of centre–local relations that is emphasised. Suffice it to say, though, that many of the smaller communes are unable to employ their own administrative staff and rely on the assistance of officials in ministerial field units for the implementation of essential services.

In recent years the role of the ministerial field services has been strengthened somewhat. In particular, a growing emphasis has been placed by successive governments on the deconcentration of state power. That is to say, there has been a move towards administrative devolution, or the transfer of service provision and policy functions from officials at the centre to those in local ministerial field services. In particular, on 6 February 1992, a law was passed which was an attempt to strengthen the principle of subsidiarity, or the transfer of decisions down to lowest efficient level of government, within the French administrative system. The aim of the 1992 deconcentration law, and a subsequent 1997 act, was to give greater responsibility to officials who are closer to the citizen, or the consumer of public goods, so that services could be provided in a way which best suited the needs of the people they most affected. Moreover, the law also aimed to break with the traditional conception of the French policy process, whereby policy was made at the centre and simply administered in the localities. It is certainly the case that the impact of the deconcentration reforms has been patchy (indeed, 70 per cent of people still see the state as 'something far away' (Sadran, 1997, p. 38)), but the principle of localisation is at least now part of the terms of the new public management in France.

Models of centre–local relations in France

There are three main interpretations, or models, of centre–local relations in France. Structured, as they are, by their competing assumptions about the resources and logics of the 'local state', these models cannot be understood without reference to the evolution of wider debates surrounding the changing nature of the French state (see Chapter 1). The first, the agent model of local government, might, like its strong state counterpart, be considered to be the 'traditional' model in that it draws upon the legalistic tradition of French political science and the assumptions of *étatisme*. The second, the model of cross-regulation, might be interpreted as the basic reply to the agent model in the sense that, like the weak state model previously, it emerged from a reappraisal of the role and an appreciation of the limitations of the French central state. This model has two variants. The first, the institutional variant of the cross-regulation model, suggests that the centre–local relationship is characterised by institutional interdependence and bargaining. The second, the sociological variant of the cross-regulation model, implies that there is an interpenetration of local and central elites. The final model, the model of local governance, might be seen, like the model of the disoriented state, as a response to contemporary challenges to traditional patterns of policy making from developments such as Europeanisation. Indeed, much like the second variant of the model of the disoriented French state, it ultimately questions the continuing pertinence of arguments upholding claims to French exceptionalism (see Chapter 8).

The agent model of centre–local relations

The agent model of centre–local relations stresses that the central state is strong and that representatives of the central state are in a position to impose their will on elected officials at the local level. Thus, it makes two key assumptions. The first assumption is that there are two units of analysis: the centre and the periphery. As such, the nature of centre–local relations can be understood simply in terms of the relative powers of the institutions at these two levels. The second assumption is that the periphery is subordinate to the centre. The powers of central government far outweigh the powers of local administrative units.

The study of local government was, until the middle of the 1960s, largely ignored by French political scientists. This was because writers tended to focus their attention on central government as the principal site of power in the French political system (Briquet and Sawicki, 1989, p. 6). Indeed, those who did write about French local government tended simply to recast the jacobin conception of centre–local relations (see above). In a relatively unexplored field of inquiry, therefore, the agent model of centre–local relations developed as the standard representation of French local government. In this way, assumptions consistent with the agent model underpinned many of the traditional interpretations of French politics generally, but these assumptions can also be identified more explicitly in the work of writers such as Ridley and Blondel (1964) and their analysis of French public administration, as well as both the Marxist school of the spatial expression of class domination (Castells and Godard, 1974) and the theory of internal colonisation (Lafont, 1971; 1973). As the dates of these works suggest, though, since the passage of the Defferre decentralisation reforms the agent model has gone somewhat out of favour. However, it is still possible to see the basic assumptions of this model in the work of, for example, de Monricher (1995) and his analysis of the post-Defferre decision-making process.

The dismissal of the influence of local actors in national policy making was initially inspired by a legal and administrative approach to the study of centre–local relations. This approach was 'long hegemonic, limiting politics at the nation-state level, according to which local communities were exclusively confined to administrative acts' (Balme *et al.*, 1994, p. 392). Indeed, local government was attributed a similar role to that of the civil service in that national politicians were deemed to be in a position to decide the content of policy which local authorities simply implemented. As such, the centre and the locality were conceptualised as two distinct and hierarchically ordered levels of government. The central state, the guardian of the general interest, determined the boundaries of national policy and exercised administrative and regulatory control over local authorities. Local interests were considered to be divisive and secondary. All told, it was more appropriate to speak of local administration rather than local government.

Historically, the legal–administrative tradition of the agent model of centre–local relations was said to be enshrined in the legacies of the process of centralised state-building undertaken by the Ancien Régime, the Revolution and the Napoleonic Empire. For example, the Napoleonic administrative reforms promoted the conception of administrative uniformity, identified the department rather than the commune as the privileged unit of local government and subjected the actions of local government to the regulation of administrative courts and government decrees rather than parliament or the civil courts. Most importantly, however, the Napoleonic Empire witnessed the appointment of prefects in each department as the local representative of central government (see above, pp. 76–7). Armed with the *a priori* power of tutelage over the decisions of local authorities, it is argued, prefects ensured and co-ordinated the implementation of national policy at the local level.

In this context, typical of the legal–administrative form of the agent model of centre–local relations is the work of Ridley and Blondel (1964). Writing about the role of local government in the early years of the Fifth Republic, they stressed that the Napoleonic model continued to underpin the system (Ibid., p. 86). This system was one in which officials were allowed to practise an 'enlightened despotism' (Ibid., p. 87) and resulted in a situation where the 'hierarchic subordination' (Ibid.) of local government to the centre still applied. They did note that even by this time representatives at local level had been given a certain amount of freedom, but they still argued that 'representatives of the central government have kept strict powers of control and in some cases play an important part in the actual administration of local services as well' (Ibid., p. 99). All told, local government was simply conceived as a another branch of the central state (Ibid., p. 100) As such, its basic task was simply to administer the services of the state at the local level rather than to engage in a process of autonomous decision making.

The legal–administrative tradition in French centre–local relations was matched by a Marxist school of urban politics. This latter school, albeit from a radically different starting point, reached similar conclusions as to the extent of the dominance of central government over local authorities. The Marxist school assumed that the state worked in the long-term interests of capital and that the changing demands of capital accumulation determined the evolution of public policy. As such, the nature and evolution of centre–periphery relations in France was subsumed within the wider class struggle of advanced capitalist systems and the policies of capital accumulation. In this way, urban politics was constructed as simply the 'spatial organisation of class domination' (Biarez *et al.*, cited in Briquet and Sawicki, 1989, p. 7). An example of such a study is provided by Castells and Godard (1974). In their work on Dunkirk they identified local politics as the outcome of struggles between class fractions and portrayed local government institutions as merely the 'relay' of the macro-level policies of the central state. The role of local government was simply to administer the macro-strategies of the central state. Indeed, the only local opposition to this overarching function came from the middle class, or bourgeoisie, which might oppose the development of a rival monopoly bourgeoisie. Whatever the struggle between the different fractions of capital, according to these accounts local government is once again little more than an agent of the central state.

In a somewhat similar vein, there was a further school of thought which stressed the relationship between the dominant centre and the underprivileged periphery. This school stressed the 'internal colonialism' of the French state (Lafont, 1971; 1973). According to this line of argument, regions were economically underdeveloped by virtue of what amounted to a 'colonial' attitude on the part of central government. In other words, the periphery was subject to the same sort of exploitation as colonies had been previously. This colonial mentality manifested itself: in the transfer of economic ownership from locally based companies to national and state-owned companies; in a concentration on industrial extraction in the regions, which meant that primary wealth was exported from the place where it was produced and that the value-added for the final manufactured product was earned elsewhere; in the ownership of both agricultural and tourism resources by those resident outside the region, notably in Paris; and in the centralisation of the distribution of goods that affected local markets and profits. All told, the central state was responsible for this situation to the extent that state-owned companies were engaged in the 'appropriation' of regional profits and that administrative organisations devised and implemented the policies necessary for its continuation.

In these ways, the agent model of centre–local relations corresponds to the traditional view of local government in France. Indeed, for the most part it represents a school of thought which, in all its manifestations, has now gone out of vogue. It is feasible, though, that this model still has a contemporary resonance. In small communes, for example, local representatives are still dependent on sub-prefects and agents of the central administration in the provision of local services because they lack the demographic and financial resources to act independently. More generally, there are contemporary analysts in the legal–administrative tradition who seem to make the same basic assumptions as those writing prior to the decentralisation reforms of the 1980s, even if the context in which they write has been transformed. In this context, as noted below on p. 93, some of those associated with the local governance model suggest that the central state retains great powers. More specifically, though, in an analysis of the Defferre reforms de Monricher (1995) argues that the role of local government has changed, that there are increasing interdependencies between central and local state organisations and that local authorities have emerged as a counterweight to the central authorities. In these respects, de Monricher presents an analysis which is typical of the first variant of the cross-regulation model of centre–local relations (see below). At the same time, de Monricher's argument is also placed in the context of a central state which, he argues, still has a key role to play in the relationship with local government. For example, he asserts that because 'the central state remains dominant, decentralization only makes local governments more powerful to achieve national policies' (de Monricher, 1995, p. 407). Similarly, he concludes that by 1994 the system of public administration was still in transition, but that its 'centralized structure and rationale has often led to strategies directed toward the conservation of old habits and privileges' (Ibid., p. 417). This argument is some way removed from the Ridley and Blondel analysis outlined above on p. 80, but it still makes assumptions which would not be out of place in the work of these writers and others.

There are a number of arguments against the agent model of centre–local relations. In the first place, it can be argued that it is an outdated model. Even if it applied prior to the Defferre reforms, it is, so this line of argument goes, no longer appropriate. Consequently, another model of centre–local relations should now be employed. Second, it can also be argued that, even prior to the Defferre reforms, it provided a reductionist conception of centre–local relations. Arguably, it always underestimated the influence of local actors and disregarded the resource dependency that united and, indeed, which continues to unite central and local state institutions. By reducing the role of local authorities to that of a 'relay' of the central state, it ignored the resources at the disposal of local government to bias the implementation of central government directives. Instead, the central state always required and, again, continues to require the organisational resources and expertise of local governments to implement policy. According to this line of argument, therefore, one or other of the variations on the cross-regulation model of centre–local relations is more appropriate (see below). Finally, it might also be argued that the agent model of centre–local relations identifies only a single mode of local government politics, whereas in practice the French system of local government is now marked by fragmentation and multi-level cleavages.

According to this school of thought, the model of local governance provides a fuller account of the contemporary role of local authorities (see pp. 90–4).

The cross-regulation model of centre–local relations

The second model of centre–local relations is the cross-regulation model (*régulation croisée*). There are two variants of this model: the institutional variant and the sociological variant. Each variant approaches the study of centre–local relations from a slightly different perspective. In this way, it is worth distinguishing between them. At the same time, though, both variants share two common assumptions and those who put forward one variant often cite proponents of the other in support of their arguments. The first assumption of this model is the same as the one made previously, namely that there are two units of analysis: the centre and the periphery. Again, therefore, centre–local relations can be understood simply in terms of the relationship between the various institutions at these two levels. The second assumption, however, is different from the one made in the previous model. Here, it is assumed that the two levels of government are interdependent, that the relationship between them is complex and that neither level is subordinate to the other. Thus, while there is a slight difference of emphasis between the two variants of this model, the essence of both can be encapsulated in the term '*jacobinisme apprivoisé*' (Grémion, 1976), or 'tamed' jacobinism.

The institutional variant of the cross-regulation model

As its name suggests, the institutional variant of the cross-regulation model approaches the study of centre–local relations from the perspective of institutional privileges. As such, it is based on the notion, first, that the central state is a powerful actor but, second, that local authorities also have a degree of autonomous influence. Thus, the centre does not simply dominate the periphery. Instead, Paris and the provinces 'are locked into a system of mutual interdependence' (Wright, 1989). This model is associated with the work of writers such as Ashford (1982a; 1982b), Eberlein (1996), Hayward (1983), Mabileau (1985; 1989; 1997), Machin (1977; 1979; 1981), Michel (1998), Schmidt (1990), Stevens (1996) and Wright (1989). As can be discerned from this list, the institutional variant of the cross-regulation model has been applied to the periods before and after the Defferre decentralisation reforms.

In his work on the role of the French prefect Machin provides a classic expression of the institutional variant of this model. He argues that prefects have 'never wielded the powers which their critics imagined' (Machin, 1977, p. 25) and that there have 'always existed important checks on the Prefects' freedom of action' (Ibid.). Indeed, the power of local *notables* was such that prefects became 'the captives of local administrative and political forces' (Ibid., p. 29). As a result, prefects rarely misused their powers of tutelage and 'sought to maintain their positions by displaying administrative excellence and gaining local support' (Ibid.). In this way, the system of centre–local relations was 'based on an uneasy alliance of elected *notables*, technical specialists in field services of ministries with traditions of independent action, and the Prefects themselves' (Ibid., p. 204), creating a relationship between these three sets of actors which was 'complex and very often confused' (Ibid., p. 205). In a later work, Machin suggested that this model was more applicable to the role of local authorities in rural areas than at the level of urban or regional government (Machin, 1981, p. 140). However, the basic thrust of the institutional argument was still to be found in his work by way of the assertion that in the French system of centre–local relations 'power was essentially dispersed' (Machin, 1979, p. 28) and that policy making took the form of collusion between officials of the central state and elected representatives at the local level (Ibid.).

In another work, Ashford also stressed the fact that prefects had to work in a co-operative manner with representatives of local government (Ashford, 1982b, p. 109). In addition, he made the further argument that the relationship of mutual dependence between the local and national levels of government is reinforced by taxation and budgetary considerations (Ibid., p. 112). He argued that local government has a crucial role to play in public works programmes. Thus, he stated, 'During a period of rapid economic and industrial expansion, the communes and departments are vitally important to national policy aims' (Ibid.). In short, the central state cannot ignore local government. In this way, he concluded that 'the complex pattern of compromise and bargaining between communes and prefects helped generate the intricate pattern of intrigue and complicity of central–local policymaking' (Ibid.). More generally, Ashford also argued that central government in France adopted a pragmatic approach to local government relations because the French system of democracy has over the years been quite fragile (Ashford, 1982a). In a historical perspective political actors at the central level have not had the authority to impose decisions on local actors against their will. What is more, local actors have themselves enjoyed considered influence and, indeed, legitimacy. Thus, Ashford argued, the relationship between the centre and the locality has not been based on exclusivity and dominance but interlocking institutional interdependence.

Another analysis which questions the traditional view of French centre–periphery relations is provided by Hayward (1983). Like Machin and Ashford, he argued that prefects and mayors have common interests which bind them together (Hayward, 1983, p. 25). The prefect must win the support of elected representatives so as to run the department effectively. Equally, mayors must seek out subsidies from the prefect so as to respond to local pressures. The result is the 'integration of local and central politics'

(Ibid., p. 24). At the same time, Hayward argued that this situation comes about because, paradoxically, the jacobin principle of equality before the law actually encourages officials to make exceptions to rules which in theory should be applied equally (Ibid.). Such is the strength of local pressure that it is only possible to maintain the system overall if concessions are made to the strict application of general rules. Thus, central state officials deal with representatives of the locality in order to maintain the very existence of the unitary and unifying system of government.

In these ways, the institutional variant of the cross-regulation model challenged the traditional view of a centre-dominated system of local government even prior to the Defferre decentralisation reforms. In addition, it has also been applied to centre–local relations in the period thereafter. For example, Keating and Hainsworth argue that the Defferre reforms marked a 'major shift in power relationships' (Keating and Hainsworth, 1986, p. 129), but that this shift 'merely reinforces existing trends' (Ibid.) which were characterised by an 'interdependent' (Ibid., p. 130) relationship between central and local government. A similar line of argument is adopted by Mabileau (1986). He states that the Defferre reforms provided 'some genuine autonomy' to French local government 'arising out of the allocation of new responsibilities to the localities' (Mabileau, 1989, p. 21). These responsibilities include the marginalisation of the prefect, the abolition of a priori tutelage, direct elections to regional councils and the devolution of executive functions to elected representatives at the departmental and regional level. Thus, he argues that the powers of the various levels of government have been clarified.

A new variation on the institutional theme is proposed by Eberlein (1996). He provides a critique of Crozier and the sociological variant of the cross-regulation model (see below). He does so by focusing on the organisational characteristics of French local government. In a study of the creation of science parks in Montpellier and Rennes, he concludes that local and regional governments 'have the authority and sufficient administrative and financial resources to initiate and formulate public policies, even though they depend on national and, increasingly, European-level funding and support' (Eberlein, 1996, p. 352). He argues that moves towards decentralisation have accentuated the presidentialisation of mayors, if not extended it to departmental and regional chairpersons, and have also facilitated both intercommunal co-operation and the professionalisation of local government officers. In addition, the increased use of joint ventures between state and local authorities has eased vertical resource dependencies. These changes have meant that 'subnational governments in post-decentralist France are capable of autonomous policy initiatives', operating as 'independent loci of governmental power and policy-making' (Ibid., p. 370). Indeed, he also argues that the pressures of electoral responsibility and the dynamics of co-operation and competition between local authorities encourage 'local authorities to take policy initiatives and to introduce them into a new, truly intergovernmental arena instead of relying exclusively on individual access to central policymaking' (Ibid., p. 354). As such, Eberlein concludes that 'France is moving toward fundamentally different patterns of territorial regulation best described as quasi-federalism in unitary disguise' (Ibid., p. 371). Thus, there is emerging a federal challenge to the unitary French state in which both local authorities and central government are key players.

The objections to the institutional variant of the cross-regulation model can be stated quite simply. In the first place, it might be argued that, despite the Defferre reforms, the centre is still in a dominant position. The fact that local actors must still seek out the prefect in order to implement policies suggests not the interdependence of centre–local relations but the continued reliance of local actors on central officials. In this case, the agent model of local government is still more appropriate. Alternatively, it might be argued that the Defferre reforms have fundamentally challenged the cross-regulation model, including its institutional variant. The system is now more fragmented and a model which concentrates on the relationship between two actors alone – central and local government – is outdated. Instead, there is great variation across the French territory which this model fails to capture. In this case, the model of local governance would appear to be more apposite.

The sociological variant of the cross-regulation model

The sociological variant of the cross-regulation model approaches the study of centre–local relations from the perspective of the interpersonal links between central and local elites and the network of socialised relationships that emerge from them. This variant of the cross-regulation model is primarily associated with the studies of the Centre for the Sociology of Organisations and, more particularly, with the work of Crozier and Thoenig (1975), Grémion (1976), Thoenig (1979) and Worms (1966). These studies drew upon the earlier work of Crozier (see Chapter 1) in their examination of the inter-organisational relations between central and local actors in France. As such, they took as their point of departure two main assumptions of the Crozier model. First, they stressed the importance of informal patterns of decision making as a necessary antidote to the inflexible hierarchical rules of the 'bureaucratic model' of French decision making. Second, they emphasised the desire of French policy actors to construct strategies of conflict avoidance. This intellectual inheritance led to the conclusion that centre–local relations were characterised by a 'beehive' (Thoenig, 1979, p. 91), or 'honeycomb' of informal networks of centre–local actors, with relationships based on interdependence, the desire for conflict avoidance and low vertical communication. Like Crozier's early works, they viewed this variant of centre–local relations in France to be distinctive, emerging from the peculiarities of French political culture.

Indeed, like Crozier, many of the writers in this school plied the thesis of French exceptionalism, at least in the context of centre–local relations (see Chapter 8). Finally, it should also be noted that, since the pioneering work of those in the Centre for the Sociology of Organisations, this variant of the cross-regulation model has been proposed by writers such as Dupuy (1985), Mazey (1990), Mény (1983; 1987a; 1987b), Rondin (1985) and Sadran (1997).

Like the institutional variant of cross-regulation model, the sociological variant rejects not only the reductionism of strong state accounts of local government, but also the tendency to view local government as organisationally distinct from central government. Instead, it argues that local elites are fully integrated into national decision-making structures and processes. Such integration undermines conceptions of unilateral policy making by either central government or local authorities, making it more appropriate to talk of the 'interpenetration' of central and local actors (Mény, 1987a, p. 63), or a system which 'is characterized more by osmosis than [the] separation' (Mény, 1987b, p. 99) of the two levels of government.

There are a number of reasons put forward to account for this phenomenon. The first concerns the existence of multiple office holding, or the *cumul des mandats*, through which politicians combine national and local offices. This tradition reinforces this integration of local and national decision-making processes. Indeed, for Mény, 'Nationally elected representatives also speak for the 'grass roots' and localism runs throughout the system, to the top' (Mény, 1987b, p. 105). In this way, he argues that, 'Despite the contradictions and conflicts inherent in the relationship between centre and periphery, the accumulation of offices helps to ensure a symbiosis and convergence of interests which breaks down only if pressures and social protest are exceptionally strong' (Mény, 1987a, p. 63). In a similar vein, Sadran argues that the essence of the peculiarly French system of local government is to be found in the role of local *notables* (Sadran, 1997). He stresses that these people are the 'obligatory intermediaries' (Ibid., p. 79) for policies which affect the local level. They are simply too strong for the centre to ignore by virtue of the executive offices they hold at both the local and the national level. As a result, quoting Grémion, he argues that 'in France power is neither decentralised or centralised; it lies in the periphery' (Ibid.).

A second reason for the interpenetration of the centre and the periphery concerns the relations of mutual dependence between the various sets of actors at the two levels. Similar to the argument in the institutional variant of this model, Dupuy stresses that elected representatives, particularly in smaller communes, seek out representatives of the state in order to receive state subsidies (Dupuy, 1985, p. 84). In this way, a socialised network of central and local actors emerges in which 'there is a certain amount of contact between people belonging to different and frequently antagonistic institutions' (Ibid., p. 81). This network combines mayors, local civil servants, general councillors, heads of the state's administrative services, local notables and prefects (see Figure 4.1).

So, for example, consistent with the institutional variant of the cross-regulation model, Dupuy argues that prefects are not merely agents of central government, but are immersed in the joint decision-making process alongside local government, even channelling local interests upwards to central authorities. Where the sociological variant differs from the institutional variant of this model is the emphasis that it places on the socialised networks that emerge from this situation, rather than simply the institutional interdependence of central and local representatives. So, Dupuy states that these 'Close interpersonal relationships lead to a lessening of the declared hostilities between the two branches of officials' (Ibid., p. 96).

Although written in the late 1960s and 1970s, various works have stressed the relevance of the cross-regulation model since the moves to decentralisation and deconcentration in the 1980s. For example, writing about the early years of the Defferre reforms, Thoenig argues that decentralisation fragmented local government and broke any uniformity of centre–local relations in France, but, at this time, he concluded that the decentralisation of local government was not 'a Big Bang' (Thoenig, 1992, p. 8). Instead, it merely 'accelerated, legitimised through law, and systematised by deepening a series of evolutions which were already ongoing in the field' (Ibid.). Thus, he concludes that the Defferre reforms have 'definitively

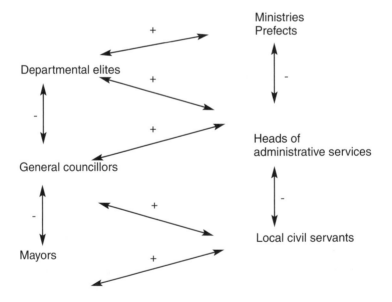

Figure 4.1   Dupuy's model of interlocking relationships at the local level

Source: Dupuy, 1985, p. 91.

Note: + and − signs indicate good and bad relationships.

broken [any] hierarchical order, while maintaining the regulatory [and tested] modes of collective games (such as the cross-regulation of politicians and state civil servants)' (Ibid., p. 13). In this way, the Defferre reforms were in no way a rupture with past practices. They merely comforted the influence of local administrative agents and notables.

In a similar way, Rondin argues that the Defferre reforms reinforced the existing influence of local *notables* (Rondin, 1985). Although the Defferre reforms might have multiplied the number of local actors and fragmented the patterns of local decision making in a manner consistent with the model of local governance (see pp. 90–4 below), Rondin argues that centre–local relations are still characterised by mutual interdependence (Rondin, 1985, pp. 287–97). Thus, representatives of local authorities still seek out the support of the prefect, their 'old partner of yesteryear' (Ibid., p. 289), in order to resolve problems. In addition, the institutional resources at the disposal of prefects, particularly the chairing of several local committees, still installs them in the role of local policy broker, co-ordinating local action programmes and resolving turf wars between different local authorities. For Rondin, this is particularly true where local authorities have little interest in being solely responsible for issues over which they have little direct control (Ibid., p. 290).

Despite its considerable intellectual heritage, the sociological variant of the cross-regulation model has been subject to a number of specific criticisms. First, Tarrow questions the very utility of applying Crozier's sociological model, a theory of organisation, to the study of centre–local relations (Tarrow, 1977). He argues that the model of cross-regulation ignores almost entirely the issue of the actual objectives and content of policies, as well as underplaying the impact of changes in the wider social and economic environment (particularly the wider distribution of power) and lateral influences on policy. Second, Schmidt implies that the sociological variant was applicable prior to the Defferre reforms, but that the institutional variant is now more appropriate. She argues that these reforms 'effectively formalized the informal powers of locally elected officials, turning the reality of informal decentralization hidden behind the rhetoric into a new formal–legal reality' (Schmidt, 1990, p. 183). A similar line of argument is adopted by Quermonne who states that the Defferre reforms ended the applicability of the cross-regulation model. It did so by enhancing the *cloisonnement*' (compartmentalisation) (Quermonne, 1991, p. 117) between territorial authorities and the prefectoral administration and the external services of the state. Third, Duran and Thoenig (1996) also argue that sociological variant provided an accurate picture of centre–local relations in the 1960s. However, they state that the system is now more 'pluralist, open and differenciated' (Duran and Thoenig, 1996, p. 590). In this way, the system of centre–local relations now resembles the model of local governance (see below). Indeed, this critique is particularly significant because Thoenig was one of those who was most closely associated with the rise of sociological variant of the cross-regulation model in the first place.

The local governance model

Inspired predominantly by the work of British, Irish and North American academics, the model of local governance argues that the common assumption of the two previous models of centre–local relations is increasingly misplaced. That is to say, the study of centre–local relations can no longer be conceived simply as the relationship between these two levels of government. Instead, it is necessary also to consider the relationship between different levels of local government, the relationship between local actors and private actors and the relationship between local government and institutions at the European level. Thus, actors at the local level are now engaged in a variety of relations, which vary from one policy area to another. The result is a fragmented system with multilevel, multi-sectoral and multifaceted expressions of political influence. In this context, Loughlin and Mazey provide a classic statement of the model of local governance when they argue that the 'French politico-administrative system is today much more "open" than hitherto and, to some extent, more "chaotic"' (Loughlin and Mazey, 1995, p. 8) and that:

> the traditional set of relationships between the different actors has changed from the old 'honeycomb' model that existed before 1982 to one that is less easily fitted into a definite pattern. In fact, there exist several different emerging patterns to the extent that ... we may also speak of a *variable geometry* in its formal constitutional structures as well as in the policy capacity across regions and departments.
>
> (Ibid.)

There is a growing body of work which recognises the emergence of patterns of local governance in France. This includes Balme (1998), Balme and Jouve (1996), Cole (1998), Cole and John (1995), Duran and Thoenig (1996); Faure (1994), Le Galès (1995), Le Galès and Harding (1998), Loughlin and Mazey (1995), Mazey (1995), Rogers (1998) and Smith (1996; 1997). What is common to these studies is the argument that the nature of centre–periphery relations has changed. What distinguishes one study from the other is the emphasis that is placed on different aspects of the new system. Thus, there is often disagreement amongst the particular proponents of this general model. So, for example, Faure argues that studies of urban politics wrongly attach the concept of governance to cities, whereas in France, following decentralisation and the Europeanisation of policy making, it is the region which best lends itself to this term (Faure, 1994). Indeed, the concept of 'governance' is itself a highly contested one. However, what is common to all of these studies is that they share the assumption that local politics is now characterised by institutional frag-mentation. In this sense, they are all consistent with the model of local governance.

One approach which can be placed under this general heading has been provided by Durand and Thoenig (1996). They argue that centre–local relations in France should now be characterised as 'the institutionalisation of collective action' (Ibid.). There are two key elements to this approach. First, they argue that the role of the central state has been undermined. The state no longer has the authority to regulate local administration on the basis of a provision of uniform services. Second, they also argue that there has been a crisis of both the economy and the welfare state which has transformed the nature of policy demands. Problems no longer simply occur in discrete issue areas, but cross-cut traditional administrative policy turfs. All told, the central state no longer has either the financial capacity or the institutional ability to regulate centre–local relations in the same way as before (Ibid., p. 592). As a result, policy making is increasingly a bottom-up rather than a top-down process (Ibid., p. 582). The state simply sets out the context within which policy responses can be drawn up (Ibid., p. 601). The precise manner in which problems are then defined and treated is open to the discretion of both public and private actors. Thus, the number of policy actors is much larger than before; there is greater differentiation between policy areas; and the management of policy issues is more flexible from one territorial area to another. In short, centre–local relations are now more sector-specific and network-based than was previ-ously the case.

A more particular version of the model of local governance emphasises the rise of urban governance. In this context, Le Galès argues that in the 1980s major French towns emerged as policy actors in their own right and that this development destabilised traditional centre–local cleavages (Le Galès, 1995). Indeed, he argues that large towns were obliged to develop in this way because of the difficulties in formulating responses to the demands for economic development and the problems of social exclusion (Ibid., p. 71). The emergence of urban governance was accompanied by a number of factors: the reinforcement of metropolitan technocracies and the growing professionalisation of municipal administration; the increasing incidence of public–private partnerships; the privatisation of urban services; the growing amount of competition between municipalities to attract economic investment; the use of contracts between the state, the municipality and social actors; the presidentialisation of the office of mayor; and, finally, the growth of links with both actors at the level of the European Union and those in other European towns (Ibid., pp. 64–7). Indeed, Le Galès argues that the operating rules and norms of actions for large urban towns are no longer set by the central state in France, but rather by the dynamics of the market and European integration. Thus, he concludes that these changes have made it impossible to speak of any single predominant form of local politics in France and, indeed, have made it necessary to leave behind the very conception of a centre and a periphery in French politics, stating that 'there is no longer a local system in France' (Ibid., p. 89).

Another example of this model can be found in the growth of local policy networks which bring together many different types of policy actors. In their comparative study of local government in Leeds and Lille, Cole and John state that 'even in a sector as conventionally statist as French education policy, new policy actors have emerged, creating new resource dependencies between central and sub-national actors' (Cole and John, 1995, p. 103). Accepting both the heterogeneity of local politics in France and the increasing fragmentation of agencies in the local policy arena, this study identifies the emergence of partnerships, both within the public sector and between the public and private actors, as well as evidence of the growing use of contracts between heterogeneous sets of actors as a means of regulation. Primarily, however, it stresses the emergence of local policy networks both as a response to the recognition by local actors of growing interdependence and as a means to ensure policy co-operation and avoid uncertainty between local actors. These networks include the traditional players in local government politics (elected local figures and state representatives) plus new actors, such as local administrators, policy experts in local and regional urban development agencies, representatives of private firms as well as university and media experts (Ibid.). Indeed, Cole and John conclude that, despite their initially different traditions of local government, policy convergence is occurring at the level of local government between France and Britain. France is adopting patterns of local governance similar to Britain. As a result, France is losing its 'exceptionalism' (see Chapter 8).

A final example of the model of local governance concerns the development of regions. The increasing importance of regions has been encouraged by both the Defferre reforms (see p. 76 above) and by the European Union. The Defferre reforms gave regions a popular legitimacy through direct election and the opportunity to draw up contracts with the state so as to foster economic development. In this context, the Brittany region has been particularly interventionist in the field of economic expenditure (Rogers, 1998). The EU raised the profile of regions both by channelling EU structural funds directly through the regional level and more generally by encouraging regional actors to negotiate directly with officials in Brussels, so by-passing central state actors in France. For example, since 1990 the Rhône–Alpes region has had a permanent office in Brussels representing its interests. That said, there is a considerable degree of consensus that regions have yet to emerge as fully fledged autonomous policy actors. So, while recognising the emergence of new actors and complex policy networks involving local and regional authorities, the state, its agents and the private sector, Guyomarch *et al.* argue that the emergence of the region should not be over-estimated (Guyomarch *et al.*, 1998, p. 212). Similarly, as Loughlin and Mazey note, most people 'agree that, since 1982, French regions have become more powerful financially, politically and economically' (Loughlin and Mazey, 1995, p. 4), but they also note that municipalities and departments still have a greater political status and policy-making importance and that 'the administrative influence wielded by Paris ministries over regional policy-making (notably the regionalized planning process) remains considerable' (Ibid.). At the same time, a strong case can still be made for the emergence of regional governance. This might be defined as '*a regionalisation of public policy, that is to say, the establishment of a regional space of interdependence and collective action among participants taking part in public policy processes*' (Balme, 1998, p. 182, emphasis in the original). Here, even in the limited number of areas where they do have policy competence, regional councils are only one set of actors, operating in tandem with domestic state officials, such as regional prefects and civil servants in regional administrative planning units, social actors and European-level administrators. In this way, even if France does not yet have a system of autonomous regional government, regional-oriented links between sets of policy actors have emerged (Guyomarch *et al.* 1998, p. 213). Again, therefore, sub-central politics is marked by varied sets of relationships, involving multiple actors in highly differentiated policy areas.

There are a number of criticisms of the local governance model. The first concerns the assumptions that lie behind the model. For example, Cole argues that the term 'governance' is useful 'since it allows a fuller understanding of the broad range of actors involved in the new governing processes' (Cole, 1998, p. 130). At the same time, he also argues that it is 'unwise to conclude that there has been a general weakening of the state' (Ibid., p. 131) because the state 'retains enormous regulatory and fiscal powers' (Ibid.). Thus, it appears as if the basic assumption of the agent model of centre–local relations lies behind this particular manifestation of the local governance model. Equally, many of those who are associated with this model often point to the emergence of new networks of local policy actors. However, it might be argued that this merely amounts to an updated and slightly reworked version of the sociological variant of the cross-regulation model, rather than a new way of looking at local politics altogether. Arguably, therefore, the local governance approach, rather like the policy network approach to state-group relations (see Chapter 7), does not truly constitute a separate model of sub-central politics, but rather new variations on old themes.

The second criticism concerns the concept of 'governance' itself. Some writers explicitly deny the validity of the term. For example, Michel argues that recent reforms have strengthened the capacity for inter-communality, or co-operation between local authorities (Michel, 1998). Thus, it is true there are now increasing examples of public–private policy networks that,

Michel argues, constitute the core of the concept of 'governance', but it is also true that inter-communality strengthens the position of local authorities in their relationship with state actors. Thus, Michel 'calls into question the concept of governance' (Ibid., p. 166) because 'Local political leaders are perfectly able to take their distance from the multi-actor system to manage their political affairs and, on the contrary, may take advantage of it when they need it' (Ibid., p. 166). This suggests that the institutional variant of the cross-regulation model may better describe the new system of centre–local relations in France. A similar point is made by Mabileau (1991; 1997; 1998). He argues that it is perhaps too premature to apply the concept of governance to centre–local relations (Mabileau, 1998, p. 64). Instead, it is best still to talk of intergovernmental relations, or the relationship between central government and the various tiers of sub-central government. In this context, he argues that France has moved towards a British-style system of local government. Indeed, he states that 'the conditions for a real system of local government according to Anglo-Saxon criteria are ... in the whole put in place' (Mabileau, 1991, p. 45). Again, therefore, it would appear as if the institutional variant of the cross-regulation model is more appropriate than the local governance model.

Conclusion

In recent years local government has been the subject of a great deal of analysis which has become more and more sophisticated. The result is that, whereas in the past there was simply one dominant model of centre–local relations, now there are a number of clearly differentiated and competing schools of thought (see Table 4.1). Therefore, as with all the other chapters in this book, the student of local government is faced with a set of scholarly dilemmas. Most fundamentally, are there two competing units of analysis or many? Is the debate about local government simply a debate which concerns public sector actors at the central and sub-central levels, or is it a debate about public- and private-sector actors both at these levels and the European level as well? Furthermore, if the debate about local government is simply a debate about the relationship between the centre and the periphery, then is the centre the dominant actor, or is there a degree of interdependence, be it institutional or sociological, between the two levels of government? As with a number of other chapters in this book, the disaggregated account of the decision-making process is currently in vogue. The local governance model has come into intellectual favour. That said, there is considerable scope for this model to be 'unpacked' and for its various assumptions to be studied in much greater detail. As noted above, at present this model ranges over those who stress the role of urban governance, those who focus on regional governance and those who consider the basic nature of centre–local relations to be

Table 4.1 Models of French local government

	Agent model	Cross-regulation	Local governance
Definition/key assumptions	1 Two units of analysis: the centre and the periphery 2 Periphery is subordinate to the centre	1 Two units of analysis: the centre and the periphery 2 Periphery and centre are inter-dependent in terms of institutional and social relations	1 Not just two units of analysis 2 Not just either dependent or inter-dependent relations between centre and periphery 3 Actors at the local level are engaged in a variety of relations
Proponents	Castells and Godard (1974), Lafont (1971), Monricher (1995), Ridley and Blondel (1964)	Ashford (1982a, b), Crozier and Thoenig (1975), Eberlein (1996), Grémion (1976), Hayward (1983), Mabileau (1985, 1989, 1997), Machin (1977, 1979, 1981), Michel (1998), Schmidt (1990), Thoenig (1979), Worms (1966)	Balme (1998), Balme and Jouve (1996), Cole (1998), Cole and John (1995), Duran and Thoenig (1996); Faure (1994), Le Galès (1995), Le Galès and Harding (1998), Loughlin and Mazey (1995), Mazey (1995), Smith (1996, 1997)
Argument/evidence	Legal-administrative framework – Jacobin and Napoleonic traditions Spatial analysis – dominant centre and under-privileged periphery Marxist analysis – centre/periphery relations in France, part of wider class struggle	*Variant one: institutional* Institutional cross-regulation strengthened by Defferre reforms, e.g., collusion between prefects and local representatives *Variant two: sociological* Interpersonal 'honeycomb' links between central and local elites, e.g., *cumul des mandats; local notables*	Large number of public and private policy actors Urban governance Local policy networks Regional governance
Criticisms	1 Outdated following Defferre reforms 2 Always underestimated the influence of local actors 3 Assumes only a single mode of local government politics – system is now fragmented	1 Variant two applies organisation theory to local level which is misleading and is not applicable after Defferre reforms 2 Variant one implies reliance of local actors on central officials which suggests agent model 3 Only a single mode of local government politics – system is now fragmented	1 Basic assumption of the agent model lies behind some versions of this model 2 The term 'governance' is misleading – institutional variant of the cross-regulation model may be more appropriate

changing in a whole set of new ways. In the future, it may well be that a debate will emerge between, for example, those who believe that regions are the driving force of sub-central governance and those who consider cities to be the main site of sub-national decision making. Indeed, it may well also be that new paradigms will emerge or that new and revised versions of old paradigms will become intellectually fashionable once more. In this sense, therefore, the debate about French local government is still in a period of transition. Indeed, the same is true for many of the other topics to be considered in this book. We will return to this point in Chapter 9.

5 Political parties

For many people in France political parties have a bad name. This is at least partly because of the common belief that the collapse of previous Republics was due to the irresponsible nature of political parties. France, it is said, was long governed by an 'assembly regime' or a 'party regime', terms with a pejorative connotation implying that political parties pursued their own petty self-interests at the expense of the common good. So, the Third and Fourth Republics were both beset by governmental instability in which seemingly irresponsible and undisciplined parties in parliament constantly threatened the exercise of executive power and the post-Liberation government was brought down when General de Gaulle resigned in 1946 stating that 'the exclusive regime of parties had reappeared' (quoted in Lavigne, 1982, p. 417).

By contrast, the Fifth Republic is often said to have cured this particular aspect of the French disease. The system was deliberately designed to reduce the influence of political parties by presidentialising and, hence, personalising the political process and promoting the role of specially trained technocrats (see Chapter 3). Even now, though, those who decry the role of political parties continue to find a sympathetic ear amongst certain sections of the population. Indeed, some political parties still refuse to call themselves by this name, most notably the gaullist Rally for the Republic (RPR), and in 1995 a total of 65 per cent of the population did not consider themselves to be well represented by political parties (Méchet and Witkowski, 1996, p. 322). That said, the role played by political parties in the political system cannot be ignored. The Constitution of the Fifth Republic officially acknowledges that parties and political groups 'can be formed and operate freely' (Article 4), all but the most marginal parties receive public funding from the state and a not insignificant proportion of the population may be classed as loyal party voters (see Chapter 6). In short, party competition continues to underpin political competition.

This chapter examines the relationship between parties and governments during the Fifth Republic. Its focus is quite specific. Rather than concentrating on broader issues such as the most appropriate classification of the party system or more micro-concerns such as the development and ideology of individual political parties, it examines the extent to which parties are able to influence the policy-making process. In so doing it touches on some of the most basic characteristics of French political parties, such as the nature of co-operation between parties, their internal organisational dynamics and the role of party leaderships. At the same time it relates these characteristics back to more fundamental questions about the nature of the state and government in the French political system. As such, this chapter serves as an analytical bridge that links institutional issues, many of which were raised in the preceding chapters, with questions of representation, which will be the primary focus of the next two chapters.

The first part of the chapter provides a brief overview of French political parties. It focuses on their main characteristics emphasising the fact that they are essentially weak, personalised and divided organisations, but also that they represent long-standing political interests. The second part of the chapter examines the extent to which parties are able to influence the policy-making process. It considers three separate models of government/party relations: the first, or presidentialised party model, suggests that parties exert little or no influence on the policy-making proces; the second, or party influence model, indicates that parties do have the opportunity to shape policy outcomes; the third, or party government model, asserts that parties are inextricably bound up with the process of governmental decision making.

French political parties

In France, there has traditionally been a wide variety of ideological opinion which has found expression in a large number of political parties. A list of the main French political parties would currently need to include the Communist Party (PCF), the Socialist Party (PS), the Greens, the left-wing Mouvement des Citoyens (MDC), the Left-Radical Party (PRG), the centre-right Union for French Democracy (UDF), Force démocrate (FD), Démocratie libérale (DL), the Gaullist Party (RPR) and the extreme-right wing National Front (FN) Mouvement national républicain (MNR) (see Table 5.1). Indeed, a fully comprehensive list of French political parties would also have to include other somewhat more marginal parties, such as the extreme left-wing Lutte Ouvrière (LO) and the Ligue Communiste Révolutionnaire (LCR), the right-wing Confédération Nationale des Indépendants et des Paysans (CNIP) and the Hunting–Fishing–Nature–Tradition Party (CPNT). Indeed, a full list would have to include other political *groupuscules*, ranging from the Natural Law Party to various micro-nationalist groups, which regularly stand candidates at elections.

This initially confusing pattern of party competition can, however, be simplified somewhat. For example, the MDC and the PRG are little more than regional off-shoots of the Socialist Party, while the Trotskyite LO and the LCR operate largely outside the normal parameters of electoral debate, even if support for them may be on the increase. Equally, the FD and the DL were long-time members of the UDF confederation. Consequently, even though the DL has now left the UDF and the UDF itself has since been transformed into a stand-alone political party, these parties can be examined as one unit. Finally, the CPNT is still little more than a pressure group for hunting interests, although support for it has recently increased, and the CNIP is now just a small extreme-right wing party *manqué*.

Moreover, this pattern of party competition can itself be simplified even further. For example, over the past thirty years there has been a considerable degree of collaboration on the left between the PS and PCF and, more recently still, between the so-called 'plural left' consisting of the PS, PCF, MDC, PRG and the Greens. Equally, for an even longer period there have been close links between the various parties of the mainstream right, most notably between the RPR and the various elements of the UDF. In this way, one of the main features of French party politics is the long-standing competition between left- and right-wing blocks of parties (see Chapter 6).

In the next chapter the electoral fortunes of these various parties will be charted. The rest of this section, though, will provide a brief introduction to the main characteristics of French political parties. Five main points will be emphasised: the recent formation of most parties; the weakness of party organisations; the personalisation of party political activity; the faction-alised nature of party competition; and the long-term patterns of party political support. The first four points suggest the fragility of French polit-ical parties. The final point, however, indicates the essential durability of party politics.

The first main characteristic of French political parties concerns their relatively recent formation. With the exception of the PCF, most political parties have been formed only relatively recently. For example, the PS was established in 1969 (and even then it was effectively re-founded in 1971), while the current manifestation of the Gaullist Party was established more recently still in 1976 (and to all intents and purposes it, too, was re-launched in 1998). In short, French political parties are comparatively quick to dissolve and reform themselves in an attempt to boost their popu-larity.

Second, political parties are organisationally weak. Most notably, they lack a large membership base. With the exception in the past of the PCF, French political parties may be classed as 'cadre', or leader-dominated, parties. For example, the PS lacks the extensive trade-union base of some of its other European social democratic counterparts, while the Gaullist Party's attempts to popularise its membership have never really succeeded. In addition, the activity of political parties is for the most part highly

Table 5.1   The main political parties in France

Name	Formation	Political trajectory
Communist Party	1920	Split from SFIO (formed 1905)
Socialist Party	1969	Merger of SFIO with small parties, including Mitterrand's CIR in 1971, plus much of PSU in 1974
Left–Radical Party	1973	Split from the Radical Party
Mouvement des Citoyens	1992	Split from PS
Greens	1984	Merger of various green movements
Force démocrate (FD) – Christian Democratic	1995	MRP (1944–66), CD (1966–76), CDP (split from the CD in 1969 until remerger in 1976), CDS (1976–95). Merged into the reformed UDF in 1998
Démocratie libérale (DL)	1997	RI (1962–77), PR (1977–97)
Union for French Democracy (UDF)	1978/1998	Formed as a confederation of non-gaullist right-wing parties. Reformed as a stand-alone party in 1998
Rally for the Republic (RPR) – Gaullist Party	1976	RPF (formed 1947), then UNR, UNR–RDT, UDV^{e}R and UDR (until 1976)
Rally for France (RPF)	1999	Split from RPR and merged with right-wing MPF party
National Front	1972	Merger of extreme-right groups. Split in 1998 into the Front national (FN) and the Mouvement national républicain (MNR)

centralised with little local branch autonomy. In some cases, particularly in the PS and the PCF, there are some strong departmental and regional party organisations and in all cases parties have their own powerful local barons, or *notables*. However, matters concerning internal appointment procedures, candidate selection and party policy are invariably decided by small coteries of national-level elites. All told, French political parties are weakly institutionalised and highly centralised.

Third, French political parties are highly personalised. The personalisation of party politics in the Fifth Republic is mainly caused by the presidentialised nature of the political system (see Chapter 2). Indeed, this feature of the political process helps to account for both the proliferation of political parties and the tendency for existing parties to be formed and re-formed at regular intervals, as individuals establish parties as vehicles for their own ambitions. As a result, the personalisation of party politics can be seen across virtually all shades of party opinion. For example, the Gaullist Party has long demonstrated a cult of personality. For many years the General was virtually infallible and his name is still revered in party circles. Jacques Chirac's reputation as the founder of the RPR was never quite so pure but for nearly twenty years the party was a monolithic entity that loyally supported its leader and undisputed presidential candidate. Similarly, the PS was dominated by François Mitterrand for nearly a quarter of a century from the time of his election as party leader in 1971. During this period, Mitterrand was not always totally in control of the party, notably in the mid-1970s and the 1990s, but his presence as leader until 1981 and then as spiritual chief while president from 1981 to 1995 meant that party business was always conducted in a highly personalised way. More generally, the UDF was created as a party-support mechanism by the then president, Valéry Giscard d'Estaing, the MDC was created mainly as a vehicle for the former socialist boss, Jean-Pierre Chevènement and the National Front has long been the personal vehicle of its founder, Jean-Marie Le Pen, even if his influence is now, arguably, on the wane. Overall, with the possible exception (at least until recently) of the Greens, French party politics has long been as much personality-based as issue-centred.

Fourth, party competition is factionalised. French parties are often internally divided. In other words, there is competition not just between parties but also within them as well. In some cases, factional competition is primarily personality-based and invariably occurs for the same reason as was noted above, namely the desire of individuals to establish a presidential profile. So, for example, there was little to distinguish the programmes of the various factions in the PS in the late 1980s and early 1990s. Instead, the party was split along personal lines as different people, including Michel Rocard, Lionel Jospin and Laurent Fabius, sought to establish themselves as Mitterrand's natural successor. In other cases, though, there is a mixture of issue-based and personality-centred factional competition. Recently, for example, the RPR has been split not just between supporters of Chirac and his 1995 presidential campaign competitor, Édouard Balladur, but also between those who have a pro-European inflexion, such as former prime minister Alain Juppé, and those who are more Eurosceptic, including Philippe Séguin and, until he left the party in 1999, Charles Pasqua. All told, there is no doubt that factionalised politics can be damaging to a party's popular image. This was one reason why the PS was sanctioned at the 1993 legislative election. However, there is also no doubt that the nature of the French political system fuels factional conflict and will continue to do so for the foreseeable future.

These first four characteristics combine to present the typical picture of French political parties as being weak organisations with little capacity to endure, mobilise support and institutionalise interests. However, this image of the French political landscape needs to be corrected somewhat by the final characteristic of French political parties, namely the long-term patterns of party political support.

There is no doubt that parties come and go with somewhat alarming regularity in the French system. However, the ups and downs of the French system mask a considerably more coherent and stable pattern of party competition. This point applies equally to the right, the left and the centrists.

In his extremely influential work René Rémond argues that three strands of right-wing thought (bonapartism, orleanism and the extreme-right) have been present in French party political life since the early nineteenth century even if they have manifested themselves through different parties at various times (Rémond, 1982). So, the bonapartist tradition of right-wing populism has been incarnated in the past few decades by the sundry acronyms of the Gaullist Party; the orleanist tradition of limited, liberal government has recently been represented by parties such as the Républicains Indépendants (RI), the Parti Républicain (PR) and now DL; finally, the extreme right-wing tradition in French politics has clearly been embodied in the FN since the early 1970s. So, the most basic divisions between the parties of the right do find expression in short-term personal and issue-based conflicts, but these conflicts also hide more long-term ideological trends.

A similar argument can be made about the parties of the left. Since 1920 the left has been split into two basic camps: the communist block and the non-communist block. The particular form of competition between these two blocks has varied from one age to another, be it outright hostility in the 1920s, the Popular Front in 1930s, the 'cold war' in the 1950s, the Union of the Left in the 1970s, or the 'plural left' in the late 1990s. Whatever the label, these different forms of competition may still be seen as separate expressions of the same basic left-wing party competition which began when the Section Française de l'Internationale Ouvrière (SFIO) split at the Congress of Tours in 1920. In short, the left is divided, but its component parts share a common ancestry.

Finally, the role of the centrist, Christian Democratic Movement has been consistent since the Liberation of France in 1944. Since this time, the Christian Democrats have attempted to define for themselves a 'third way' between socialism, on the one hand, and capitalism, on the other. For the most part, this has proved impossible and the centrists have usually chosen to ally with the right. And yet, the Christian Democrats, from the Mouvement Républicain Populaire (MRP) to the FD, have been faced with the same strategic dilemma and the same party political choices for over fifty years now.

Thus, there is no doubt that French political parties are fragile creations, but it is also true that for the most part they represent long-term political interests that find expression through whichever party label that is currently in vogue.

Models of government/party relations in France

The rest of this chapter is concerned with the role that parties play in the policy-making process. Are parties able to influence the process or are they excluded from it? Are they simply government-support organisations or do they exert an independent control? Do they invade the state or are they separate from it? In this context three models of government/party relations can be identified. The first, or presidentialised party model, suggests that parties are weak political actors that are unable to shape the political process; the second, or party influence model, asserts that on occasions parties have exercised a degree of external control; the third, or party government model, indicates that party and governmental institutions are largely indistinguishable and that neither operates autonomously of the other.

The presidentialised party model

The presidentialised party model asserts that political parties are able to exert little or no influence on the policy-making process and that the process is dominated by governmental institutions which themselves are dominated by the president. Against this background, one writer has provided a neat summary of the role of political parties under this model: 'French political parties (except the Communist Party) have been transformed into 'presidential machines' which carry out two successive duties: first of all, they serve as an organisational springboard for a candidate at the presidential election, and then they serve as an organisational relay for the President of the Republic ("the president's party")' (Thiébault, 1993, p. 283).

The presidentialised party model is the most widespread interpretation of government/party relations in France. It is supported by a number of prominent writers including people such as René Rémond (1993) and Jean-Louis Quermonne (1980; 1986). In addition, as the title of this model implies, there is a clear overlap between the presidentialised party model of government/party relations and the presidential government model of core executive politics (see Chapter 2). Thus, many of those who support the presidential government model also make the same basic assumptions as those who assert the validity of the presidentialised party model. As a result, as with its core executive counterpart, this model represents the traditional interpretation of government/party relations in the Fifth Republic.

Two key elements underpin the presidentialised party model. The first of these elements is that the government and the party (or parties) which supports (or support) the government are separate analytical units. They both have different institutional interests. They both have individual political identities. As such, it is logically possible to consider the influence that the one has on the other. The second element is that the supporting party has very little influence over government policy. In this way, the supporting party is deemed to be the subordinate component of the government/party relationship and the government is said to be the dominant partner. In short, the supporting party is treated as simply '*un parti de godillots*', or a party of bootlickers. Against this background, Rémond provides a classic expression of this model. Speaking about François Mitterrand, he states:

> the decisive test is knowing who, in the case of a difference of opinion between the majority party and the executive, has the last word. Well, after eleven years at the head of the state of a man who has not denied his socialist leanings and nine years in power where socialists were in the majority, the answer is not in doubt: decision-making power is still at the Elysée Palace.
>
> (Rémond, 1993, p. 139)

The first reason which is put forward to justify the presidentialised party model is the argument that the president is somehow placed above political parties (see, for example, Quermonne, 1980). The president enjoys such a position as a result of the 1962 constitutional amendment instituting the direct election of the president. The effect of this reform is said to be threefold. In the first place, the direct election of the president means that the head of state is not dependent upon the parliamentary majority for his/her appointment. Thus, the president has a personal mandate which is separate from the party political mandates in the legislature. As such, presidents have their own independent and unimpeachable source of popular authority. Second, candidates need to win more than 50 per cent of the vote in order to win the presidential election. Given that no political party in the Fifth Republic has ever won this amount of votes on its own, the presidential majority is always more than a single-party majority. Presidential candidates are obliged to construct their own personalised majority from a combination of sometimes rather disparate political forces. Finally, presidential elections are essentially candidate-centred contests. Candidates draft their own programmes and so, once elected, the government is obliged to enact the president's priorities rather than those of the party. Indeed, when he was elected in May 1981, Mitterrand was quick to insist on this point, stating that 'my promises constituted the government's charter of action' (quoted in Avril, 1982, p. 117). As Cole notes, this 'deprives parties of the critical policy-making capacity essential for a genuinely independent existence' (Cole, 1993, p. 64).

The second justification of this model is the argument that the system as a whole has become presidentialised. It is here that the link with the presidential government model of core executive politics is at its strongest. As Duhamel notes (again writing about the first Mitterrand presidency), presidents have adopted 'the pyramidal conception of the Fifth Republic, one in which the President dominates the government and the government, in turn, dominates Parliament' (Duhamel, 1987, p. 144). So, for example, the president, and not party representatives, is responsible for appointments to the government. These include not just the prime minister, as the Constitution indicates, but government ministers as well. The result, then, is a government which is constructed by and is loyal to the president. The same, it might be argued, is also true for the relationship between the president and the parties in the National Assembly (Avril, 1994, p. 46). In 1969, 1974, 1981 and 1988 the contours of the government's majority changed not as a function of a parliamentary election but because a new president entered office. In the first two cases this was because opposition parties rallied to support the new president. In the last two cases it was because the president immediately dissolved the National Assembly. As a result, the parties which comprise the parliamentary majority have, somewhat confusingly, come to be referred to as the 'presidential majority' (Avril, 1979). What is more, if there are ever tensions between the government and the parliament, the former can use its arsenal of constitutional powers to subdue the latter (see Chapter 2). Within this framework, the president is the principal decision maker in the system and political parties have no room to act as independent forces in the policy-making process. The president controls the government and the parliamentary majority is dominated (Quermonne, 1986). Indeed, this is why Quermonne, who was one of the principal proponents of the administration and politics model of the French bureaucracy (see Chapter 3), is associated with this model rather than the party government model. He believes that, even though party representatives have colonised the administration (see p. 115 below), both the executive and the system of parties in France are dominated by the president. Thus, there is a politico-administrative class, but the members of this class operate within a policy-making process that is governmentalised, presidentialised and, hence, personalised.

The third justification for this model emphasises the essential weakness of French political parties that was outlined in the previous section. Under the Constitution of the Fourth Republic the fragility of political parties caused them, somewhat paradoxically, to dominate the political process. As Criddle notes, they were unable to aggregate political demands into coherent policy programmes and, instead, acted more like interest groups in a system which allowed them access to executive power (Criddle, 1987, p. 137). The result was governmental instability. By contrast, in the Fifth Republic the weakness of political parties has caused them to be excluded from the political process. Since 1958, political parties have come to operate as little more than presidentialised electoral machines (Criddle, 1987). This rule applies equally to the gaullist presidential rally-type party (or, perhaps more appropriately, the catch-all-type party) from 1959 to 1974, to the giscardian cadre-type party from 1974 to 1981 and to the socialist mass-type party after 1981 (Cole, 1993, pp. 50–3). The party's image overlaps with the president's image and the party's internal decision-making process is presidentialised. Indeed, this latter point is true even when long-time party leaders, such as Mitterrand and Chirac, have formally stood down from their party positions after being elected as president. On these occasions the president was still careful to appoint a loyal lieutenant to the position of party leader. As Thiébault states:

> The formal leader ... is effectively appointed by the President himself with the formal methods of selection only serving to ratify the President's choice. The formal leader's authority and legitimacy depends on the President. He is often a political figure of the second order, non-presidential candidate, former minister or not. He must never appear as a competitor to the President.
>
> (Thiébault, 1993, p. 287)

In these ways, the nature of French political parties is such that in a presidentialised system they are organisationally unable to serve as an independent influence on decision making.

The evidence to support the presidential party model is to be found, so it is argued, in all of the presidencies since 1958. So, for example, Michel Debré, the first prime minister of the Fifth Republic, very clearly emphasised the subordinate role of the Gaullist Party (then known as the Union pour la Nouvelle République, or UNR) when he said that '[t]he UNR has no value, the UNR has no meaning, the UNR has no legitimacy except to the extent that its action is totally in tune with the political directives of General de Gaulle' (quoted in Charlot, 1986, p. 315). Similarly, Giscard d'Estaing frequently made it plain that he considered himself to be above the party political fray and argued that: 'My role as President of the Republic is to allow none of these parties to take the slightest step towards the weakening of the institutions particularly those which exercise executive power' (quoted in Avril, 1979, p. 56).

However, perhaps the most significant example to back up this model concerns the role of the PS after Mitterrand's 1981 election victory. Prior to the election, party representatives criticised the haughty and authoritarian manner in which executive power had been exercised since 1958. And yet, in office the exercise of executive power closely resembled previous administrations and the party, it has been argued, was unable to influence the decision-making process. This led Duhamel to insist that there was not 'a single instance when the Socialist Party leaders, or its parliamentary group, imposed a policy decision on the government' (Duhamel, 1987, p. 152). The most high-profile example of the party's weakness came with the so-called 'amnesty of the generals' affair in 1982. Here, the government introduced a bill to restore the career rights of the generals who were involved in the 1961 Algerian rebellion. However, the party objected and amended the bill so as to remove this provision. The president, though, insisted on the original version and the government used the constitutional powers at its disposal to overturn the party's demands (see Favier and Martin-Roland, 1990, p. 540). Indeed, this, it might be argued, is not an isolated example. The party as an independent actor was excluded from the major decisions concerning nationalisation policy in 1981 and then economic austerity in 1982 and 1983. As Bell and Criddle note:

> the potentially troublesome relationship between Government and Party was secured by weekly meetings between President Mitterrand, Prime Minister Mauroy and Party leader Jospin, with the latter's role soon defined as one closer to apologist for the government than spokesman for activist hopes.
>
> (Bell and Criddle, 1988, p. 253)

Indeed, it might be noted that this formulation of government/party relations is not considered to be confined merely to the early years of the Mitterrand presidency. For example, Cole notes that in the post-1988 period: 'no commentator would seriously deny that [the Socialist Party] remains the subordinate partner in the president–government–party triptych' (Cole, 1989, p. 21). In short, the Socialist Party, it is contended, was unable to influence the main decisions of the Mitterrand presidency. In this way, the PS proved itself it to be *'un parti de godillots'* just as other presidential parties had been previously.

The basic problem with this model is the same one that was identified previously in relation to the presidential government model of core executive politics (see Chapter 2). The presidentialised party model, so it might be argued, provides little more than a caricature of government/party relations. It does so for two reasons.

First, it might be argued that it overestimates the power of the president to influence the policy-making process. Is there really not a single instance when the party or the parliamentary party group has influenced the president's decision? Is it really the case that party representatives are happy to play the role of presidential apologists or, worse, bootlickers? Even the Gaullist Party in the mid-1960s, at the time when this model first came into vogue, was, it might be argued, more than simply a blindly loyal presidential support machine. There were, for example, problems within the party concerning Algerian policy as well as more basic institutional rivalries between the government and party organisations that had to be managed. Thus, the evidence might, arguably, suggest that this model misses the mark.

Second, it can be asserted that this model underestimates the extent to which the president is reliant upon party political forces. Indeed, nothing more clearly illustrates the fact that presidential power is party-dependent than the experience of 'cohabitation'. As soon as the president faces a hostile parliamentary majority, then the source of presidential power disappears. It is wrong to suggest, therefore, that the president is above party politics. On the contrary, so the argument goes, the president is a hostage to party fortune.

For these reasons, then, even if the presidentialised party model is the most common interpretation of government/party relations, it is still open to the criticism that it provides a simplistic and essentially inaccurate account of this relationship.

The party influence model

In contrast to the presidentialised party model, the party influence model of government/party relations indicates that parties do have the opportunity to shape the policy-making process. It can be acknowledged that French political parties are organisationally weak, that they are highly personalised and that they may be internally divided, but it is also asserted that they still occupy a strategic position within the decision-making arena. As such, when the circumstances are right, party representatives do have the ability to shape policy outcomes. Thus, neither the government nor the president is always dominant. Instead, there are occasions when senior party officials have the means to influence the decision-making process.

With the advent of the Fifth Republic the proponents of the party influence model have been outnumbered by those who support the presidentialised party model. In this way, the party influence model is in general terms a less common interpretation of government/party relations than the previous model. Nevertheless, the party influence model is supported by a not insignificant number of people. For the most part, those who propose this model point to its emergence during the first socialist period of government after 1981 (see, for example, Portelli, 1989; and Avril, 1982). However, it is also said to be relevant to the gaullist period of office in the 1960s (Charlot, 1971; 1986) as well as to the political system of the Fifth Republic more generally (Borella, 1990).

As with the presidentialised party model, the party influence model is underpinned by two key elements. The first element is the same as the one before, namely that the government and its supporting party (or parties) are separate analytical units. As before, both have different institutional interests and individual political identities. Again, therefore, it is possible to consider the influence of the party on government policy. The second element, though, is different from the one in the previous model. Here, it is argued that the supporting party does indeed have the capacity to exert a degree of influence over government policy. This is not to say that the supporting party is necessarily considered to be the dominant partner in the relationship with the government nor even that it is considered to be an equal partner. It is simply to say that the supporting party is more than merely '*un parti de godillots*' and that it is an independent actor with at least the opportunity to shape policy decisions.

The rationale for the party influence model is threefold. First, unlike the previous model, political parties are considered to be somewhat more than mere electoral machines that unswervingly support presidential candidates. Instead, parties have programmes that they seek to promote and defend. They have members whose worries and concerns they wish to articulate. They have leaders and senior representatives who have their own career interests to promote. These characteristics set parties apart from governments. Governments have national concerns to consider. They have procedural norms to follow. Government members have their own ministerial careers to advance. There is, then, a basic conflict of interests and an institutional tension between government and party organisations. This means that parties feel the need to influence government policy and that governments feel obliged to resist the proposals of party organisations.

Second, again in contrast to the previous model, here the president is not considered to be above party politics. It is certainly the case that presidential elections are the defining moments of the political system, but, it is argued, political parties are intimately associated with the presidential electoral process. Despite de Gaulle's own beliefs, 'parties play a role which is a lot more central than the founder of the Fifth Republic would probably have wished. They appear notably to be an inevitable channel for those who aspire to become president' (Schonfeld, 1992, p. 285). Presidential candidates invariably emerge from political parties. They need party sponsors in order to stand for election. They use established party networks in order to build up support for their campaign. They gain support because they represent a particular party or political tradition. All told, presidential elections are party elections just as much as they are personalised campaigns. The result, as Borella points out, is that 'the president, to the extent that he exercises power, is a man of the forces which support him, the interests which he represents and the aims that he wants to achieve. He is a party instrument' (Borella, 1993, p. 50). In this way, the successful presidential candidate may claim to speak on the nation's behalf but in reality the president is little more than the spokesperson for a particular coalition of party forces.

Third, as the previous quote from Borella suggests, the presidentialised nature of the decision-making process is somewhat downplayed. As such, there is no quasi-automatic link between this model of government/party relations and the presidential government model of core executive politics. In the party influence model the president is not treated as some sort of virtually omnipotent being who hands down policy decisions from on high. Instead, the policy-making process is said to be characterised by various forms of interaction between representatives of the government and party organisations. The party is integrated, willingly or unwillingly, into the decision-making process. Similarly, in this model the strength of the executive with regard to the legislature is noted, but the role of party representatives in the National Assembly is still emphasised. So, for example, King underlines the role of the government/backbencher relationship, acknowledging the limited influence of the latter, also stating that 'the Government may have a majority but it depends on that majority's votes and is bound, therefore, to some degree at least, to defer to its opinions' (King, 1976, p. 22). The result is a policy process which is more pluralistic, and essentially less presidentialised, than the one which was described in the previous model.

There is plenty of evidence to support the party influence model. Indeed, Machin has made the general argument that, as party competition has become more fluid and presidential influence has decreased, so 'Presidents and their governments have been growing more willing to accept criticisms and modifications from parliament in general and the deputies of their own parties in particular' (Machin, 1993, p. 138). Be that as it may, Charlot has argued that party influence dates right back to the early years of the Fifth Republic. He asserts that: 'In reality the dominant gaullist party was a lot less "godillot" than people have suggested' (Charlot, 1986, p. 314). For Charlot, one manifestation of the party's influence can be seen in the relationship between Gaullist Party representatives in the executive and legislature. He argues that: 'In the course of time a whole web of relations has been woven between the gaullist group and the government, a network of men on Christian-name terms with friendships dating back over twenty-five years' (Charlot, 1971, p. 151). This network of contacts facilitated the management of government/party relations but it also provided at least the opportunity for parliamentary party representatives to have an input into the policy-making process. So, publicly the party was a presidential support mechanism. However, in the background, as Charlot states, 'the party and the [parliamentary party] group alert, by internal channels, the government to any errors and omissions in its policies' (Charlot, 1986, p. 316).

A further example of party influence concerns the role of the Socialist Party during the Mitterrand presidencies. Contrary to the assertions that were made in the previous model, there is evidence to suggest that the party was involved in the policy-making process and, so, was in a position to shape the outcomes of that process. For example, the former prime minister Pierre Mauroy boasted that 'probably never in the history of the Fifth Republic has a party been so closely associated with the elaboration of the executive's policies' (Mauroy in *Le Monde*, 30 November, 1982). Over and above this perhaps somewhat partial political rhetoric, Portelli has argued that: 'the balance sheet of the first [Mitterrand] term in office was clearly characterised by a considerably increased role for parties within the set of political institutions' (Portelli, 1989, p. 63). Indeed, one of the writers who is most closely associated with the presidentialised party model acknowledged that, at least in the immediate aftermath of Mitterrand's victory, 'what is new is that [the president] has brought into the frame one actor who up to now has been absent from the picture: the party' (Avril, 1982, p. 123).

The influence of the Socialist Party from 1981 to 1986 and from 1988 to 1993 was derived, it might be argued, from the various types of formal and informal contacts that it established with the government. The most celebrated example of the former was the government/party seminar which took place on 16–17 July 1982. Here, the prime minister and government ministers met senior Socialist Party representatives not simply to exchange information, but to debate what role the party ought to play in the policy process. It was decided that the party should play a more pro-active role in the formulation of government policy. Consequently, several working groups were set up with the task of drawing up policy proposals which could be put to the government with the aim of institutionalising government/party contacts. Similarly, government and party representatives regularly met to discuss particular policy issues. For example, from 1988 to 1993 such meetings were held on an almost annual basis to discuss the details of the budget, and particularly its fiscal component, before its presentation to parliament. To this end, a meeting was held on 17 October 1989 to discuss the 1990 budget. At the meeting, the party accepted the Finance Minister's proposal for a reduction in corporation tax in return for an increase in the wealth tax, an increase in the tax on the appreciation of assets held by individuals and companies and a reform of the *taxe professionnelle*. In addition to these formal contacts, there were also informal contacts. The most celebrated example of these was the so-called 'elephants' breakfast', which took place every Tuesday morning from 1981 to 1986 at the Elysée Palace, the president's residence, and from 1988 to 1993 at Matignon, the prime minister's residence, in the absence of the president. Here, the president, the prime minister, the leader of the party and the president's chief adviser would meet to discuss the burning political issues of the day. It is difficult to provide tangible examples of party influence because of the confidential nature of these meetings. However, it might be argued that these meetings involved more than just the exchange of information, that the party leader emerged from them as more than just an apologist for the government (see above) and that, instead, they were policy-making meetings that provided an opportunity for the party to shape the most important policy decisions of the government.

The final period of party influence, it might be argued, concerns the 1997 government. The five-party 'plural majority' is an heterogeneous collection of left-oriented political parties. The nature of this coalition has meant that the prime minister has been subject to criticism from some of his government partners and has been obliged at least to acknowledge these criticisms and, arguably, to take them on board. This was perhaps most apparent during the protest action by the unemployed in January 1998 when representatives of both the Greens and the Communist Party objected to the government's handling of the affair, resulting in a shift in government policy. Similarly, the Greens' representative in the government, Dominique Voynet, has been careful to report back regularly to her party organisation. This allows the minister to justify her actions in government and maintain the support of the party. It also allows the party to voice its concerns and maintain control of her. More generally, it indicates to the prime minister that the Greens' membership of the 'plural majority' is not unconditional and that if the party is unhappy with the government's policies then it will leave office. In this way, it is another example of the extent to which government policy cannot simply be decided in isolation from party political considerations and so provides further evidence to support the model of party influence.

The main criticism of this model centres around the argument that the evidence to back it up is unconvincing. Rather like the criticism of the shared government model of core executive politics, it may be argued that the opportunity to participate in the decision-making process is not the same as the capacity to influence that process. With relation to the party influence model, it might be asserted that just because representatives of government and party institutions happen to meet on a regular basis does not necessarily mean that the latter actually have the ability to shape the ideas of the former. Instead, such meetings, it might be argued, are simply a façade. After all, it would certainly take a great leap of analytical and empirical faith to believe that the General was really in hock to Gaullist Party representatives in the legislature. Similarly, it would be perhaps naive to suggest that anything tangible really emerged from meetings such as the government/PS seminar in 1982. All told, it can be conceded that it is certainly the case that governments need to maintain the support of parties in order to survive and that they cannot simply ignore the demands of the supporting party altogether. However, it is also the case, it might be argued, that the number of occasions when the party manages to influence the government action is so small that the model which best captures the nature of the government/party relationship is the presidentialised party model.

The party government model

The party government model indicates that parties are inextricably bound up with the process of governmental decision making. Here, it is argued that it is not simply the case that in the right circumstances political parties may have the opportunity to influence policy. Instead, it is argued that the policy-making process cannot be understood without reference to the influence of political parties. Parties have colonised the governmental system such that the boundaries between the two supposedly separate institutions are blurred to the point of being indistinguishable.

The party government model is the least common interpretation of government/party relations. This is at least partly because the model is derived from work in the field of comparative government rather than French politics *per se*. However, this comparative work can happily be applied to the French case and, indeed, the French system has been the explicit focus of some recent work (see, for example, Morel, 1996; and Reif, 1987). As a result, in order to identify the main elements of this model it is necessary both to draw upon French-centred studies and to extrapolate from comparative work.

Again, there are two key elements to this model. The first of these elements clearly distinguishes this model from the two previous ones. Here, the government and its supporting party (or parties) cannot be considered as separate analytical units. They do not have different interests. Instead, they have common identities. This means that it is not logically possible to consider the influence that the one has on the other. The second element follows on from the first. In this model, the party and government are inter-linked. They are indissociable. There is a blurring of the separation between government and party powers. When there has been party government, as Elgie and Griggs note, 'The boundaries between [party and government] faded away' (Elgie and Griggs, 1991, p. 27).

In the comparative politics literature the presence of party government is associated with various factors (see, for example, Blondel, 1995; Blondel and Cotta, 1996; and Katz, 1987). In the French context three such factors should be emphasised. The first factor concerns the colonisation of govern-ment and state organisations by party representatives (see Chapter 3). When they win power, parties move into government. That is to say, party members are appointed as government ministers. They are appointed as advisers to government ministers in ministerial *cabinets*. They are appointed to positions in the central administration. They are appointed to positions of influence in the wider public sector. In short, parties invade the state. A large percentage of the most senior people in both govern-mental and state organisations are, thus, party members. They are people who previously belonged to party organisations. They are people who have come through the ranks of the party. They are party representatives. As such, the party does not simply exist as an autonomous government-supporting institution. It is simultaneously part of the governmental and state machine as well.

The second factor associated with the French model of party govern-ment concerns the complementary interests of party and government representatives. Unlike the implication of the previous models, ministers do not simply have institutionalised ministerial interests that are separate from party interests. On the contrary, even though ministers undoubtedly have their own ministerial interests, they also have party interests as well. They want their party to do well at elections. They want to maintain the support of party representatives in the legislature. They want to move up the ranks of the party hierarchy. In this way, ministerial interests and party interests are not independent. They are closely linked. The same point applies to party representatives outside the governmental or state struc-tures. For example, party representatives in the legislature undoubtedly have their own party-centred concerns. At the same time, though, they also have government-centred concerns. They want to see the government succeed. They want to see the government create the most favourable conditions for their re-election. They may also aspire to government office themselves. In these ways, then, the same people exhibit both government and party interests simultaneously. The two sets of interests are not autonomous.

The third factor concerns the organisation of political parties. Political parties have increasingly become cartel parties (Katz and Mair, 1995). According to Katz and Mair, cartel parties represent a new type of political party, replacing old-style 'cadre' parties, 'mass' parties and 'catch-all' parties. Cartel parties have emerged over the last three decades. They are characterised by close relations with state structures (see p. 105 above). They are characterised by ideological proximity. They are characterised by collusion between ostensibly opposing party organisations. This means that all political parties, or at least those with a governmental vocation, identify common party political interests. This may take the form of the promotion of state subsidies or the development of a patronage system. Finally, they are characterised by the domination of professional politicians. The result is that parties still compete against each other but that they also share many of the same concerns. They are concerned with managing the social system rather than reforming it. They are concerned with ensuring their place within the state system rather than acting as an external force to change it. They are concerned with their professional careers rather than their ideological motivations. These characteristics are not out of place in the French context.

The evidence for the party government model can be found in the party background of government members, the extent of party patronage and the financial advantages parties gain from the state.

First, Fifth Republic governments have been dominated by party representatives. All presidents have been *de facto* or even *de jure* party leaders at the time of their election. All prime ministers, with the exception of Georges Pompidou and Raymond Barre, have been party figures at the time of their appointment. The vast majority of government ministers have had a party background. So, for example, in his study of party government in the Fifth Republic, Reif calculates that in the very early years of the regime 39 per cent of government ministers were not recruited from parliament and, in this sense, did not have a party background (Reif, 1987, p. 62). This reflected de Gaulle's anti-party sentiment. However, by 1968 (still under de Gaulle's presidency) this figure had fallen to 3.2 per cent and by the first government of the Pompidou presidency it had fallen to zero (Ibid.). The same party political background of government ministers can be seen during the socialist administrations. The PS forbids government ministers from simultaneously holding a party post. However, when the party won office in 1981 a large percentage of those who were holding senior party positions simply transferred to the government. Equally, the new party executive was largely chosen by Mitterrand himself. As Morel notes, therefore, 'not only was the division between party executive and government rather artificial during the Mauroy cabinet, but the independence of party appointments was also rather more formal than real' (Morel, 1996, p. 44). Those entering the government took with them party concerns (including the desire to advance the interests of their own faction). Those entering the party's executive did so in the knowledge that their appointment was governmentally inspired. Furthermore, Portelli asserts that it was 'with the victory of the right at the March 1986 legislative election that the osmosis between institutions and parties reached a sort of apogee' (Portelli, 1989, p. 62). This was due to the fact that the government contained all the party leaders of the mainstream right. Indeed, this is remarkably similar to the situation under the current administration where only the Communist Party Leader, Robert Hue, remained outside the government. All told, then, competing party interests are not separate from the government. They are present at the very heart of the governmental machine.

Second, party representatives have also colonised the wider state machine. There are two main manifestations of this phenomenon. The first concerns the percentage of party representatives in ministerial *cabinets*. For example, 15 per cent of all *cabinet* members in 1981 and 9 per cent of all *cabinet* members in 1988 came directly from party or other political associations (Dagnaud and Mehl, 1989, p. 142). This figure, though, underestimates the total number of party members in the sense it only includes those whose profession immediately prior to appointment was with a political party. The second concerns the percentage of party representatives in the administrative and commercial public sector. Each new government takes advantage of its patronage powers to replace many of the most senior people in the 'permanent' administration, such as prefects, ambassadors, heads of public sector companies and so on. The net result of these patronage powers is that the state becomes associated with the party in power. So, in the 1960s there were criticisms of the so-called UDR-state (or gaullist state). In the mid-1970s the penetration of UDF representatives increased with the election of Giscard d'Estaing. The 1980s saw the rise of the PS-state. This was epitomised by the call at the 1981 Party Congress for administrative heads to roll and for socialist appointments to be made. The alternation in power in 1986 led to complaints of an RPR-state which were mirrored by similar complaints in both 1993 and 1995. For example, the 1986 period is almost unique in that the incoming government dismissed the most senior civil servant in the country, the Secretary General of the Government, because he was considered to be politically suspect. There is, then, a spoils system in France which ensures party representation in the upper echelons of the state system.

Third, parties gain considerable financial advantages from being in government. For example, since 1988 the amount that candidates can spend on presidential elections has been limited but in return the state has reimbursed a substantial part of the costs incurred. Perhaps more importantly, once in office parties benefit from the state's regulatory functions (Morel, 1996, pp. 56–8). The state has the power to authorise a whole range of decisions. In the past, the quid pro quo for these authorisations was very often a donation, either directly or indirectly, to party coffers. The systematic nature of this type of political financing has been well documented and criticised by Mény (1992). The effect has been to tie government and party interests even more closely together. The party needs to be in office in order to finance its activities and the government uses its time in office in order to forward its party's interests. These points apply to all parties equally. They suggest that there is a close imbrication of party and government interests. In this way, they indicate the presence of party government.

The main criticism of the party government model concerns the assumption that the government and supporting party (or parties) should not be considered as separate analytical units. This assumption, it might be argued, is unrealistic. In fact, government and party interests should be treated as being quite distinct. Both operate according to their own institutional logics. Both have their own separate goals. As a result, when party representatives move into government they do not simply maintain their party identity. Instead, they take on board a new identity and follow the logic of their host institution. In this way, they adopt a governmental role. Thus, party representatives do not 'invade' the state, they are 'captured' by the state. Similarly, when ministers leave office and re-enter party organisations they divest themselves of the governmental culture that they have acquired. They regain their party identity and reassume a party mantle. Once again, they adopt a party role. In this context, the relationship between the government and the supporting party is an essentially conflictual one. As such, the nature of government/party relations can only be captured by either the presidentialised party model, on the basis of evidence that the will of the government prevails, or the party influence model, on the basis of evidence that the will of the party prevails.

Conclusion

The study of government/party relations involves making two fundamental choices (see Table 5.2). The first choice concerns the very nature of government and party institutions. The presidentialised party model and the party influence model both assume that the two institutions have separate interests. By contrast, the party government model assumes that they have common concerns. There is no halfway house between these two assumptions. There is no compromise position. There is simply a stark choice to be made between two mutually exclusive alternatives. The second choice concerns the evidence which is presented to support the various models. The presidentialised party model emphasises the hegemonic position of the government and, in particular, the president. The party influence model stresses the potential importance of party organisations. The party government model affirms the invasion of state structures by party representatives. Again, there is little common ground between these three positions. Each corresponds to a very different interpretation of events. In this context, therefore, the decision as to which is the most appropriate model of government/party relations is a reflection of the way in which people view the fundamental position of government in the Fifth Republic and the role of political parties since 1958. In turn, this same decision is also a reflection of certain more general themes, such as the strength or weakness of the French state (see Chapter 1), the nature of the bureaucracy (see Chapter 3), the relationship between the government and social forces (see Chapter 7) and the basic characteristics of the French policy-making style (see Chapter 8).

However, what is perhaps most noticeable about the debate in this chapter, especially in contrast to those examined in the previous chapters, is that a truly disaggregated account of government/party relations has yet to emerge. The majority of observers continue to support the traditional model, the presidentialised party model, while a smaller number maintain their support for its still relatively long-standing competitor, the party influence model. It is precisely for this reason that the party government model needs to be explored in more detail. The great merit of this model is that it has the potential to enliven a sometimes rather moribund discussion between the two more established schools of thought and it certainly demands a more diversified and, arguably, more rewarding research agenda. Moreover, it is not without its own contemporary salience. The effort expended by the current prime minister, Lionel Jospin, in keeping together the 'plural left' alliance is, seemingly, only matched by the equivalent effort that has been expended by the president, Jacques Chirac, in helping to construct, destroy and now rebuild the various party political alliances on the right.

In short, parties are, and always have been, central to the functioning of the political process. Moreover, they are central in a way which is simply ignored by those who promote the presidentialised party model and which is perhaps downplayed by the supporters of the party influence model. Overall, this is one area where there needs to be a greater amount of academic inquiry and where new modes of analysis need to be applied more systematically. The debate about the relationship between parties and the state is a fundamental one, but it is also one which, in the French context, needs to be revitalised.

Table 5.2 Models of party/government relations in France

	Presidentialised party	Party influence	Party government
Definition/key assumptions	1 Government and parties are separate analytical units with different institutional interests 2 Parties are able to exert little or no influence on the policy-making process which is dominated by the president	1 Government and parties are separate analytical units with different institutional interests 2 Parties do have the opportunity to shape the policy-making process	1 Government and parties are not separate analytical units with different institutional interests. 2 Blurring of the separation between government and party powers 3 The policy-making process cannot be understood without reference to the influence of political parties
Proponents	Avril (1979), Duhamel (1987), Quermonne (1980, 1986), Rémond (1993), Thiébault (1993)	Avril (1982), Borella (1990), Charlot (1971, 1986), Portelli (1989)	Elgie and Griggs (1991), Morel (1996), Reif (1987)
Argument/evidence	President is above political parties Political system has become presidentialised French political parties are organisationally weak Evidence: gaullist, giscardian and socialist periods in office	Parties are more than electoral machines which exist to support presidential candidates President is not above party politics Political system has not become presidentialised Evidence: gaullist and socialist periods in office	Colonisation of government and state organisations by party representatives Complementarity of party and government interests French parties have increasingly become cartel parties Evidence: from Pompidou presidency onwards
Criticisms	1 Overestimates the power of the president 2 Underestimates the extent to which the president is reliant upon party political forces	1 Overestimates the power of parties	1 Government and parties are separate analytical units with different institutional interests 2 Parties do not 'invade' the state they are 'captured' by it 3 When ministers leave office they adopt a party role

6   Voting behaviour

The origin of French electoral studies can be traced back to 1913 and the publication of André Siegfried's seminal work of electoral geography, *Tableau politique de la France de l'Ouest sous la Troisième République*. The aim of this work was to demonstrate the long-term stability of the main ideological tendencies, or *tempéraments politiques*, of nineteenth-century French political life. Siegfried's essentially cartographic approach, identifying and interpreting maps of regional political support, was subsequently adopted by some of the most eminent names in French electoral studies, such as François Goguel (see, for example, Goguel, 1981) and Alain Lancelot (1986a). Indeed, a similar type of analysis has also been adopted in more recent work by Emmanuel Todd whose anthropological slant has led him to stress the importance of long-standing regional and family traditions in the formation of political attitudes (Todd, 1990).

Even though the cartographic tradition of electoral studies has a long history in France, for the most part this tradition has now been superseded by studies that use survey data to understand voting. In this context, one of the main features of the French electoral studies is the prominence of private opinion polling organisations. There are currently five such organisations (the BVA, the CSA, the IFOP, Louis Harris and SOFRES), the oldest of which, the IFOP, was founded in 1938. They are all extremely professional and their results regularly form the basis of election-night analysis on radio and television and in the print media. By contrast, academic electoral surveys have been few and far between. From 1958 to 1988 inclusive there were only four French-sponsored national election studies of this sort covering the 1958, 1962, 1978 and 1988 elections (Ysmal, 1994, p. 369). This means that the data used in French electoral studies have overwhelmingly come from either one-off research projects or from information provided by the private polling organisations. This is not to imply that these data are somehow suspect. It is simply to say that specially constructed longitudinal data series are not available in France unlike the situation in, say, Britain and the US (Ibid., 1994, pp. 369–70).

This chapter will focus on the debates generated by survey data studies. It will do so partly because this is now the dominant mode of analysis and partly because many of the qualitative aspects of the cartographic approach, such as the continuing strength of particular ideological tendencies in certain regions, can also be identified in the work that uses survey data. In the first part of the chapter the basic patterns of French voting behaviour since 1958 will be presented. In the second part, the competing interpretations of French voting behaviour will be assessed. There are three schools of French electoral studies: the sociocultural school, which contains two variants – the sociological model and the party identification model; the strategic school, which also contains two variants – the model of the new voter and the econometric model; and the interactionist school, which itself contains two variants – the demand and supply model and the politometric model.

Trends in Fifth Republic voting behaviour

Since the foundation of the Fifth Republic, the electoral context within which the French have gone to the polls has changed. In particular, there has been an increase in both the frequency of elections and the variety of electoral systems.

Over the last forty years the frequency with which elections take place has increased. In 1959 elections were held to only three levels of government: cantonal elections which elected departmental, or general, councils; municipal elections which chose town councils; and legislative elections which returned deputies to the National Assembly. Since this time, though, three more levels of elections have been introduced. In 1962 the Constitution was amended to allow for the direct election of the president with the first election taking place in 1965. In 1979 the first direct elections to the European Parliament were held. Finally, in 1986 the members of regional councils were elected for the first time. Indeed, this list of national consultations might be extended even further to include referendums, seven of which have been held since 1959. As a result of this proliferation of electoral choice, there was only one election-free year from 1981 to 1989 inclusive and only two such years from 1992 to 1998 inclusive. There is in France, therefore, what amounts to a continuous election campaign.

Just as the number of elections has increased over the last forty years so, too, has the variety of electoral systems. From 1964 to 1979 elections at all levels were held under the two-ballot majority system. Here, voters have one vote. If a candidate receives more than 50 per cent of the vote, s/he is elected. However, if no candidate receives this figure, then there is a second ballot at which the person who receives simply the most votes cast is elected. In general, this type of system encourages voters to vote for larger parties and for parties to form electoral alliances. (For the mechanics and effects of this type of system, see Elgie, 1996; and Elgie, 1997c.) After 1979, though, different types of more proportional (or PR) electoral systems were progressively introduced. In 1979, the first set of

European elections was held under a national PR-list system with a 5 per cent threshold. Then, in 1982 the method of election to municipal councils was revised with a 'dose' of proportional representation being introduced. Furthermore, in 1986 both regional and legislative elections were held under a departmental PR-list system with the highest average formula and a 5 per cent threshold, although legislative elections did revert back to the two-ballot majority system in time for the 1988 election. In short, the two-ballot majority still predominates and across all levels of elections competition is skewed towards larger parties and coalitions of parties. However, there is no doubt that the overall effect of the introduction of PR since 1979 has been to render the French political game 'more open and more complex' (Mény, 1989a, p. 147).

In the last chapter the persistence of a long-term system of left/right party competition in France was noted. In the medium and short term, however, there appears to be a tremendous amount of electoral volatility. The basic patterns of French voting behaviour do change. Indeed, the period from 1958 to 1998 saw the transformation, or, more properly, transformations of the French party system. During this time three general periods can be identified: first, the rise of gaullism and the divided left from 1958 to 1971; second, the consolidation of two-block, four-party politics in the mid-1970s; and, third, the scattering of party preferences in the 1980s and 1990s. (For an overview of French party politics, see Grunberg, 1985a; and Machin, 1989.)

The period from 1958 to 1971 was marked by the strength of the Gaullist Party on the right and the divided nature of the left. (See Chapter 5 for a brief history and overview of French parties.) The first legislative election of the Fifth Republic pointed the way for subsequent consultations. On the right, forces that had come to prominence under the Fourth Republic were weakened to the advantage of the Gaullist Party. So, for example, whereas the Christian Democratic vote remained stable at 11 per cent, the extreme-right-wing *poujadiste* party won less than 2 per cent of the vote at the 1958 election compared with 13.2 per cent in 1956. Furthermore, the Gaullist Party won 17.96 per cent of the vote in 1958, compared with 3.9 per cent in 1956, so establishing it as the strongest single force on the right. By the late 1960s this pattern had been confirmed. In 1967 the extreme right had disappeared, the Christian Democrats won 14.09 p er cent of the vote and the gaullists won 31.37 per cent, making it by then the largest party in the system overall. Indeed, such was the strength of the Gaullist Party and such was the reaction to the events of May 1968 that the Gaullist Party was able to win 37.28 per cent of the vote in the legislative election in June of that year and with it an overall majority of seats. In a French context, this was a startling event.

On the left, the situation was complicated. In 1958 the Communist Party was still the largest single party in the system, winning 18.89 per cent of the vote. This figure, though, represented a decline of 7 per cent in the party's support in just two years. Support for the parties of the non-communist left stood at 26.34 per cent, the greatest proportion of which was gained by the SFIO winning 15.48 per cent. By 1962 the left was more divided still and support had shifted amongst its various components. The communist vote increased to 21.87 per cent but the vote for the non-communist left declined to exactly the same figure with the SFIO winning a mere 12.43 per cent of the total vote. For the rest of the 1960s this was the pattern. In 1968, for example, the communists won 20.02 per cent of the vote and the non-communist left won a total of 20.50 per cent, with the largest proportion going to the federation of left-wing parties and groups, the FGDS, which totalled 16.54 per cent. At this time, then, the right was dominant and the Communist Party was the strongest single movement on a divided left.

The second main period of the French party system came during the 1970s. This period was characterised a simplification of party forces and a harmonisation of support for the left- and right-wing blocks. On the left, there were three major developments. First, by 1971 the vast majority of the non-communist left had come together in one party, the Socialist Party, led by François Mitterrand. Second, the communists and the socialists agreed to form an electoral pact in 1972. The 'union of the left' was agreed for pragmatic reasons but it was more than just a marriage of convenience, spawning a joint programme which the two parties were committed to implementing if elected to power. Even though the pact broke down prior to the 1978 election, it showed that the left now had a serious governmental ambition. Third, by 1978 the Socialist Party had outstripped the Communist Party as the major force on the left, winning 22.79 per cent of the vote compared with 20.61 per cent. This demonstrated that within the left the Socialist Party was now the main force.

On the right, the gaullists' position was threatened. Indeed, Valéry Giscard d'Estaing's victory at the 1974 presidential election triggered a realignment of forces on the non-gaullist right. By the mid-1970s all of the different components in this area came together under the heading of the UDF to provide support for the newly elected president. As a result, whereas in 1973 the gaullists won 24.02 per cent of the vote compared with a total of 16.67 per cent for the non-gaullists, by 1978 the gaullists could muster only 22.54 per cent as against 23.89 for the non-gaullists. The period of gaullist hegemony on the right was over.

Overall, the various left- and right-wing realignments in the 1970s produced a party system which Maurice Duverger (1992) called 'a bipolar quadrille'. This implied that there were two political poles, one on the left and one on the right, within each of which there were two forces, the communists and socialists on the left and the gaullists and the UDF on the right. Each of the two blocks won roughly the same amount of support (46.79 per cent for the left and 46.73 per cent for the right in 1978) with the same being true for each of the two parties within the two blocks (see the voting percentages above). In this context, the right's governmental supremacy was threatened as only a small shift in the vote would cause the left to win which it did, resoundingly as it happened, in 1981.

The third period of party competition began in the early 1980s and is still continuing. This period is marked by disillusionment with the four parties in the bipolar quadrille and the rise of other party political forces. On the left, the 1981 presidential election was the last that the communists contested as a serious competitor to the socialists. By 1986 the party won only 9.7 per cent of the vote. It support has since stabilised but it still gained only 9.9 per cent of the vote in 1997. The 1981 election also marked the high point of Socialist Party support when it won 36.05 per cent of the vote. Since this time, it declined to a low of 14.5 per cent at the 1994 European elections but then increased to a more respectable 25.7 per cent in 1997. On the right, both the gaullists and the UDF have seen their fortunes fluctuate. In 1988, when they lost, they could only manage 38.0 per cent of the vote between them. In 1993, when they won, the parties combined support was still only 39.9 per cent. Most recently, though, in 1997, when they lost again, together they scraped only 31.4 per cent. In short, the bipolar quadrille is a thing of the past.

In its place is what has variously been described as a 'quintille quadripolaire' (Habert, 1990, p. 29), meaning a four-pole, five-party system, or a 'sextuor cacophonique' (Habert, 1992a, p. 25), implying a rather disorganised six-party game. During this period, the two most prominent forces to have emerged are the FN and the ecologists.

The FN first came to prominence in a series of by-elections in the early 1980s, but its first successful national electoral performance came at the 1984 European elections when it won 11.0 per cent of the vote. Two years later it won 9.7 per cent at the legislative election, benefiting from the reformed electoral system to return over thirty deputies. Since this time, its vote has varied between 10.5 per cent of the vote at the 1994 European election and 15.2 per cent at the 1997 legislative election. With the exception of the 1986 election, this level of popular support for the FN has not been translated into a large number of parliamentary seats, although it has continued to win seats at European and local levels. Overall, though, what is significant about its electoral performance is that the FN, unlike the *poujadistes* in the Fourth Republic, has proved that it is not a 'flash party', suggesting that there is a part of the electorate that is not just tempted by but is also loyal to an extreme-right-wing neo-fascist party.

The ecologists have also showed that they can win and maintain a degree of support. Although they began to gain attention in the early 1980s, their first main success came at the 1989 European election when the ecology list won 10.59 per cent of the vote. In fact, this score was somewhat anomalous because, for once, the ecologists managed to put forward a united front. For the most part, the most distinctive feature of French ecologism has been its divisions, which have severely hampered the movement's electoral success. Still, there is a proportion of the electorate which is clearly mobilised by environmental issues and to the extent that the movement is now finally dominated by one major party, the Greens, its electoral future looks at least relatively assured.

Over and above the FN and the ecologists various other parties and groups have done well at one election or another. For example, the dissident left-wing list of the soon-to-be-incarcerated business and football mogul, Bernard Tapie, came close to beating the Socialist Party's score at the 1994 European election. One year later, the extreme-left candidate, Arlette Laguiller, won nearly 5 per cent of the vote at the presidential election. Even the Hunting–Fishing–Nature–Tradition list has proved that it can win a respectable level of support at European elections. In addition to these forces, there are other dissident left- and right-wing groups which serve to complicate the electorate game and make both pre- and post-election alliance building all the more difficult.

Models of French voting behaviour

Those who study voting behaviour try to explain changing levels of electoral support across a series of elections and also seek to account for particular levels of support at individual elections. In short, those who specialise in voting behaviour seek to explain a dependent variable, the level of the vote for a party or group of parties, in terms of one or more independent variables, such as class, religion, party identification, government economic performance and so on. Needless to say, different people stress different independent variables which results in both a variety of overarching schools of electoral studies and separate models of voting behaviour in each school.

There are three overarching models of French voting behaviour. (For an overview, see Mayer, 1996.) The first, or sociocultural, school focuses on the importance of sociological variables and party identification in explaining why people vote the way they do. The second, or strategic, school considers the voter as an individual who is influenced to vote in a particular way by factors such as campaign issues, the nature of the contemporary political context and the state of the economy. The third, or interactionist, school synthesises the two previous approaches and generates models in which a variety of long- and short-term factors are simultaneously influential in shaping political preferences.

The sociocultural school

The first school of French electoral studies may be classed as the sociocultural school. The basic assumption of this school is that people from different class, religious and/or cultural backgrounds will identify with certain parties. In particular, the proponents of this school tend to assert that by virtue of their social background people will develop a general identification with either a particular party or with the left or the right more generally.

There are two main expressions of this school. The first can be found mainly in the work of French scholars. By the 1970s there was a clearly identifiable French model of voting behaviour. Variously called the 'deterministic model', the 'sociological model' (Mayer, 1997, p. 11), the 'psycho-sociological model' (Mayer and Perrineau, 1992b, p. 125), the 'French variant of the Michigan paradigm' (Mayer and Perrineau, 1992b, p. 82) and a combination of 'the ecological tradition and the Michigan paradigm' (Gerstlé, 1996, p. 735). This model, which here will be called the 'sociological model', was intellectually dominant in France until the mid-1980s (see, for example, Michelat and Simon, 1977). The second expression of this school can be found in the work of American scholars, notably Converse and Pierce (1986) and Pierce (1995). Whereas French writers established a peculiarly Gallic version of the Michigan paradigm, American writers tended, perhaps unsurprisingly, to prefer the original to the copy. This model, the party identification model, has been proposed by only a limited number of none the less extremely influential people.

The sociological model

The sociological model is associated with the work of virtually all of those who studied French electoral behaviour in France up to the end of the 1970s. It comprises three main elements: left/right identification, social class and religious affiliation. In its most basic form this model indicates that non-practising Catholics who belong to the working class are likely to be associated with the left (both communist and non-communist) and that practising Catholics who belong to the middle class are likely to be associated with the right (both gaullist and non-gaullist).

The first element in the sociological model concerns the salience of the left/right dichotomy in French political life. This salience can be demonstrated by the fact that over the years surveys have consistently shown that a vast majority of the French can place themselves at some point on the left/right spectrum. For example, in a study of a representative national sample of 4,507 voters at the 1978 legislative election only 4 per cent of people refused to place themselves on such a spectrum (Capdevielle *et al.*, 1981, p. 257). Indeed, since the time when the standard seven-point SOFRES measurement of left/right identification was first introduced in 1964, the number of people refusing to locate themselves anywhere on the spectrum fell from 10 per cent to only 6 per cent in 1988 (Michelat, 1993, p. 66). Clearly, during the course of this period the popular meaning of the terms 'left' and 'right' may have changed but, nevertheless, it is apparent that the terms still mean something to most people and that they still help to distinguish between the different opinions that people hold.

What is more, the salience of the left/right dichotomy is reinforced by the finding that a left/right identification emerges both at a very early stage in a person's political development and that by and large people place themselves at the same point on the left–right spectrum as their parents. So, for example, Percheron found that in 1989 a majority of 16–18-year-old children would place themselves somewhere on the seven-point left–right spectrum (Percheron, 1989, p. 74) and that 64 per cent of people in this age group (excluding those not replying to the question) placed themselves at the same point on the spectrum as their parents (Ibid., p. 80). Finally, the salience of the left/right dichotomy is confirmed by the fact that most people who place themselves on the left tend to vote for left-wing parties and that most people who place themselves on the right tend to vote for right-wing parties (see Table 6.1).

Table 6.1   Relationship between party vote and left–right self-placement (per cent)

		Self-placement				
		Left	Centre	Right	None	Total
Vote	Extreme left	82	10	4	4	100
	Communist	91	6	2	1	100
	Socialist	74	19	5	2	100
	Ecologist	40	36	16	8	100
	UDF (non-gaullist right)	5	40	53	2	100
	RPR (gaullist)	5	32	61	2	100

Source: Adapted from Capdevielle *et al.*, 1981, p. 257.

Table 6.2   Relationship between profession and left–right self-placement (per cent)

100% →	Extreme left	Left	Centre	Right	Extreme right
Manual workers	26	32	18	15	5
Intermediate professions	21	30	23	18	5
Employees	20	31	22	18	6
Salaried farmers	19	30	24	19	3
Upper managers and liberal professionals	16	23	29	23	5
No profession/retired	14	23	29	21	9
Heads of industry and commerce	6	18	36	29	6
Farmers	6	10	37	35	8

Source: Lancelot, 1985, p. 380.

Table 6.3   Relationship between religion and voting behaviour in 1978

	Left	Right	Total
Regularly practising Catholics	18	82	100
Occasionally practising Catholics	38	62	100
Non-practising Catholics	61	39	100
No religion	86	14	100

Source: Adapted from Boy and Mayer, 1997a, p. 105.

The second element in the sociological model concerns the extent to which social class tends to determine a person's self-placement on the left–right dichotomy. In short, manual workers, members of intermediate professions and employees are more likely to identify with the left than the right and, conversely, upper managers, members of the liberal professions and heads of industry and commerce are more likely to identify with the right than the left. The findings of the 1978 legislative election survey demonstrate this relationship, even if the findings are less strong than the previous relationship between left/right self-placement and party support (see Table 6.2). The results of survey data at the 1986 legislative election produced similar results (Mayer, 1986, pp. 153–7).

The third element in the sociological model concerns the influence of religion on voting behaviour. In this case, practising Catholics are more likely to identify with the right whereas non-practising Catholics and those without any religious affiliation are more likely to identify with the left. This observation is one of the most long-standing features of French electoral studies. Indeed, Siegfried's aforementioned study of nineteenth-century politics emphasised the extent to which religious affiliation structured the vote. More recently, the 1978 election study showed the link between religiosity and voting behaviour (see Table 6.3). In a similar vein, Mayer's study of the 1986 legislative election provoked the unequivocal conclusion that 'religion remains the primary explanatory factor' (Mayer, 1986, p. 151) in determining voting behaviour.

The importance of religion to the sociological model lies not only in its direct impact on the development of a left/right identification but also in its interrelationship with the class factor. (This is shown diagramatically in Figure 6.1.) As Ysmal notes, 'social cleavages act on left–right orientations through religion as a 'Weltanschauung', a 'culture' or a more or less consistent belief system which concerns not only the political domain but also life in general' (Ysmal, 1994, p. 372). The importance of the religious factor lies not merely in the idea that right-wing practising Catholics will mobilise to defend Church interests against the left-wing anti-clericals, although they will, but in the notion that they will mobilise to defend a general set of social and economic values against the left. In this way, class and religious factors are said to reinforce each other and create separate left/right belief systems. On the one hand, there are Catholic-conservatives (Lancelot, 1981, p. 11) who are both economically liberal, promoting the free market and economic freedom, and culturally illiberal, stressing law and order, traditional moral values and national identity. On the other hand, there are working-class atheists who are economically illiberal, wanting to see the state intervene in the economy to reduce inequalities, and culturally liberal, tolerating permissiveness, multiculturalism and unconventional behaviour. Overall, the result of the relationship is such that when class and religious factors are combined the correlation with voting behaviour is even stronger. So, in 1988 a total of 55 per cent of all voters chose Mitterrand at the second ballot of the presidential election and yet only 32 per cent of non-working class practising Catholics voted for Mitterrand whereas 70 per cent of non-self-employed, non-practising Catholics did the same (Boy and Mayer, 1993, p. 176).

One of the implications of the sociological model is that voting patterns are relatively stable. As Mayer notes, 'because voting is a social act it demonstrates regular and permanent characteristics' (Mayer, 1997, p. 16). To the extent that voters are locked into separate belief systems, voting becomes both an expression and a reaffirmation of cultural identity. As a result, those who vote for a particular party at one election are likely to vote for the same party at the next election. This can be seen with the figures for left- and right-wing voter loyalty at the 1984 and 1986 elections (see Table 6.4). At the same time, though, if the social and attitudinal underpinnings of the belief systems undergo fundamental change, then the model will predict that aggregate voting patterns will also change. So, for example, as a result of the changing working patterns, most notably a rise in salaried workers, as well as the increasing influence of cultural

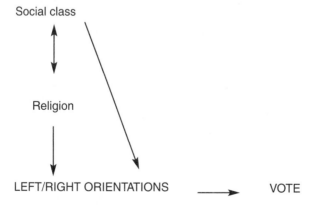

Figure 6.1   The sociological model of voting behaviour
Source: Ysmal (1994, p. 371).

liberalism, proponents of the sociological model predicted in the early 1970s that the left's vote would increase (Lancelot, 1986b, p. 257) which was of course the case.

The zenith of the sociological model came in the mid-1970s when there seemed to be a clear fit between the theory and the practice. From this point on, though, the predictive capacity of the model began to weaken and the basic model, as presented here, was called into question. For example, the model suggested that the left should have won the 1978 election, but it lost, hence the title of the book *Left-wing France Votes Right* (Capdevielle *et al.*, 1981). Consequently, the model was adjusted to include the importance of personal capital (*l'effet patrimoine*) in the class side of the equation and account was taken of the special circumstances of the election, namely the last-minute collapse of the 'union of the left'. Similarly, even though the model successfully predicted the left's victory at the 1981 election, it then failed to account for the left's defeats at both the 1982 cantonal and the 1983 municipal elections. Accordingly, the model was further adapted to include the proviso that incumbent parties will naturally suffer mid-term losses (Parodi, 1983). Finally, the results of the 1986 election suggested that a distinction needed to be drawn between public-sector salaried workers and private-sector salaried workers, the former being more likely to vote for the left than the latter (Mayer, 1986, p. 155; and Boy and Mayer, 1997a).

The problem with the basic version of the sociological model is that it provides only a 'fairly rudimentary model of electoral explanation' (Mayer, 1995, p. 43). In particular, as Table 6.2 itself suggests, even at the height of the sociological model, the relationship between class and voting behaviour was much less strong than the equivalent relationships concerning left–right self-placement and religion. Indeed, subsequent attempts to refine the explanatory power of the model to include factors such as mid-term elections merely reinforce the impression that the model itself is inherently flawed. Moreover, the sociological model may have appeared more attractive in the 1970s and very early 1980s when there was a degree of electoral stability and when only small percentage shifts of

Table 6.4   Electoral stability in France, 1984–6 (per cent)

		1986 vote				
		Left	*Right*	*Green*	*Abstention*	*Total*
1984 vote	*Left*	90	8	0.5	1.5	100
	Right	4	96	0	0	100
	Green	46	21	24	9	100
	Abstention	44	51	3	2	100

Source: Adapted from Dupoirier, 1986, p. 170.

votes resulted in victory of defeat for left- and right-wing formations. By the 1990s, however, when electoral volatility was on the increase, its focus on long-term factors of electoral stability appeared misplaced. In this context, the sociological model continues to have its proponents, even though their support is perhaps now less than wholehearted. So, for example, one set of writers concluded quite modestly that the basic model merely 'retains a basic scientific quality: a capacity for taking measurements within relatively well established limits of precision' (Boy and Mayer, 1993, p. 182). In this context, revised sociological models of voting behaviour, such as the one proposed by Boy and Mayer (1997b), increasingly resemble formalised versions of demand and supply models (see below, p. 138).

The party identification model

The party identification model is derived from work that was pioneered by researchers at the University of Michigan in the 1950s and 1960s. The essence of this model is that the variable that best predicts voting behaviour is a person's identification with a particular party. Voters become emotionally attached to a particular party that leads them to vote for that party consistently. Indeed, the strength of the attachment is such that if they do decide not to vote for the party at one election, then the likelihood is that they will vote for it again at the next election. This model, then, places great emphasis on the concepts of 'brand' loyalty and electoral stability. In fact, this model suggests that durable electoral change is only likely to occur if there is a profound upheaval of the economic and social system that provokes a once-and-for-all realignment of party loyalties.

By virtue of its intellectual origins, the party identification model has been applied most frequently to the study of elections in the US. However, it has also been exported, although not without some intellectual resistance, to the study of elections in other countries and France is one such example. In the French context this model is associated with the work of Philip E. Converse and Roy Pierce. In particular, it is based on the findings of two sets of election surveys, the first covering the three presidential and legislative elections in the period from 1967 to 1969 (Converse and Pierce, 1986) and the second covering the presidential election of 1988 (Pierce, 1995). The result is an explanation of French voting behaviour which is similar to the sociological model but which varies as a function both of the importance it places on party identification rather than left–right self-placement and the extent to which takes some account of short-term factors.

The first distinction between the sociological model and the party identification model is the focus on partisan identification rather than left/right self-placement. Converse and Pierce state that there are three reasons why in the past writers might have wished to focus on left/right identification rather than individual party identification in the French context (Converse and Pierce, 1986, p. 14). This was because of the large number of parties in the party system; the transience of individual political parties; and the fact that within the family unit parents were reticent to communicate their own political attitudes to their children. They argue, though, that, even in the 1960s, the focus on left/right identification was somewhat misplaced. This is because people only had a sketchy understanding of what was meant by the terms 'left' and 'right'. They state:

> we do not have to go very far beneath the surface to learn that many of these self-placements are of questionable pedigree, since the individuals involved often have but a limited understanding of what the labels 'left' and 'right' mean politically.
>
> (Converse and Pierce, 1986, p. 149)

Indeed, they go on to argue that, even though the brute levels of party identification in the late 1960s were not great (59.5 per cent in 1967, 48.7 per cent in 1968 and 45 per cent in 1969), the figures suggested that, if anything, 'party attachments lend significantly more continuity and organization to popular political behavior in France than do feelings of location on a left–right continuum' (Converse and Pierce, 1986, p. 150). What is more, in Pierce's subsequent study of the 1988 presidential election he found that the level of party identification had increased. By this time 71 per cent of people reported a discrete party identification (Pierce, 1995, p. 43). For the most part this increase was said to be caused by both a simplification of the overall party system and an increase in political interest. Whatever the reason, it led to the preliminary conclusion that 'to the extent that the competing roles of ideological positioning and partisan attachments can be couched in racetrack terms, the two basic attitudes run neck and neck in France' (Pierce, 1995, p. 74). When more sophisticated calculations were made the finding was that 'party identification predominates over left–right positioning as a factor in the first-ballot vote' (Pierce, 1995, p. 130). In sum, Converse and Pierce, both jointly and separately, go to great lengths to suggest that party identification is at least as important a factor as left/right identification in the determination of French voting behaviour if not more so.

The second distinction between the sociological model and the party identification model concerns the account which is taken of short-term factors. The party identification model is based on the argument that party identification determines the long-term structure of the vote, but it is also argued that short-term factors shape the way people vote as well. For example, if an opposing party campaigns on a particularly salient policy issue or fields an exceptionally popular candidate, then voter loyalty may waver at least temporarily. Consistent with this line of reasoning, Converse and Pierce build the importance of short-term factors into their model. Consequently, they find that in the late 1960s somewhat more than 5 per cent of all voters were influenced by the parties' issue positions (Converse and Pierce, 1986, p. 341). Similarly, Pierce finds that in the late 1980s in addition to partisanship, candidate evaluations affected voter choice, although issue positions were less important (Pierce, 1995, p. 144). The result is a model that roughly approximates one of the interactionist models of voting behaviour to be discussed below. Nevertheless, the Converse and Pierce model is still distinguished by the overall emphasis that it places on the role of party identification and, hence, belongs in the sociocultural school of electoral studies.

The main critique of the Converse and Pierce model is that it fails to capture the specificity of the French case. In a system where parties come and go with alarming regularity, party identification has, so it is argued, little meaning. In this context, left/right self-placement, as proposed in the sociological model, is more appropriate. In addition, a more general critique has been provided by Zuckerman (1989). This is a trenchant piece that attacks not just the specificities of the French case but also the very concept of party identification generally. For example, Zuckerman argues that the empirical basis of the Converse and Pierce model is weak. He states that the level of party identification is not high in comparative terms nor is the level of brand loyalty from one election to the next (Zuckerman, 1989, p. 481). In addition, he also argues that the theoretical utility of the concept of party identification is weak. He notes that the notion of party identification:

> may mean psychological attachment ... but also short-term commit-
> ment, relative preference at a particular point in time, an attachment
> to a negative assessment of alternative parties, as well as an identifica-
> tion while being positive or indifferent to the other parties, usual vote
> choice and a host of other meanings.
>
> (Zuckerman, 1989, p. 482)

On the basis of these criticisms and others he concludes that 'Converse and Pierce have written an epitaph for their approach to the analysis of polit-ical behavior' (Zuckerman, 1989, p. 483). Even if Zuckerman's conclusion is a little harsh, there is certainly a sense in which the party identification model has now become *démodé* everywhere and not just in France, although there are still some fervent partisans of the model in the US. Nevertheless, it is still explicitly championed by Pierce in the French case and at least a reasonable case can be made for it.

The strategic school

The second school of French electoral studies is the strategic school. The central difference between the sociocultural school, particularly the socio-logical model, and the strategic school is that in the former, the unit of analysis is essentially collective whereas in the latter it is essentially individual. The sociological model stresses the importance of social structures. Correspondingly, the focus of attention is the members of a social class, those with a particular religious affiliation, or those with a certain partisan sympathy. By contrast, the models in the strategic school centre on the individual. The unit of analysis is the individual voter and the motivations of such a voter. Within this school, though, there are rival explanations. Indeed, once again there are two separate and distinct models. The first may be called the model of the 'new' voter and the second is the set of econometric models of voting behaviour.

The model of the 'new' voter

Inspired by work that was originally carried out in the US as a reaction to the Michigan paradigm, the model of the 'new' voter examines the individual motivations of 'new', 'strategic, 'rational', or 'calculating' voters. In France, it emerged on the intellectual scene in the mid-1980s and is associated theoretically with Georges Lavau (Lavau, 1986) and empirically with the work of the late Philippe Habert and, quite significantly as he was once one of the main supporters of the sociological model, Alain Lancelot (see, for example, Habert and Lancelot, 1988). It suggests that increasingly high levels of electoral volatility have rendered existing sociocultural models redundant, that the most volatile voters in the system now have a distinct sociological, political, ideological and participatory profile and that these voters are particularly responsive to short-term factors, such as candidates and campaign issues.

As early as 1984, election results suggested to some at least that the sociological model was scarcely applicable any longer (Lancelot and Lancelot, 1987, pp. 91–2). One feature of elections at this time was that voter volatility was increasing. For example, one writer noted that slightly over 50 per cent of people had failed to support the same party at both the 1981 presidential and the 1984 European elections (Grunberg, 1985b, p. 438) and that as a result it was necessary to revisit the whole question of electoral behaviour (Ibid., p. 444). In 1988, the issue of electoral volatility became even more salient by virtue of the fact that Mitterrand was comfortably re-elected in the May presidential election but that the Socialist Party failed to gain an overall majority at the June legislative election. For Habert and Lancelot this volatility 'illustrates to the point of caricature the inadequacy of traditional models of interpreting electoral behaviour' (Habert and Lancelot, 1988, p. 16). By 1992, it appeared as if voter mobility had become an established feature of French political life. Indeed, high levels of mobility were occurring both across time (over 50 per cent of people failed to vote for the same basic political formation at both the 1988 legislative election and the 1992 regional election) and at a single point in time (34 per cent of people voted for different parties at the

1992 regional and cantonal elections which were held simultaneously) (Habert, 1992a, pp. 27–8). To the extent that sociocultural models were associated with either electoral stability or a once-off realignment of party preferences, then the dealignment of voter choice suggested that these models were outdated.

Apart from noting the extent of volatility in the 1980s and 1990s, the model of the 'new' voter was significant because it suggested that these voters shared distinctive characteristics. The first characteristic, somewhat paradoxically, was a common sociological profile (Habert and Lancelot, 1988, p. 21). (See Table 6.5.) The typical 'new' voter was predominantly young, male, middle class, salaried and well educated. The second was a shared political centrism. On the left/right scale, 41 per cent placed themselves at the centre compared with only 27 per cent of the population as a whole (Ibid.). This political centrism was reflected in the fact that these voters preferred power sharing rather than one-party government. The third characteristic was an ideological centrism. This conclusion was reached by observing that 'new' voters tended to take an intermediary position between loyal right- and left-wing voters on ideological questions (Ibid., p. 22). The fourth characteristic was a high level of political autonomy. The 'new' voter had a low level of party identification. Indeed, 71 per cent replied that they were only 'slightly close' or 'not at all close' to a political party. At the same time, the 'new' voter did not take refuge in abstention. Only 3 per cent abstained at the first ballot of the 1988 presidential election compared with 17 per cent of the population as a whole. In all, the 'new' voter was less likely to respond to established political signals and more likely to make up his/her own mind independently.

The final element of the 'new' voter model concerns the motivations of such voters. Habert found that 26 per cent of the people who voted for François Mitterrand at the first ballot of the 1988 presidential election failed to vote for the Socialist Party list at the 1989 European election (Habert, 1990). Moreover, he found that nearly two-thirds of those who switched and voted for the right in 1989 cited as their main reason for doing so 'the person who headed the list' compared with only 27 per cent who stayed faithful to the socialists (Ibid., p. 22). In addition, he also found that 82 per cent of those who switched and voted for the ecologists in 1989 stated that the 'environment' was among the most pressing problems of the day compared with merely 23 per cent of loyal socialists (Ibid., p. 23). In this way, the 1989 election showed that the 'new' voter was affected by short-term factors: issues, personalities, the electoral game at stake and the political environment. The significance for the 'new' voter of factors associated with the short-term electoral conjuncture led Habert to conclude his analysis of the 1992 Maastricht referendum by saying that an 'electoral decision is never anything but the provisional result of a series of choices between numerous factors amongst the most important of which are the nature and the importance of the issue at stake' (Habert, 1992b, p. 880).

Table 6.5 The sociological profile of the 'new' voter, 1988 legislative election (per cent)

		All	Loyal left	Loyal right	New voters
Sex	Men	48	49	49	51
	Women	52	51	51	49
Age	18–24	15	8	9	20
	25–34	20	20	12	23
	35–49	25	28	28	24
	50–64	22	24	30	21
	65 +	18	21	21	13
Prof.	Farmer	4	2	10	2
	Businessman	6	3	9	8
	Professional	5	6	4	5
	Intermediate prof.	8	7	7	12
	Employee	11	11	9	11
	Worker	16	20	12	18
	No profession/retired	51	53	50	44
	(of which retired)	20	24	24	15
Sector	Independent	10	7	15	10
	Employer	6	3	15	6
	Salaried public	23	28	14	22
	Salaried private	39	40	33	46
Rel.	Reg. pract. Cath	17	9	32	12
	Occas. pract. Cath.	30	28	32	45
	Non-pract. Cath.	34	42	27	24
	Other	19	21	9	19
Shares	Yes	19	12	30	20
	No	81	88	70	80
Educ.	Bac. and higher	24	19	28	30

Source: Adapted from Habert and Lancelot, 1988, p. 17.

In the late 1980s and early 1990s the rise of the 'new' voter model caused quite a stir amongst those studying French electoral behaviour. At this time, for some at least, 'everything seems as if this group is the advanced guard in a process of recomposition which may progressively attain the whole of the system' (Habert and Lancelot, 1988, p. 21). Since then, though, the model has been criticised. For example, some writers have acknowledged the rise of a distinctive 'new' voter but have argued that 'his/her specific weight among the total unstable voters is too inconsequential to be identified using quantitative analysis' (Boy and Dupoirier, 1993, p. 164). Equally, Bréchon states that: 'The paradigm of the rational voter perhaps functions for some electorates or categories; but the model appears doubtful for categories of population having both a strong ideological and religious structure' (Bréchon, 1997, p. 28). Thus, people have stressed either the continuing salience of the models in the sociocultural school or have incorporated the accounts of the 'new' voter in the interactionist school. As a result, in its pure form at least, as presented here, the model of the 'new' voter now has few followers.

Econometric models

Inspired, once again, by a methodology which was developed in the US, there has been an interest in econometric models, sometimes known as politico-econometric models or politometric models, of French voting behaviour for over two decades now. These models have two characteristics: first, they apply models generated in the field of economics to the political realm and, second, they assume that individuals vote rationally, meaning that they wish to maximise benefits and minimise costs. The net result is that those who put forward econometric models usually propose a link between the perceived economic performance of the incumbent government and the percentage of the vote which is cast it. To the extent that different writers emphasise the importance of different macro-economic indicators of government performance, then there are different econometric models of voting behaviour. Nevertheless, to the extent that all such writers focus on the extent to which a government's economic performance shapes the vote, then these different models can all be considered under a single heading.

Econometric models calculate what might be termed the 'vote function', or the likelihood that people will vote for a particular party or political forces, or, alternatively, the 'popularity' function, when party support is being assessed, on the basis of economic variables. They do so by proposing an equation which at its most basic can be expressed in the following manner (Servais, 1997, p. 137):

$$V = F(var1, var2, etc.)$$

where V is the vote function, var1 is the first variable to be considered, var2 is the second variable to be considered and so on, and F is the relationship to be proposed between the different variables.

Such models differ according to the particular variables which are taken into consideration and the precise relationship which is proposed between them. For example, Rosa and Amson considered the relationship between support for the left and the rate of inflation, levels of personal income and unemployment, concluding that high levels of inflation and unemployment are favourable to the left, whereas a high level of personal income is not (Rosa and Amson, 1976, pp. 1110–11). By contrast, Raymond Courbis calculated the support for the incumbent government as a function of the growth of disposable household spending power six months prior to the election. The higher the growth, the more likely it is that the government will do well (Courbis, 'L'équation du vote', in *Le Figaro*, 13 April 1995, p. XV.). Similarly, Lafay and Servais proposed a relationship between support for the governing coalition and two variables: first, the extent to which people were optimistic about future economic conditions; and, second, whether the government still benefited from a 'honeymoon' effect which gradually dwindled over a six-month period (Jean-Dominique Lafay and Marie Servais 'Des sondages préélectoraux aux modèles politico-économétriques', in *Le Figaro*, 4 May 1995, p. XV). Again, the greater the optimism and the sooner the election, the more support the governing coalition is likely to win.

The enticing aspect to econometric models of voting behaviour concerns the extent to which their calculations successfully account for past election results and whether or not they correctly forecast future ones. So, for example, Rosa and Amson found a significant correlation between their model and previous election results over a 50-year period up to 1973. More recently, Courbis predicted prior to the election that in the event of a contest between Chirac and Jospin at the second round of the 1995 presidential election Chirac would win and that he would obtain between 54 and 56 per cent of the vote. In reality, Chirac did, of course, win and by a margin of 52.8 per cent to 47.2 per cent. As a result of findings similar to these, Lafay and Servais felt confident enough to state that: 'currently it is difficult to escape the simple but robust conclusion that in the left–right battle the popularity of the two coalitions and their electoral results are scarcely anything other than a "referendum on the past economic management of the majority in power" ' (Lafay and Servais, 1995).

For the most part, though, the application of econometric models to the study of French voting behaviour is still in its infancy. This is partly because of the lack of formal training in this area in the French academic system. It is also partly because of lack of fit between models which are based on economic indicators alone and actual electoral results. For example, one writer was obliged to make a rather embarrassing public apology for a model which overestimated the left's vote at the first round of the 1988 legislative election by as much as 10 per cent. More generally, econometric models are open to the criticism that they provide a naive picture of voter motivations. In other words, the assumption that people vote rationally can be challenged. Some people vote irrationally. That is to say, they support a party or group which would appear to be pursuing policies that go against their own self-interest. Furthermore, other voters may vote on the basis of other types of non-economic performance-related rationality. In all, then, econometric models are subject to both empirical and theoretical objections.

The interactionist school

The third school of French electoral studies is the interactionist school. What is common to the models in this school is that they combine the most salient elements of the models in both the sociocultural and strategic schools. Accordingly, the writers in the interactionist school emphasise long-term, short-term and on-the-spot factors. They consider the role of social, economic and political variables. This synthesis of seemingly opposing models is nicely encapsulated by Mayer and Perrineau when they state that: 'the voter is neither a prisoner of the yoke of sociological variables nor an unattached 'fidget' reacting to the circumstances of the moment' (Mayer and Perrineau, 1992b, p. 110). As before, it useful to distinguish between two separate models in this school: first, the demand and supply models and, second, the politometric models.

Demand and supply models

The origins of the various demand and supply models of French voting behaviour can be traced back to the early 1970s (Ysmal, 1994, p. 376). For the most part, though, these models were not conceptualised in their current form before the mid-1980s and then came to prominence only in the late 1980s and early 1990s. All told, these models provide a critique of both the sociological model and the 'new' voter model. In their place, they stress that there are two distinct influences on individual voting behaviour. The first influence is the role played by the most basic sociological variables, such as the by now familiar importance of class position and religious practice, as well as party identification and left/right orientation. These variables constitute the demand side of the model and are equivalent to long-term factors that engender a degree of electoral stability. They are a reflection of what the voter wants. The second influence is the role played by the contemporary electoral environment, such as the equally familiar influence of candidates, issues, government performance and so on. These variables constitute the supply side of the model and are equivalent to short-term factors that encourage a degree of voter mobility from one election to the next. They are a portrayal of what the voter is offered at the election.

The demand and supply models criticise the sociological model for its basic inability to explain electoral volatility. For example, even during the supposed heyday of the sociological model one study suggested that 39 per cent of people changed their voting intention in the period from December 1980 to April 1981 in the run-up to Mitterrand's victory at the presidential election. As Ysmal quotes: 'such findings ... could not be interpreted in the terms of the old wisdom since neither left–right identification, nor social class and religion had changed during the electoral campaign' (Ysmal, 1994, p. 378). Instead, it was argued that voting was influenced by short-term campaign-oriented factors. The demand and supply models also criticise the model of the 'new' voter and for two main reasons (Mayer and Perrineau, 1992a, p. 87). First, it is argued that the 'new' voter does not have the distinctive profile that was outlined by Habert and Lancelot. Rather, electoral mobility tends to be confined to the less well educated and to those who are less interested in politics. Second, it is also argued that the number of left/right vote-switchers is small. Instead, most people who do not support the same party as they did at the previous election simply prefer to abstain rather than vote for the opposing electoral block. The demand and supply models, then, criticise the other main models of voting behaviour. At the same time, though, they are themselves constructed from the basic principles of these self-same models. In this way, what is common to all of the various demand and supply models is the account that they take of both long-term social factors and short-term circumstantial factors.

One person who has been associated with the demand and supply approach is Alain Lancelot. On this occasion he argued that the vote is structured by a combination of three general factors (Lancelot, 1986b, pp. 259–60). First, there is a long-term factor, which he calls 'political predisposition', and which he defines as 'the individual political orientation of the voter such as it is formed – and sometimes transformed – over the course of his/her life' (Lancelot, 1986b, pp. 259). This predisposition is derived from the person's perception of his/her objective social position as it is filtered through a system of cultural interpretation which is maintained by the school system, the Church, the press, party messages and so on. This process means that the voter will naturally be associated with a particular political tendency and will be predisposed to vote for the group which represents that tendency. Second, there is the configuration of the electoral supply (Ibid.). This factor consists of the system of candidatures, the personality of the candidates and whether or not they have a local notoriety. Third, there is the voter's strategy when faced with the stakes of the particular election in question (Ibid., p. 260). Here, voters may be motivated by a party's programme, or by a desire to see the post-electoral institutions operate in a particular way. The combination of these three factors results in an approach which can be seen in Figure 6.2.

Other writers associated with the demand and supply approach are Mayer and Perrineau (see Figure 6.3). They state that the 'heavy variables still form the contours of the French electoral landscape' (Mayer and Perrineau, 1992b, p. 91), meaning social class and religion. At the same time, though, they argue that these variables merely predispose the individual to vote for a particular party or group but that this predisposition only becomes concrete when the circumstances of the election are taken into consideration. In this respect, Mayer and Perrineau focus on three general factors. First, they outline the importance of the election itself, taking into account the office at stake (presidential, parliamentary and so

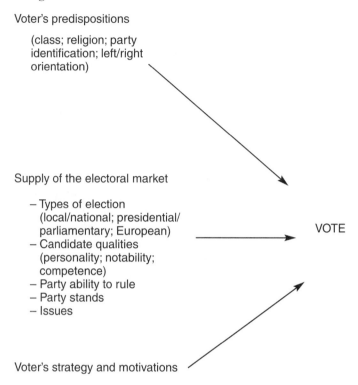

Voter's predispositions

(class; religion; party
identification; left/right
orientation)

Supply of the electoral market

– Types of election
(local/national; presidential/
parliamentary; European)
– Candidate qualities
(personality; notability;
competence)
– Party ability to rule
– Party stands
– Issues

VOTE

Voter's strategy and motivations

Figure 6.2   The Lancelot interactionist model of voting behaviour
Source: Adapted from Ysmal, 1994, p. 380.

on), the local dimension of the election and the type of electoral system which is being employed (Mayer and Perrineau, 1992b, pp. 93–6). Second, they consider the constraints of the electoral supply, focusing on the choices made available through the party system, the candidates who are standing and the issues which are salient (Ibid., pp. 96–104). Third, they take account of the electoral campaign, stressing the role of television and the media generally as well as the impact of opinion polls (Ibid., pp. 104–10). In this last respect, their approach is similar to the one proposed by Jacques Gerstlé who states that party preferences are shaped by the conduct and the dynamic of the campaign (Gerstlé, 1996, p. 745).

In the same way that the sociological model was the dominant model of the 1970s, the demand and supply model has become the dominant model of the 1990s. Its main attraction is that it eschews reductionist explanations and emphasises that 'in order to understand electoral choices, it is necessary to examine the totality of the process' (Mayer and Perrineau, 1992b, p. 111). Its main problem, though, is that it is an essentially retrospective

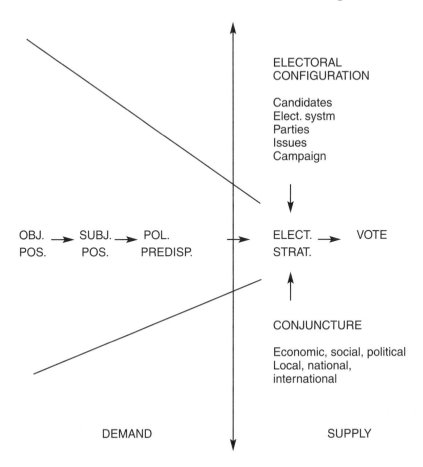

ELECTORAL
CONFIGURATION

Candidates
Elect. systm
Parties
Issues
Campaign

OBJ. → SUBJ. → POL.   ELECT. → VOTE
POS.   POS.   PREDISP.   STRAT.

CONJUNCTURE

Economic, social, political
Local, national,
international

DEMAND   SUPPLY

Figure 6.3   Mayer and Perrineau's demand and supply model of voting behaviour
Source: Mayer and Perrineau, 1992b, p. 111.

model of voting behaviour that fails to discriminate between the various factors that it considers. The predictive capacity of the demand and supply model is almost zero. To the extent that it emphasises the impact of factors such as the electoral system and the campaign, it implies that the final result is open until the very last vote is cast. In addition, it tends to lump all of the different factors in together and fails to establish the extent to which long-term factors are decisive or the likelihood that short-term factors will challenge established predispositions. In this way, it encourages a narrative approach to the study of election campaigns which, it might be argued, is a poor substitute for an analytical model of electoral behaviour that can provide at least an approximate forecast of electoral outcomes.

Politometric models

By their very nature, politometric models are closely related to econometric models. Both apply economic models to political life. At the same time, though, politometric models are sufficiently different for them to be considered separately. They are different because there is a sense in which econometric models are not actually providing an explanatory model of voting behaviour at all. All they are doing is simply registering the impact of economic conditions on aggregate voting trends (Lewis-Beck, 1983, p. 356). By contrast, politometric models take account of other social and political variables and so build up a picture of all of the salient factors that motivate the individual to vote in a particular way.

The person who is most associated with a politometric model of voting behaviour is Michael S. Lewis-Beck (1983; 1993; 1997). He argues that individuals are particularly affected by economic conditions and that economic performance-related voting does occur in France (Lewis-Beck, 1993, p. 10). He states that:

> microlevel analysis demonstrates that economic conditions help determine the vote in French legislative elections. Individual perceptions of personal economic hardship, such as inadequate income or joblessness, and national economic difficulties, such as rising inflation or unemployment, move the French voter to the Left opposition.
>
> (Lewis-Beck, 1983, p. 357)

At the same time, though, he also argues that 'nontrivial numbers of people do not appear able to go against the voting propensities dictated by their social and ideological attachments and choose strictly on the basis of their calculations about the economy' (Lewis-Beck, 1993, p. 8). In other words, as with the supply and demand models, this politometric model merges the basic characteristics of two seemingly opposing models: the sociological model and the econometric model.

In their article on the influence of economic conditions on the left-wing vote, Rosa and Amson hinted that both economic and non-economic variables should be taken into consideration (Rosa and Amson, 1976, p. 1119). Nevertheless, it is Lewis-Beck who makes explicit the need to consider both sets of factors. For example, he states that an 'elaborated model of the French voter' (Lewis-Beck, 1993, p. 10) might be expressed in general terms as follows (Ibid.):

vote = religion + class + ideology + economics

When the calculations are made, Lewis-Beck asserts that such a model 'explains the legislative voting behavior of the French electorate rather well' (Lewis-Beck, 1983, p. 357) and is statistically significant. The result, then, is an analytical model of electoral behaviour that does indeed provide an approximate forecast of electoral fortunes.

The main problem with politometric models is similar to the equivalent problem with econometric models. That is to say, politometric models are based on the assumption that some voters vote rationally and yet such an assumption can be challenged. In this way, models of voting behaviour, such as the sociological school or the demand and supply model, which eschew rational or strategic motivations, are perhaps to be preferred. (For a good discussion of this model, see Cayrol *et al.*, 1997).

Conclusion

It is clear, then, that there are many competing explanations as to why people vote the way they do. As with many of the debates in this book, it is also clear that the dividing line between the different models is sometimes fuzzy. For example, Pierce's 1995 version of the party identification model results in something approaching a demand and supply model of voting. Similarly, the caveat that is introduced at the end of Rosa and Amson's econometric model suggests that their analysis resembles a politometric approach. Nevertheless, the overall result is a rich and eclectic area of study in which there are clearly identifiable schools of thought (see Table 6.6).

What is more, from the evaluation of these schools, it is clear that there is a certain convergence as to which independent variables are most appropriate in explaining voting behaviour. These include social position, ideology and left–right self-placement, campaign factors, the economic and political environment and so on. However, where scholars still differ is in both the emphasis that they place on the importance of the particular variables, particularly whether long-term social or short-term campaign factors are the most significant, and also the method by which the importance of the factors is to be calculated. Therefore, the student of voting behaviour is still faced with various choices.

The fact, however, that there is a degree of intellectual convergence means that it might be tempting to conclude that the models in the interactionist school are generally superior. These models, be they demand and supply models or politometric models, appear to eliminate the reductionism of the sociocultural and/or strategic schools and at the same time they also capitalise on the strengths of these same models. However, demand and supply models should also be viewed with a certain degree of scepticism. For example, they seem to suggest that the voter is influenced by almost everything apart from the proverbial kitchen sink. At one level, this is, of course, correct. At another level, though, it is also unhelpful. We should not expect models of voting behaviour to predict elections down to the last vote. However, we should expect them to provide some sort of indication as to the likely success or failure of political forces. In this way,

Table 6.6 Schools of French voting behaviour

	Sociocultural	Strategic	Interactive
Definition/key assumptions	1 People from different class, religious and/or cultural backgrounds will identify with certain parties 2 The identification is a long-term one 3 Voting patterns are relatively stable	1 The unit of analysis is the individual voter 2 Voting behaviour is motivated by individual utility calculations 3 Electoral volatility may occur	Combines the most salient elements of the models in both the sociocultural and strategic schools
Proponents	Capdevielle *et al.* (1981), Dupoirier (1986), Lancelot (1981, 1985), Mayer (1986), Michelat (1993)	Habert and Lancelot (1988), Lancelot and Lancelot (1987), Lavau (1986)	Lancelot (1986b), Gerstlé (1996), Lewis-Beck (1983, 1993, 1997), Mayer and Perrineau (1992b)
Argument/evidence	*Variant one: sociological* Electoral behaviour is associated with left/right identification, social class and religious affiliation *Variant two: party identification* Voters become emotionally attached to a particular party. Party identification is more important than left/right identification	*Variant one: 'new' voter* The typical 'new' voter is predominantly young, male, middle class, salaried, well educated and politically centrist and is affected by short-term factors *Variant two: econometrics* Assume individuals vote rationally. Usually propose a link between the perceived economic performance of the incumbent government and the support it gains	*Variant one: demand and supply* Two influences: long-term factors, such as social position and left/right identification; short-term factors, such as candidates, issues and government performance *Variant two: politometrics* Individuals are particularly affected by economic conditions but are still influenced by their social and ideological attachments
Criticisms	1 Variant one provides only a rudimentary model of electoral explanation 2 Variant two fails to capture the specificity of the French case where levels of party identification are low 3 Both variants are outdated	1 Variant one correctly identifies the profile of a 'new' voter, but there are very few of them 2 Predictions made on the basis of variant two do not fit electoral outcomes 3 Variant two assumes voters vote rationally, which is naive	1 Variant one encourages a narrative approach to electoral campaigns 2 Variant one provides an essentially retrospective model of voting behaviour 3 Variant two assumes voters vote rationally, which is naive

revised versions of models in the sociocultural and strategic schools, however rudimentary their ability to forecast elections may be, might yet represent a more discriminating method of explaining voting behaviour. Therefore, as with the situation with regard to all of the debates covered in this book, we should not see the study of French voting behaviour as having reached some sort of end point where one particular model must now necessarily dominate. On the contrary, there is still the opportunity for a great deal more debate to occur in the future, for alternative models to be reworked and for new models to be proposed.

7 Interest groups

At the turn of the Fifth Republic, Lavau (1958) and Meynaud (1962) bemoaned the paucity of studies of interest group politics in France. Moreover, even those few studies that did exist were soon undermined by the changing patterns of interest group politics that emerged following the demise of the Fourth Republic. Indeed, the presidentialisation of politics in the Fifth Republic and the reinforcement of the powers of the executive over political parties and the National Assembly rid interest groups of the legislative veto points that they had exercised during the Fourth Republic. In this context, despite the appeals of Lavau and Meynaud for further work, it is not surprising that for a long time the study of state/interest group relations in France was largely 'ignored as a subject of systematic research in France' (Mény, 1989a, p. 388) and that it continued to suffer from what Wilson characterised in the mid-1980s as 'information gaps' (Wilson, 1987, p. 5). Indeed, Wilson's own 1987 empirical, system-level analysis, now somewhat dated, has not been repeated. Work still remains divided into the three categories which he bemoaned: general studies focusing on the main interest groups but which provide few broad hypotheses on their political function; studies of individual groups or specific sectors; and, finally, case studies showing the involvement of interest groups in more visible and significant decisions.

Somewhat paradoxically, though, even if less emphasis has been placed on the study of interest groups in France when compared with elsewhere, there has nevertheless been a long-running and relatively clear-cut debate about the nature of interest group involvement in the French system. This chapter considers this debate. It does so by focusing on the characteristics of state/interest group mediation in France and the management of groups within the policy process. The first section offers the reader a brief overview of contemporary developments in the organisation of interest group politics in France, leaving to one side, however, the flourishing *vie associative* of clubs and societies which, for the most part, remain outside the political domain. The second section then examines attempts to theorise the nature of state/interest group relations in France. It maps the competing assumptions of four mainstream approaches: pluralism, corporatism, the untidy reality model and policy network theory. As in the case of the models presented in other chapters, these approaches sometimes overlap and those who put forward essentially the same model often do so in slightly different ways. All the same, these four models neatly capture the fundamental differences between the various protagonists in the debate about the nature of interest group politics in the French political system.

Interest group politics in France

Interest group politics in France has traditionally been shaped by a number of interlocking factors. These include the mistrust of interest groups, low rates of group mobilisation, the ideological fragmentation of representative associations and the internal division of group confederations. These factors have resulted in a situation in which organisational life is weak but protest movements are strong. In addition to these traditional features, recent developments have generated new patterns of interest group behaviour based around autonomous associational activity, the decline of protest politics and the rise of new social movements.

Traditionally, there has been a mistrust of interest groups in the French system of government. For the most part this stems from the conception of the role of the state that predominated from the time of the French Revolution in 1789. As noted in Chapter 1, this conception was based around Rousseau's belief that the state should stand above the political process. It should do so because the state was said to embody the general will, the will of all the French, rather than the particularistic concerns of interest groups, or political parties for that matter. Thus, it was the duty of the state to avoid being captured by such groups in order for the will of the people to flourish. Indeed, this conception of the state's role was not simply an abstract one confined to the French equivalent of the 'chattering classes'. The Le Chapelier law of 1791 outlawed interest groups and professional associations and certainly stifled the development of the labour movement until its repeal in 1884. Equally, the right to free association was only enshrined in legislation as late as 1901. More recently still, the founders of the Fifth Republic exhibited a marked hostility towards civil society and its representative intermediaries, favouring, instead, technocrats and the role of the state as a directive force. In all of these ways, then, the development of interest group activity was hampered by the elite conception of the proper role of the state.

The role of interest group politics in France was further affected by the supposedly individualistic aspect of French political culture. The French, it has long been claimed, do not join groups. Thus, associational life in France has been weak. There are, of course, problems with this broad-brush political-culture approach and, indeed, it has been argued that associational life in France is flourishing (Hall, 1990a, pp. 78–9). However, it is clear that rates of group mobilisation in France are still comparatively low.

For example, trade union membership is the weakest of any state in the European Union and the OECD, having declined from around 25 per cent in 1974 to around 8 per cent in 1992 (Groux and Moriaux, 1996, p. 175). Indeed, in their comparative study of educational policy making in America and France, Baumgartner and Walker (1989) argue that French interest groups have smaller staffs and less funding than American groups, with the budgets of French groups appearing 'minuscule' in comparison to their American counterparts (although differences are reduced when state subsidies of seconded staff are included in calculations).

Additionally, the main economic and social interest groups in France have been highly fragmented. In France, trade unions are not so much differentiated functionally under one umbrella organisation, such as the TUC in the UK. Instead, industrial workers in France are mobilised within five main peak organisations, which are divided on ideological grounds. So, there is the communist-leaning Confédération Générale du Travail (CGT), the socialist-oriented Confédération Française Démocratique du Travail (CFDT), the less partisan but still left-inspired Force Ouvrière (FO), the Catholic-dominated Confédération Française des Travailleurs Chrétiens (CFTC), as well as the right-wing Confédération Française du Travail (CFT). These federations are divided by long-established ideological disputes. For example, the anti-communist FO broke away from the CGT in 1948, whereas the CFTC broke with the CFDT after its decision in 1964 to end its Catholic associations. All told, these confederations sometimes seem more concerned to compete with each other rather than forming a united front which might forward their collective interests more efficiently.

Furthermore, even when group representation is channelled through large functionally oriented confederations, such organisations have themselves been internally divided. For example, for many years there was one main teaching union, the Fédération de l'Éducation Nationale (FEN). In 1952, the FEN grouped together 77 per cent of all employees in national education and, despite a steady decline in its rates of mobilisation, still represented 62 per cent of all employees in the national education system in 1970 and 48 per cent of all employees in 1985. However, the individual trade unions grouped within the FEN were always divided by tensions born of ideological conflict between different left-wing tendencies as well as the competing interests of secondary and elementary teachers. These divisions turned the federation into something of a 'battlefield' (Baumgartner and Walker, 1989). Indeed, the problems associated with these internal cleavages came to a head in 1992 when the FEN leadership expelled the two communist unions representing secondary and physical education teachers. As the FEN transformed itself into the Syndicat des Enseignants, the expelled unions went on to create the Fédération des Syndicats Unifiés (FSU). The emergence of the FSU simply exposed the cleavages running through the teaching profession and underlined the internal problems within the previously monolithic federation.

All of these factors would tend to support the view that interest group activity in France is weakly structured. Indeed, as noted above, France is typically portrayed as a country in which associational life is underdeveloped. However, even if this is the case, this is not to say that the pattern of state/interest group relations in France has necessarily been harmonious. On the contrary, there is also a strong tradition of protest politics in the French system. In fact, the number of working days lost through strikes has typically been greater in France than, say, the UK. At the same time, the pattern of strike activity tends to be different in the two countries. In France, for example, the ideological division between the various trade union confederations has meant that there has rarely been any overarching collaboration between them. In addition, there is also a long tradition of violent protest in the French system. Such protests are rarely organised by the established interest group actors themselves. Instead, they are usually the product of fringe groups or, more usually still, the result of rank-and-file activity over which established leaderships have little control.

Over and above these established features of organisational activity in France, recent trends have served to change the interest group environment somewhat. First, traditional patterns of bargaining by group leaderships have lost further ground to *coordinations*, or campaigns led by rank-and-file activists. These *coordinations* were first spawned in the nursing strikes against the Rocard government in 1988. Here, nurses at the grassroots created their own structures and organisation to determine demands and the direction of protests. They rejected traditional hierarchies and operated outside the influence of established group leaderships. Similar movements and protests have occurred in agriculture, where farmers have mobilised nationally through the interactions of local activist networks.

Second, the recourse to protest politics and strike action is in decline. High-profile strike actions by trade unions, such as public sector train and underground workers and more recently truck drivers, continue to force concessions from the French government. In 1995 demonstrations against the prime minister's plan to reform pension policy, particularly with regard to the railway sector, resulted in the largest wave of demonstrations since 1968 and brought much of the country to a standstill. In 1997 truck drivers paralysed the French transport network in order to win improvements in their own working conditions. In this sense, protest politics is not dead, far from it. However, the number of popular mobilisations and intersectoral strikes, which were typical of the 1960s and 1970s, have declined in number. This is particularly true in the private sector. Indeed, the single private-sector dispute of any significance in the first half of the 1990s was at the electronics firm Alsthom in Belfort in 1994 (Hewlett, 1998).

Third, the last thirty years have seen the rise of different types of groups, usually known as 'new social movements'. These are groups that represent new forms of social interests. They include feminist groups, such as the Mouvement de Libération des Femmes which was particularly active in the 1970s; anti-racist movements, such as SOS Racisme which came on the scene in the mid-1980s; and gay advocacy and AIDS activist groups, such as Act-Up and ARCAT-SIDA which emerged mainly in the 1990s. These movements have formal structures, but they mobilise people who might otherwise have been outside the mainstream of protest politics. Moreover, it might also be added that some previously unmobilised groups are now organising themselves in spontaneous, more informal, uncoordinated but still extremely successful forms of collective action. The most notable case here concerns associations of the unemployed whose members occupied local employment agencies in January 1998 in order to try to change the government's labour policy.

In all of these ways, then, it is quite conceivable that new forms of state/interest group relations are supplanting, and perhaps have already supplanted, old forms of the same.

Models of state/interest group relations

The study of state/interest group relations has, in a comparative perspective, generated a veritable cottage industry of case studies, typologies and intellectual paradigms. Even though in France the study of interest groups has perhaps not received quite the same attention as in some other places, there is still a number of competing approaches to the study of state/interest group relations. For example, Vincent Wright distinguished between four such interpretations: the domination crisis model; the endemic and open conflict model; the corporatist and concerted politics model; and the pluralist model (Wright, 1989, pp. 257–74). Frank L. Wilson also distinguished between four models: pluralism; the marxist model; corporatism; and the protest model (Wilson, 1987, 18–44). In this chapter, four approaches to the study of state/interest group influence will be singled out. The first, the pluralist or state pluralist account, assumes that a large and fluid number of groups, with varying resources, compete for influence in a comparatively open and fragmented policy arena in which the state shapes but does not simply determine policy outcomes. The second, the corporatist or meso-corporatist account, suggests that policy making is a closed process of mutually dependent bargaining between state managers and a limited number of privileged interest groups. The third, the untidy reality model, refutes the existence of any single, unified approach to explain the different forms of interest intermediation in France. The fourth, policy network theory, argues that policy making takes place within relatively closed and varied networks of government departments, interest groups and professional bodies and stresses the disaggregation of policy making and the fragmentation of the state.

Pluralism and state pluralism

The pluralist model of state/interest group relations has a considerable intellectual history. For the most part it is associated with US writers and with studies of the US policy process. However, the US paradigm has also been said by some writers to characterise the dominant pattern of interest group activity in France. One prominent writer has provided a thorough definition of the pluralist model. He states:

> The pluralist model describes power as widely distributed among numerous, autonomous groups representing social and political forces in the society. These groups confront government and each other in constant but shifting patterns of competition and cooperation that determine public policy. The state moderates among the conflicting demands presented by the interest groups as it determines official policy.
>
> (Wilson, 1987, p. 18)

In the French case, the pluralist model usually has a slightly different inflexion from its US counterpart. As noted in Chapter 1, a strong state is often said to be one of the main features of French political life. In terms of state/interest group relations, this means that many writers prefer to tailor the classical pluralist account to suit this feature of the French political system. As a result, the French version of the pluralist model is often called 'state pluralism', indicating a situation where the state does not simply moderate interest group competition but at least partly shapes the outcome of the policy process over and above the demands of the competing social forces.

There is a certain degree of support for the pluralist or state pluralist model of interest group activity in France. In the first place, the early works on French interest groups were clearly marked by the basic assumptions of orthodox pluralism (Lavau, 1958; and Meynaud, 1962). Even though these writers acknowledged the role of the state, pluralist assumptions were reflected in the recognition of both the fragmentation of interest groups in France and the strategies employed by those groups. Subsequently, the French version of the pluralist model has been proposed by other writers (for example, Safran, 1991), the most notable of whom is Frank L. Wilson (Wilson, 1987). Wilson recognised the deviations of French interest group politics from the orthodox model of pluralist interest group relations (Wilson, 1982, p. 199) and, again, emphasised the role of the state, but he also maintained that the predominant pattern of state–interest group mediation in France remained fundamentally pluralist (Wilson, 1983, p. 907). It should be noted, though, that in some of his later work, Wilson has reassessed his position and questioned the applicability of pluralism to the French case (Wilson, 1986).

In the orthodox model of pluralism the ability of groups to mobilise and influence the policy process is taken for granted. Such confidence in the significance of interest groups rests upon three primary sets of assumptions. First, the state is viewed as a neutral, relatively passive and fragmented actor. Access to decision making is, thus, open with no one interest having privileged, or 'closed', relations with state actors. Second, there are few barriers to prevent the mobilisation of groups of disgruntled individuals. An absence of mobilisation is taken as evidence by orthodox pluralists not of the difficulties of collective action and interest group formation but of consent or satisfaction with the status quo. The theory of countervailing powers even implies that should one group come to dominate a policy issue, an opposition group will emerge to counterbalance its influence in the policy process. Third, pluralists assume that there is a wide and fluid distribution of power and resources throughout society. While not equal, interest groups mobilise different resources, with no group possessing a monopoly of such resources. In other words, power is non-cumulative, with interest groups employing a variety of strategies from lobbying members of parliament through to writing petitions and organising mass demonstrations. Overall, therefore, orthodox pluralist conceptions of the policy process accentuate the influence of large numbers of interest groups in decision making, whereby groups mobilise and present demands to a neutral and passive state that largely responds to the fluctuating alliance of groups within society. Policy outputs mirror the balance of societal forces as registered by the passive state.

In the French case, there is some basic evidence that suggests that the political system conforms to a pluralist mode of analysis. For example, a law passed in 1901 makes it relatively easy to set up an interest group. Simply by going along to the departmental prefecture, the official representatives of the new group can register its existence and the organisation then becomes protected and regulated by the law. This means that there are a large number of interest groups in the French system. In addition, there is also competition between the different groups in a particular sector. For example, as noted in the previous section, there is not just one single, confederal structure in the trade union sector like the TUC in Britain. Instead, there are individual and competing union confederations that vie with each other for support of workers generally. Finally, the activity of French pressure groups is also considered to be typical of the activity of groups under a situation of interest group pluralism. That is to say, interest groups lobby the government to try and influence legislation. They engage in publicity campaigns, which are designed to attract the public's attention to their particular cause or demands. They will organise mass demonstrations to publicise their demands and they will often resort to violence as a way of attracting attention, such as the burning of foreign meat by French farmers protesting against imports. All of these strategies are typical of pluralist interest group activity.

Against this background, the earliest work on interest group activity in

France was replete with the assumptions of orthodox pluralism. This work was initially centred on the Fourth Republic (1946–58) which was denounced by many as a *régime d'intérêts*. So, for example, Philip Williams argued that small, unrepresentative, but politically very significant interest groups were able to determine the outcome of public policy during this time (Williams, 1964). In particular, he pointed to the powerful North African lobby, which stifled constitutional change and promoted its own interests very successfully. He also pointed to the alcohol lobby, particularly the large numbers of small wine-growers who resisted attempts to change their comfortable situation. To a large extent, these groups did not represent large, national interests (such as the trade unions, for example). Instead, they were small, sectional interests. However, their votes were also crucial to certain small parties in the National Assembly which, more often than not, were also partners in the governmental coalition and which could not afford to ignore the demands of their client interest groups. The result was that these small parties were often willing to bring the government down so as to satisfy the demands of groups that represented only a small fraction of the population. Interest groups under the Fourth Republic, therefore, were often economically marginal but politically significant.

The experience of the Fourth Republic influenced those who were writing at the beginning of the Fifth Republic in 1958. Typically, for example, Lavau isolated the standard pluralist strategies open to pressure groups. These ranged from mobilising public opinion and writing letters to candidates through to exploiting networks with parliamentarians and members of the administration and even financing candidates' campaigns (Lavau, 1958). Indeed, in keeping with the pluralist assumptions of the fluid and wide distribution of power throughout society, he argued that the influence of pressure groups was not fixed or cemented but was determined by a series of factors, including financial power, the number of members, the discipline of the organisation, relations with political parties and the presence of well-organised rivals. Most importantly, interest groups were not said to be totally subsumed by an overbearing French state. Lavau acknowledged that: 'The administration itself, even if the minister – a politician – does not bring pressure to bear on it, cannot remain completely indifferent to the argument of numbers' (Lavau, 1958, p. 76). Indeed, the heterogeneous partisan nature of French governments at that time was said further to have facilitated pressure group influence as groups were able to exploit party rivalries and gain access to the minister's personal advisers.

Even though these early studies were clearly influenced by orthodox pluralist assumptions, they also recognised the uneasy match between some of the theoretical assumptions of classical pluralism and the actual practice of state–interest group politics in France. In particular, both Lavau and Meynaud acknowledged that the role of the state was stronger in

France than was normally understood in other pluralist accounts. For example, Lavau pointed to the role played by the state in attributing legal recognition to groups as well as the emerging growth of professional power in consultative committees. Moreover, Meynaud went so far as to argue that the American pluralist school failed to explain the practice of interest group politics in France because of the autonomy of the state (Meynaud, 1962). The French state, he argued, frequently acted independently of any coalition of interest groups, pursuing its own policy preferences in the absence of external pressure from interest groups (Ibid., p. 398). Such state autonomy undermined the fundamental pluralist assumption of the neutral state that acted upon the dominant policy preferences of interest groups within society. Meynaud argued that ultimately the relatively passive conception of the pluralist state meant that when 'applied to contemporary France, this position [classical pluralism] was untenable' (Ibid.). To back up his point, Meynaud, writing at the outset of the Fifth Republic, drew attention to the burgeoning number of consultative committees, as, although neither a new practice nor isolated to France, this meant that the state was increasingly integrating interest groups into the decision-making process (Ibid., pp. 237–9). Such consultative committees and specialised commissions, he argued, further weakened the relevance of classical pluralism to interest group politics in France. They attributed privileged access to certain groups over others and meant that 'at least within certain limits, the administration no longer decides alone: it shares its managerial *facultés*' (Ibid., p. 246). Similarly, Lavau argued that such consultative committees blurred the boundaries between public and private as 'interest groups become administrators, take over administrative functions and assume (not as such, but within these organisms and in close co-operation with the civil servants belonging to them) certain prerogatives of the state' (Lavau, 1958, p. 82). In doing so, these technical committees, Lavau alleged, were introducing into the French state a sectional or 'particularistic spirit' which undermined its embodiment of the 'general will' (Ibid.).

In this way, then, even the early studies of pluralism emphasised the privileged position of the state in the decision-making process and so can be classed as examples of the state pluralist model. Later pluralist works, such as those by Safran (1991) and Wilson (1983), are consistent with this line of thought. Indeed, Safran identifies seven reasons why pluralism is applicable to the French case (see his list on the following page). For his part, Wilson accepted as deviations from classical pluralist thought the active and dominant role of the state, the distinction that government draws between 'friends and foes', the frequent recourse to protest politics and the ultimate absence of consensus over the rules of the decision-making process. However, he also maintained that the basic pattern of state/interest group mediation in France remained pluralist, albeit what he terms 'limited pluralism' (Wilson, 1983, p. 909). Significantly, he argued that interest group leaders did not perceive groups and their functions as interwoven with the state or threatened by the state. Rather, they interpreted decision making as open to influence, understanding inequalities in access as the result not of privileged relations between the state and certain groups but as the result of the groups' own weaknesses in numbers and mobilisation. With neither representational monopolies nor inter-group accommodation, the strategies employed by groups were wide-ranging and located within the pluralist framework (Wilson, 1983).

Safran's model of pluralism in France

1 Groups themselves have asked for, and helped to develop, regulations regarding any formalised relationship with the government.
2 There is hardly an economic or professional interest that is articulated by a single interest.
3 The leadership of organised interests is chosen not by the government but by the rank-and-file.
4 'Incorporated' groups may freely boycott formal meetings with the government.
5 Privileged links between groups and the government exist in all countries, including archetypal pluralist countries, such as the US.
6 Most groups exhibit 'plural' forms of behaviour depending on the policy issue.
7 Groups continue to engage in classical pluralist activity, such as lobbying, collective bargaining and strikes.

Safran, 1991, pp. 121–2

In fact, although pluralist writers in France have adopted a state-centred approach and have acknowledged, for example, the presence of state-sponsored consultative committees, these writers have also generally dismissed these committees as being ineffective, toothless and erratic arenas of pressure group politics (Wilson, 1983, p. 907). According to this line of argument, the committees are deemed to be far from institutionalised, relying ultimately upon the strategies of state officials, their personal relations with elite leaders and the capacity of groups to present their arguments. (Wilson, 1983, p. 907; Ehrmann, 1971). Indeed, Meynaud argued that the influence of consultative committees appeared far from consistent and had yet to usurp other channels of pressure group activity despite the decline of parliament under the Fifth Republic (Meynaud, 1962, pp. 246–7). More importantly, pluralist writers often stress that interest groups and governments wish to retain their autonomy. They do not want to form privileged, institutionalised contacts. As Wilson notes, the politics of protest in France derives from difficulties of elite/follower relations and the fragmentation and competition between groups that prevents group leaderships from becoming too aligned with government because of the threat of rank-and-file discontent (Wilson, 1987).

It is apparent, then, that there are some cogent arguments in favour of the state-dominated pluralist model of state/interest group relations in France. Indeed, it might be argued that the changing nature of French politics in the last two decades or so has increased the potential viability of this model. For example, Peter Hall has pointed out that in recent years there has been a proliferation of interest groups in France (Hall, 1990a). As such, the French, far from being reluctant to join groups, are now doing so in considerable numbers. Thus, there is an increasing opportunity for competition among groups to occur which is a fundamental characteristic of pluralist studies. At the same time, the role of the state has declined somewhat. The state can no longer be considered to be 'above' society. Moreover, in the cases where the state has institutionalised consultation procedures with interest group representatives, then many of these consultative bodies exist, Hall argues, 'primarily for show' (Hall, 1990a, p. 80). Overall, he concludes that 'a number of convergent trends have enhanced the pluralism of French politics in recent years and shifted some political emphasis away from the state towards civil society' (Ibid., p. 92).

At the same time as there are seemingly good arguments in favour of pluralism, there are also potential weaknesses. The first weakness is theoretical. The recognition by pluralist writers of the autonomy and capacity of the French state to shape policy arenas might be said to detract from the fundamental assumptions of the role of the state in pluralist theory. In other words, it might be argued that the French version of pluralism is so far removed from the classical version of this model that it is no longer merits the pluralist label at all. In short, there is a question mark as to whether pluralism *à la française* is really pluralism at all. Indeed, this point is neatly illustrated by Wilson's rather perplexing assertion that the 'French experience suggests that corporatist patterns of interest-group–government interaction may simply be a form of pluralism to which government and interest groups may have recourse for specific issue areas of certain periods' (Wilson, 1983, p. 909). Here, it seems as if even Wilson himself might be arguing that other schools of thought, in this case corporatism, capture at least as accurately as pluralism the predominant configuration of interest group activity in France.

The second weakness is empirical. Much has been made of the inadequacies of Wilson's methodology and the failure of the pluralist school to acknowledge developments in policy sub-systems such as agriculture (Keeler, 1985). In practice, it is argued, the state has developed privileged relationships with particular client groups in certain areas. In these areas, competition between groups does not really exist, consultative committees are not toothless and policy outputs are a product of the ongoing, institutionalised relationship between the state and 'insider' organisations. Overall, corporatists argue that pluralism can only cope inadequately with the 'privileged' integration of key groups into the policy-making process, and that such developments are evidence of the moves in advanced capitalist societies towards the development of corporatist ties between interest groups and the state. It is to this model of state/interest group relations that we shall now turn.

Corporatism and meso-corporatism

As with pluralism, the corporatist model of state/interest group relations also has a considerable intellectual history. In this case, though, the contemporary theory of corporatism is not primarily a US creation. Instead, it emerged in the 1970s and early 1980s from work carried out mainly on European countries. The concept of corporatism, though, is polymorphic (Jobert, 1996, p. 22). That is to say, it has always had a number of particular meanings often expressed by way of a range of different adjectives and prefixes. So, we find reference to, for example, 'state' corporatism, 'societal' corporatism, 'liberal' corporatism, 'neo-corporatism' and 'meso-corporatism'. All the same, the standard definition of the term has been provided by Schmitter, who states that it consists of:

> a system of representation in which the constituent units are organized into a limited number of singular, compulsory, non-competitive hierarchically ordered and functionally differentiated categories, recognized or licensed (if not created) by the state and granted a deliberate representational monopoly within their respective categories in exchange for observing certain controls on their selections of leaders and articulation of demands and supports.
>
> (Schmitter, 1974, pp. 93–4)

In the French context, Lawson has amended one element of Schmitter's definition so as to emphasise the point that in a corporatist system state and interest group representatives meet together in one or more official organs of government in order to arrive at policy outputs (Lawson, 1983, p. 347). Indeed, this institutionalisation of contacts in formal arenas of government is at the heart of the corporatist model.

The corporatist model of interest group activity in France has been championed by a number of prominent supporters. Most notably, these include William D. Coleman (1993), Bruno Jobert (1989), Bruno Jobert and Pierre Muller (1987), John S. Keeler (1981; 1985; 1987) and Kay Lawson (1983). The early proponents of corporatism in France were keen to take issue with their pluralist counterparts. For this reason, a clear and explicit debate emerged between two rival camps – most notably between Wilson on the pluralist side and Keeler for corporatism. More recently, however, this debate has subsided. Now, the corporatist school is represented

by a highly influential school of thought which has been championed primarily
by Jobert and Muller and which came to dominate French-language
studies of state/interest group relations by the early 1990s. That said, what
is perhaps most striking about all of these studies is that they tend to
propose, once again, a peculiarly French version of the classical corporatist
model.

For many of those associated with this model, France is identified as
demonstrating the essential characteristics of corporatism, but is also said
to exhibit certain distinctive features that set it apart from other countries.
In a comparative context, traditional corporatist accounts have tended
primarily to concentrate on the tripartite negotiations between state
managers and the leaders of peak interest organisations, especially the
umbrella organisations of labour and capital. These closed negotiations
were said to thrive on the low fragmentation of interest groups, the high
density and rates of mobilisation and the hierarchical internal organisation
of these groups. In this context, the high fragmentation and low rates of
mobilisation of French labour unions (see above, pp. 147–8) were said to
mitigate against the pursuit of traditional corporatist mechanisms in
France. As a result, interest representation in France was shown to be
different from the strong corporatist features prevalent in Sweden and
Austria or the moderate corporatism of (West) Germany. Consequently,
proponents of the corporatist model in France retreated from the endorse-
ment of fully fledged corporatism, recognising that the attribution of an
across-the-board corporatist designation of French interest group politics
was a misguided exercise (Keeler, 1987). As such, the corporatist school
that developed in France was primarily that of meso-corporatism, or 'neo-
corporatism' in Keeler's terminology', which acknowledged both that
state/interest group relations varied from one policy sub-system to another
and that it was possible to talk of 'corporatism without labour'. In other
words, in France corporatism was deemed to be sectoral (Muller, 1992b,
pp. 279–80), operating in certain policy areas but not others, including,
most notably, labour relations.

Meso-corporatists characterise policy making as a closed process of
mutually dependent bargaining between state managers and privileged
interest groups, with the outcomes of this process implemented through
the channel of interest group leaderships who police their rank-and-file
membership. Blurring the boundaries between state and civil society, meso-
corporatists argue that the advanced capitalist state is increasingly obliged
to attribute monopoly representation to a limited number of functional or
producer groups in exchange for their co-operation in the formulation and
implementation of public policies. In return for monopoly access, interest
group leaderships undertake to provide the state with organisational
resources such as expertise and information and, more importantly, to discipline their membership during the implementation of agreed policy measures.
These positive-sum games provide state managers with the co-operation

and expertise necessary for policy implementation. They also provide group leaderships with the capacity to influence policy and with the resources that are essential to them both in their competition with other groups and in the creation of selective benefits for their members to over-come the temptation to free-ride (the situation where people gain the benefits of group membership without incurring the costs). Such mutual dependency leads society-centred meso-corporatists to recognise that producer groups place marked constraints upon the actions of state managers. However, state-centred liberal corporatists argue that state elites can recognise, licence and grant representational monopolies to certain groups over others. Indeed, the incorporation of groups into the decision-making process can lead groups to undertake the state's dirty work by disciplining their own members' demands and channelling their mobilisa-tion within the policy process.

In the French case, there is some compelling evidence to suggest that the sectoral corporatist model provides the most salient explanation of interest group activity. In general terms, it is certainly the case that individual groups come close to having a monopoly in different areas. For example, there is a series of groups which represent farmers. However, the Fédération Nationale des Syndicats d'Exploitants Agricoles (FNSEA) is by far and away the largest of these groups and is the one which is said to enjoy a privileged relationship with the government. Similarly, there is a single, dominant employers' group, the Mouvement des Entreprises de France (Medef), which was previously known as the CNPF. It represents the interests of the business sector as a whole and negotiates with the government on its behalf. This was seen in 1997 with regard to the then CNPF's privileged (but ultimately unsuccessful) role in discussions concerning the introduction of the thirty-five-hour working week. In addition, it is also the case that there are a great many different committees, commissions and councils where representatives of these groups formally negotiate with the members of the government. The most obvious example of such an organisation is the Economic and Social Council, which is formally mentioned in the 1958 Constitution. The Economic and Social Council is an example of functional representation consisting of a range of members appointed by both interest groups and the government whose main task is to draw up reports about economic and social policy which are then presented to the government for consideration. Further examples of corporatist-type arrangements are the so-called modernisation commissions, which meet to draw up the five-year economic plans and which bring together representatives of the state and interest groups to discuss economic priorities for the years ahead. All told, in the corporatist model of interest group activity it is argued that these councils, committees and commissions have a positive role to play in the policy process and that policy outputs are the result of ongoing state/interest group interaction.

More specifically, Keeler argues that neo-corporatism best explains the development of the collusive relations between the FNSEA and the

Ministry of Agriculture throughout the Fifth Republic. The emergence and sedimentation of these corporatist relations were facilitated by the transition to the Fifth Republic, the state's requirement of a partner to manage the implementation of structural change within the farming community and the capacity of the agricultural group leaderships to discipline and control grass-root farmers. In fact, in his study of the changing relations between agricultural trade unions and the state, Keeler identified the typical developments associated with a pronounced degree of corporatist decision making. First, the state eased policy implementation through its exploitation of the capacity of agricultural trade unions to police their members. Second, the FNSEA became, for Keeler, a state-supported official union which exercised a considerable degree of hegemony in the agricultural policy sub-system because of its privileged access, both informal and formal, to the decision-making process, its devolved authority and in addition, its state subsidies (Keeler, 1987). Finally, this biased influence and competitive advantage over its rivals provided sufficient incentive for farmers to join the FNSEA, thereby ensuring a 'successful effort by the state to act as the architect of syndical order' (Keeler, 1981, p. 205).

In a similar vein, Jobert and Muller have outlined the presence of sectoral corporatism. They argue that corporatism and the professional regulation of social activities is a fundamental element of the delivery of French public services, but that the nature of the corporatist relation varies from one sector to another (Jobert and Muller, 1987, pp. 171–206). They distinguish two models of sectoral corporatism: technical and social. The technical model involves the take-over of the management of the policy sub-system by a technostructure of elite civil service *corps* (see Chapter 3). In contrast, the social model delegates control to professionals who face an administrative hierarchy with little prestige. Here, the development of sectoral corporatism is not necessarily founded upon the organisational resources associated with the low fragmentation and high rates of mobilisation commonly associated with corporatist state/interest group politics. Rather, the strength of the interest group actors emanates from their cultural authority over other policy actors and the wider parameters of French society. As such, interest group actors are able to dominate other actors through ideological corporatism as it is their unified vision of the world that dominates the preferences and policy instruments of other actors in the policy sub-system.

For example, in the French health policy sub-system, Jobert and Muller recognise the apparent weakness of the sectoral corporatist approach because of the fragmentation of the representative organisations of the medical profession (Jobert and Muller, 1987, p. 184). They acknowledge that interest group fragmentation is compounded by low membership and the inability of professional elites to discipline the rank-and-file members. These organisational weaknesses enable medical elites to mobilise defensively against external threats to its self-regulation and expertise, but leave them unable to take charge of the regulation of the health care system as expected within corporatist bargaining structures. However, Jobert and Muller conclude that the strength of the medical profession lies not in its organisational resources but in its cultural authority over other policy actors and wider French society. As such, the French medical profession provided the dominant *référentiel*, meaning terms of reference or policy discourse, in health policy making. The dominance of such a policy discourse provided the foundations of this particular '*corporatisme à la française*'. That said, it should be noted that in more recent work Muller has pointed to the crisis of French corporatism. This is the result of the increasing role of the market in the public policy process and the fact that France is more and more dependent on the international economic environment at the expense of internal state-led economic policy management (Muller, 1992b, pp. 289–91).

Whatever the arguments in favour of corporatism, the model is still open to criticism. As with pluralism, the first criticism is theoretical. For example, the essence of Keeler's argument is that interest group politics varies from one policy sub-system to another. He argued that state/interest group relations in any given sector could be placed on a continuum ranging from strong pluralism, structured pluralism through to weak corporatism, moderate corporatism and strong corporatism (Keeler, 1985). In this context, though, Mény argues that 'Keeler's neo-corporatist model is quite far from that originally defined by Schmitter' (Mény, 1989b, p. 93). The result, it might be argued, is that, as with the pluralist model, the concept of corporatism is stretched so far in the French case that it loses any analytical force. As Mény notes, 'one can only wonder what validity remains in using the neo-corporatist concept, which had a substantially different definition at the outset' (Ibid.). Consequently, it is better, so it might be argued, to adopt an alternative model of state/interest group relations, such as policy network theory (see below, pp. 164–8), where the degree of conceptual stretching is, arguably, not so pronounced.

The second criticism is, once again, empirical. The response of some writers to the claims of meso-corporatists is to point to the evidence of the weakness of groups and the ineffective nature of consultative committees. So, Cox and Hayward emphasise the point that neo-corporatism is almost completely absent from French economic policy (Cox and Hayward, 1983). More generally, Wilson argues that his empirical findings suggest that neither classical corporatism nor the more restricted notions of meso-corporatism, nor sectoral corporatism, are applicable to the French case (Wilson, 1986, p. 405). Instead, he states that leaders perceive a clear division of responsibility between representatives of the state and interest groups and that both jealously guard their autonomy from each other (Wilson, 1982, p. 199). Echoing these critiques, Culpepper even questions the capacity of the FNSEA to serve as a privileged corporatist partner within the agricultural policy community, particularly after the disruptions of the first *septennat* of François Mitterrand (Culpepper, 1993). He refutes the bipolar nature of corporatist group dynamics in agriculture, allowing for both multiple groups (which is recognised by Keeler) and muted competition between these groups. Both of these points run counter to the corporatist model and Culpepper proposes, instead, a version of the policy network model.

The untidy reality model

At first sight, it might appear as if the untidy reality model is scarcely worthy of being designated a model at all. This is because it is almost an anti-model in the sense that it is deliberately designed to refute the notion that one overarching theory can accurately capture the complexities of state/interest group relations in the French system. The essence of this approach, therefore, is that 'it is misleading to speak of state–group relations and more accurate to think in terms of relations between a particular public decision-maker and a specific group. There is, in truth, an infinite and bewildering variety of situations' (Wright, 1989, p. 290). Nevertheless, to the extent that the basic assumptions of this approach are different from those presented in the three previous models, then the untidy reality interpretation deserves both to be considered and, moreover, to be considered as a separate and distinct account of state/interest group intermediation.

The untidy reality 'model' of state/interest group relations is associated with Vincent Wright. In his classic textbook on the French political process, Wright presents four models of the relations between the state and interest groups (see above, p. 150) and concludes by dismissing all four and by proposing his own interpretation of interest group politics (Wright, 1989, pp. 254–93). To the extent that Wright is most closely associated with this model, his work will provide the focus of attention here. However, there are also echoes of Wright's approach in the work of other writers. For example, in one article Yves Mény argued that 'no model will do' (Mény, 1989b, p. 99). However, Mény has also provided a case for the policy communities approach and so his work will be considered under the policy network model. Perhaps most notably, though, Sonia Mazey (1986) has presented a somewhat similar line of argument which, even though it has been called 'hyper-pluralist' by one critic (Hayward, 1988, p. 114, n. 4), contains many of the themes that can also to be found in Wright's work. Finally, some of the most recent literature on new social movements in France is also worth considering in the general context of this model (for example, Waters, 1998a; 1998b).

As noted above, the untidy reality model does not take refuge solely in a unidimensional explanatory approach. Instead, recognising both the fragmentation of groups and the interventionism of the French state in shaping the group universe, this model highlights the existence of more than one form of interest intermediation in France, invoking multiple models of state/interest group relations, which include variants of pluralism and liberal corporatism. Thus, Wright argues that it is misleading to try and pronounce some kind of general characterisation of interest group politics in France. He concludes:

> To appreciate fully the complex and shifting nature of the relationship between the state and the groups requires an intellectual eclecticism and tolerance ... it is clear that no general theory suffices. Perhaps the only statement that can safely be made is that the relationship between the fragmented state and the no less fragmented groups during the Fifth Republic is like the rest of government – infinitely complex, intrinsically untidy and constantly changing.
>
> (Wright, 1989, p. 293)

Similarly, although Mazey is writing more generally about the French policy style, she presages Wright when she argues that 'public policy-making is too varied and complex a process to be encompassed within a single schema. In practice, the specific nature and severity of constraints encountered by governments differ according to the policy area in question' (Mazey, 1986, p. 413).

There are two main elements to the untidy reality model. The first is the assertion that the state is fragmented (see Chapters 1 and 3). Consistent with the fragmented model of the French civil service, both Mazey and Wright assert that the state is not monolithic. For example, Wright argues that 'both government and administrative institutions are riddled with functional, ideological and personal divisions' (Ibid., p. 274). This means that the state cannot act concertedly. Instead, there is competition between the different components of the state machine. The second aspect of this model is the argument that interest groups themselves are equally fragmented. As Wright notes, 'the term "pressure groups" hides an infinite variety of situations, for they differ in size, structure, strategy, tactics, aims and power' (Ibid.). All told, there is 'variation in state–group relations' (Mazey, 1986, p. 425), or, as Wright puts it, the end result is not a situation in which there is either state pluralism, meso-corporatism or policy networks, but a situation in which 'the relationship between the different organs of official decision-making and the various groups – ranges from domination to subservience, from collusion and complicity to baleful and begrudged recognition and even outright hostility' (Wright, 1989, p. 293). Thus, state/interest group relations are multilevelled, multidimensional and multifaceted.

It is in this context that the impact of new social movements (NSMs) can be integrated into the account of state–group relations. Although most of the people who study NSMs are not concerned with the traditional pluralist/corporatist debate, the rise of new social movements might seem to fit the pluralist account of state–group relations. This is because there are a great many such NSMs covering a wide range of policy concerns with little formalised access to government and which engage in many of the traditional forms of pluralist protest, such as large-scale demonstrations. And yet, it is the very heterogeneity of these groups which suggests that the untidy reality model is the most appropriate intellectual home for their work. So, for example, Waters argues that NSMs operate in political spaces which 'are flexible, diffuse and horizontal, operating without overarching structures or dominant influences' (Waters, 1998a, p. 502). Indeed, she claims that some NSMs do not 'explicitly seek political access as a means of furthering their aims' (Waters, 1998b, p. 171). Instead, they engage in symbolic acts, they operate at the community level and they build relationships with other non-government actors. In these ways, NSMs provide a good contemporary example of the diversity of interest group politics in France. For this reason, they can usefully be considered under the heading of the untidy reality model.

The problem with this model, so it might be argued, lies precisely in the fact that it is not really a model at all. The acceptance of heterogeneity means that this interpretation tells us little about the mechanics of policy making and the variables that explain the different patterns of interest group politics across policy sub-systems and throughout the different steps of the policy process as a whole. Indeed, the essential strength of this model, namely the recognition of the diversity of patterns of interest group politics in France, might actually be said to weaken its capacity to establish any general assumptions which can explain the dynamics of policy making, apart from the acceptance of diversity and the absence of any general prescriptions. Thus, this model risks becoming overly descriptive, with the capacity merely to outline the specific dynamics of interest group politics from one case study to another. As such, it retreats from establishing general assumptions or predictive lessons as to the nature of state/interest group intermediation. In short, what some may see as its basic strength others may view as its fundamental flaw.

Policy network theory

The policy network model is a comparatively recent account of state/interest group relations. Derived from work carried out both in the US and, perhaps more systematically, in the UK, policy network theory emerged during the course of the 1980s and early 1990s. As Cole and John note, the policy network approach 'is based on the idea that, in a complex policy environment of most liberal democracies, decision making is rarely limited to key actors in a single organisation; rather it involves bargains and agreements made between actors across many bodies' (Cole and John, 1995, p. 90). Extrapolating from this assertion, the essence of the policy network model is that policy making takes place within relatively closed networks of government departments, interest groups and professional bodies, or, as Cole and John put it, 'policy networks are regularised patterns of linkages between decision-makers in public and non-governmental organisations' (Ibid.). In the French case, the policy network approach 'has stressed the role of individuals – whether top ranking civil servants or political *notables* – in mediating the complex relations between local and national state, quasi-state and group actors in policy making' (Ibid., p. 93).

In the case of France, there is little specific literature on policy networks, although parallels have been drawn between established UK-centred policy network theory and the work of French writers such as Crozier and Freidberg (1977) and Jobert and Muller (1987), all of whom underline the formulation of public policies within stable networks marked by common values and frequent interactions (Jouve, 1995, pp. 132–3). Instead, the literature of French policy networks tends to be confined to sector-specific studies. In this sense, there are intellectual links between this model and the previous one. However, some of the policy network studies do go on to build up a more expansive account of the policy process as a whole. In this way, there is a fundamental difference between the two. So, those associated with the policy network literature in the French context include Cole and John (1995), Culpepper (1993), Fontaine, 1996), Giuliani (1991), Hayward (1986), Josselin (1995) and Mény (1989a). The sectors considered include local government, agriculture, banking and the financial services and economic policy generally.

In their UK-based study of policy networks, Marsh and Rhodes identify two primary meso-level policy networks – policy communities and issue networks, which emphasise structural relationships between organisations at the sectoral level rather than relations between individuals (Marsh and Rhodes, 1992). 'Policy communities' are characterised by stability, frequent consultation between members, restricted memberships, high levels of consensus and a balance of power among members. 'Issue networks' are atomistic, lack stability, have a large fluctuating membership with limited interdependence and have an unequal spread of resources between members.

Marsh and Rhodes argue that policy networks are brought together through resource dependency, with their boundaries determined by breaks in the resource structure, as identified by the 'centre' or produced by external pressures. Networks subsequently emerge in policy sub-systems such as health, where governments are dependent upon professionals for information and expertise and where decision-making is ultimately biased towards policy implementation. The unsatisfactory quality of coercion as a regulatory tool in the instances where the state depends upon groups for resources obliges governments to exploit the tools of exchange and shared norms and values. However, policy networks are also integrated through shared expertise or common belief systems. In a similar vein, Haas points to epistemic communities, unified by common expertise and sharing normative and causal beliefs and common policy solutions (Haas, 1992).

Equally, Sabatier identifies advocacy coalitions in which groups and organisations share common basic values and belief systems, and operate with the same causal assumptions, problem perceptions and preferred policies (Sabatier, 1988).

In the French case, consistent with the previous model, policy network theory stresses the disaggregation of policy making and the fragmentation of the state. Indeed, similar to Keeler's assumption about neo-corporatism and Wright's argument that reality is untidy, networks are said to vary across policy sub-systems with no consistent policy style or pattern of interest intermediation. Thus, state–group relations under policy network theory are marked by heterogeneity. However, unlike the previous model, this heterogeneity is formalised in terms of a specific theoretical approach.

The essential assumptions of the policy network literature can be identified in a number of policy sub-system areas. For instance, Culpepper argues that the dynamics of agricultural policy making are best encapsulated by competitive policy collaboration whereby multiple independent groups operate in a privileged policy community marked by muted competition (Culpepper, 1993, p. 302). Agricultural groups with technical expertise exercise discretion over policy implementation, particularly at the sub-national level. However, the 'ambit of group policy-making competence is limited, and the importance of the national consultative institutions is erratic' (Ibid.). As such, state actors remain dominant as the role of groups in policy formulation is unlikely to go beyond that of an advisory capacity. In a similar vein, Hayward argues that the image of the homogeneous and highly centralised French state is simplistic (Hayward, 1986, p. 23). Instead, the state is itself fragmented and compartmentalised to the extent that 'power is dispersed among semi-autonomous subsystems, each pursuing its own policy objectives, with its own industrial clientele' (Ibid.). The result is an 'economic policy community', which may be defined as 'a network of identifiable actors engaged in an interactive process by which aims are implemented' (Ibid., p. 7). The main characteristic of a such a system is a situation where the:

> policy-making process is conceived as operating within semi-pluralistic, elitist decision-making communities, which in the case of economic and industrial policy give pride of place to the discretion of actors in the major business firms, to the public and private bankers, and to the politico-administrative leaders, exercised within a framework of domestic and international constraints.
>
> (Hayward, 1986, p. 38)

A more general account of policy networks is provided by Mény (1989a). He argues that the most important element of French policy communities is the power and influence of the French administrative elite (Ibid., p. 390). Members of this elite have a quasi-monopoly of representation in their areas of expertise and they also penetrate the political class by their involvement in ministerial *cabinets* and, indeed, by their recruitment to party political posts. A further component of French policy communities concerns the privileged place reserved for representatives of certain interest groups (Ibid., pp. 391–2). More particularly, the state chooses its partner groups, thus legitimising their role and establishing 'professional oligopolies' (Ibid., p. 393). The result is a highly sectoral policy process in which there is a situation of mutual dependency and relatively fixed state/interest group relations.

Finally, Giuliani provides a more popular, if not populist, account of French policy networks in his study of the lobbying industry (Giuliani, 1991). He, like Mény, stresses the overwhelming importance of the elite administrative training schools that produce graduates who naturally build up a network of personal and professional contacts. Indeed, he argues that 'the old boys network ... is one of the strongest elements of French society' (Giuliani, 1991, p. 90). He also stresses the importance of political networks, sometimes based on factions within individual political parties (Ibid., pp. 93–4). In this context, lobbyists (and the populist tone of the book stems largely from the pejorative nature of this term in the French language) seek out representatives of these networks and build up an address book of indispensable contacts. The nature of these sorts of policy networks is more informal, fluid and open than the ones suggested by Mény's analysis, but the result is essentially the same. Representatives of interest groups interact with state actors in specific issue areas to generate mutually beneficial policy outcomes.

There are two main criticisms of the French version of policy networks. The first criticism concerns the very appropriateness of policy network theory itself. It might be argued that those who employ the term 'policy networks' might just as well use other more formalised models of state–group relations. For example, it is noticeable that Hayward himself describes his policy community approach as a 'semi-pluralistic' account of the decision-making process (Hayward, 1986, p. 38). In a similar vein, there are seemingly close links between some policy network accounts and the meso-corporatist approach to policy making. For example, even if Mény's description of policy making is intellectually compelling, it would not be too unfair to suggest that what he is actually providing is a description of meso-corporatist decision making rather than a new and distinct approach based around a policy communities framework. Equally, it is noticeable that Jouve included Jobert and Muller's account of sectoral corporatism as being in the tradition of French policy network analysis (Jouve, 1995). According to this line of argument, then, there is little to justify a separate theory of policy networks. Instead, policy network theory can be replaced by other more traditional models of state–group relations.

The second criticism is empirically generated and has been provided by

Epstein (1997). He argues that the negotiations to secure a successful world trade agreement during the 1991–3 GATT talks demonstrates the inadequacy of the policy communities approach. He assumes that the agricultural policy-making sector is a good example of the policy communities approach. He then shows that when it was clear that an agreement on the agricultural issue was a prerequisite for agreement in other areas of the GATT talks, the cosy nature of the traditional agricultural policy network was undermined:

> as interest group leaders and high-ranking officials at the [Agriculture ministry] found themselves playing second fiddle to those closer to the power centre of the French government, specifically to the offices of the president and prime minister, and the finance, industry and foreign ministries.
>
> (Epstein, 1997, p. 357)

As a result, he argues that: 'Studies of the French agriculture sector invariably link the policy process to the policy community model, but cannot provide an explanation for the internalized framework that the government adopted during the agriculture crisis' (Ibid., p. 366). In this way, policy network theory, it might be argued, provides at best only a partial account of state/interest group relations.

Conclusion

Despite suffering over time from certain 'information gaps', the study of state/interest group relations in France has spawned a number of high-profile debates, not least that which divided pluralists, such as Wilson, from corporatists, such as Keeler (see Table 7.1). Those participating in this debate must make a fundamental choice as to whether they seek to make macro-level judgements about the nature of state/interest group relations or whether they wish to adopt a meso-level approach that recognises the supposed array of relationships between the state and interest groups across distinct policy sectors. Whatever the choice, all students face a similar set of investigations into issues such as the number of groups within and across policy sectors, the resources at the disposal of these groups, the open or closed nature of decision making and the nature of state intervention in the management of the group universe. Within the academic community, recent studies have tended to favour a meso-level composite approach that recognises the diverse nature of state/interest group relations across a variety of policy sectors. All told, there is no doubt that the pluralist and corporatist paradigms have been largely superseded by the studies associated with the composite approach, most notably policy network theory. Indeed, the policy network model is now intellectually dominant both in France and elsewhere.

Table 7.1 Models of interest group politics in France

	Pluralism	Corporatism	Untidy reality	Policy networks
Definition/key assumptions	1 Power is widely distributed among numerous, autonomous groups 2 The state, however, does at least partly shape the outcome of the policy process	1 State and interest group representatives meet together in one or more official organs of government in order to arrive at policy outputs 2 Institutionalised contacts in formal arenas of decision making	1 Rejection of overarching explanations 2 State/group relations are particular to each policy area	1 Policy making takes place within relatively closed networks of government departments, interest groups and professional bodies 2 Senior individuals mediate the complex relations between local and national state, quasi-state and group actors
Proponents	Hall (1990a), Lavau (1958), Meynaud (1962), Safran (1991), Wilson (1982, 1983, 1987)	Coleman (1993), Jobert and Muller (1987), Keeler (1981, 1985, 1987), Lawson (1983), Muller (1992b)	Mazey (1986), Wright (1989), Waters (1998a, b)	Cole and John (1995), Culpepper (1993), Giuliani (1991), Hayward (1986), Josselin (1995), Mény (1989a)
Argument/evidence	It is easy for interest groups to be formed. There is competition between groups. Groups engage in classical pluralist activity	State is obliged to attribute monopoly representation to a limited number of groups in exchange for their co-operation in policy formulation and implementation. Evidence: agriculture, education	The state is not monolithic. Groups differ in size, structure, strategy, tactics, aims and power. State/interest group relations are multilevelled, multidimensional and multifaceted	Policy making is disaggregated and the state is fragmented. Networks vary across policy sub-systems with no consistent policy style or pattern of interest intermediation
Criticisms	1 The model departs too much from classical pluralism 2 Ignores developments in policy sub-systems where groups have privileged access	1 The concept of corporatism is stretched so far in the French case that it loses any analytical force 2 Groups are weak and consultative committees are ineffective	1 Scarcely merits the term 'model' 2 Fails to have any explanatory power	1 Corporatism and policy networks are a different description of the same basic phenomenon 2 The state is still dominant

The move towards a composite approach to the study of state/interest group relations is based on the acceptance of France as a differentiated polity characterised by multiple resource dependencies in which the state is only one actor among many. However, the recognition of the varied nature of interest group politics in France is not without its difficulties. Most notably, it runs the risk of providing students of French politics with little more than 'thick' descriptions of patterns of decision making in particular policy sectors. There is, thus, a tendency towards hyper-empiricism. However, the great merit of policy network theory is that it has helped to establish a new research agenda. This agenda is based on longitudinal case studies across different policy sectors in France as well as comparative case studies across similar policy sectors in France and elsewhere. Indeed, some of the best contemporary work on interest group activity in France has taken this form (see Cole and John). Over time, policy network theory will no doubt be challenged and alternative paradigms will emerge. However, there is also no doubt that, as with the contemporary debate about, for example, local government, the study of state/interest group relations represents one of the more stimulating areas of French political studies at this time. As a result, studies in this area may provide valuable lessons not only for students of French politics but for students of comparative policy making as well.

8 Europe and the French policy-making style

There is no doubt that one of the most important influences on the functioning of the French political process over the last four decades has been the development of the European Communities/European Union (EC/EU). Although the pace of European integration has been uneven since the signing of the Treaty of Rome in 1957 and although the extent of Europeanisation still varies across the different aspects of the policy-making process, there is now scarcely any aspect of French politics that has not been touched at least to some degree by the impact of European integration. That said, there continues to be disagreement as to the overall effect of Europe on the French political system. There is a debate about the extent to which France has become Europeanised. This debate is the focus of this chapter. It examines the extent to which European integration has changed the French policy-making style. More specifically, it addresses the issue of whether there is a style of policy making that is uniquely French in its operation or whether policy making in France now takes place under essentially the same conditions and manifests itself in basically the same way as policy making elsewhere in Europe.

The chapter begins by briefly charting the impact of European integration on various aspects of the French political system. It then goes on to identify in some depth three separate models of the French policy-making style: the model of French exceptionalism, the model of French conformity and the model of bounded singularity. It should be appreciated right from the outset that this chapter is designed to provide a general overview of the French political process. As such, it deals with a number of topics that have been examined so far, such as the role of the state and local government. It also addresses a number of the themes that have been present throughout the course of the text, such as the transformation of social forces and the representation of popular interests. In this way, this chapter is constructed so as to complement the other chapters in the book, rather than to act as a stand-alone account of the French decision-making process. In practical terms, this means that the reader will often be invited to refer back to previous arguments, so dispensing as far as possible with the need for unnecessary repetition.

France and Europe

Since 1957 the pace of European integration has not been constant and the impact of the EC/EU on the politics of member states has been uneven. In particular, after a period of stalemate in the 1970s the transformation of the EC/EU began in earnest only in the mid-1980s and the 1990s with the signing of the Single European Act (1986), the Maastricht Treaty (1992) and then the Amsterdam Treaty (1997). Moreover, even in recent times moves towards European economic integration have advanced much more rapidly than equivalent developments in the realm of foreign and defence policy making. All the same, however, there is no doubt that the EC/EU has had an impact across an extremely broad range of areas. In the case of France, it is useful to outline the effect of the EC/EU in three such areas: institutions, political representation and policy issues.

Institutions

The EC/EU had had a clear impact on the institutional architecture of French politics. For example, membership has fundamentally affected the functioning of the French legal system. By joining the EC, France agreed that European law would take precedence over domestic law if the two came into conflict. As a result, France in effect agreed to acknowledge the supremacy of the European Court of Justice (ECJ) – the highest court of arbitration within the EC/EU system – over judicial institutions in France. True, it was only in the 1980s that domestic French courts, most notably the Council of State, explicitly recognised the ultimate authority of the EU, but there is no doubt that over the years decisions made by the ECJ have helped to accelerate the process of European integration both in France and across the EC/EU more generally. Another example concerns the role of the country's central bank, the Banque de France. One of the requirements of Economic and Monetary Union (EMU) was that all participating countries had to have an independent central bank – a bank that was free from government influence. For over 50 years, however, the Banque de France had been subservient to the demands of the French government (see Elgie and Thompson, 1998). During this time the government was able to control interest rates and manage monetary policy in the way that it wished. Prior to the introduction of EMU, though, the French government had to give up this power. The government was obliged to introduce legislation and undertake a major institutional reform. As a result, since 1994 the Banque de France has been independent and since 1 January 1999 the power to alter interest rates has rested solely with the European Central Bank (ECB).

In these cases the consequence of EC/EU membership has weakened the sovereignty of domestic decision makers. In other areas, though, the impact of Europeanisation has been somewhat different. For example, it has been argued that the intergovernmental nature of EC/EU bargaining (see below, p. 175) has helped to underpin the presidentialised nature of the French political system (Guyomarch *et al.*, 1998, pp. 45–50). Since de Gaulle, Europe has been considered to be part of the president's 'reserved domain' (see Chapter 2) with the effect that, outside 'cohabitation', the president has been in a privileged position to determine France's position in relation to key issues of European integration. Conversely, however, it might also be argued that in recent times moves towards greater European integration have helped to rehabilitate somewhat the role of the French parliament. As a result of pressure from deputies, the Constitution was amended in 1992 to oblige the government to submit legislative proposals made by the European Commission to parliament for scrutiny. This reform has not fundamentally altered the position of parliament in the system – it remains both weak and peripheral (see Chapters 1 and 2) – but it has allowed deputies to exert at least a greater degree of influence than before over this increasingly important aspect of policy making. A similar example concerns the relationship both between and within member states. On the one hand, the EC/EU has helped to promote the role of the central state and national leaders within the European system by focusing attention on domestic policy positions – what is the French position on enlargement, institutional reform of the EU and so on and how does it differ from, say, the German view or the British view? On the other hand, though, it has also been instrumental in developing the role of sub-national governments in the policy-making process. Indeed, as noted in Chapter 4, the emergence of a regional 'policy space' is at least partly a result of European initiatives regarding the administration of structural funds and other forms of development aid. Thus, European integration has served to strengthen domestic institutions in some cases.

Political representation

In addition to its impact on the institutional aspect of French politics, European integration has also profoundly affected the nature of both party politics and interest group representation in France.

In the case of party politics, Europe has affected the relationships both within and between left- and right-wing political parties, helping to Europeanise parties but often creating a distinct anti-European sentiment as well (see Chapter 5). On the left, problems over Europe at the time of the debate on the Maastricht Treaty were the main motivation for a split within the Socialist Party (PS) and the creation of the Mouvement des Citoyens (MDC). Since the early 1980s the majority of the PS has been in favour of European integration. The MDC, however, is a small anti-European party which has promoted a jacobin-style, state-centred approach. Similar problems have marked the relations between the PS and the Communist Party (PCF). The PCF continues to regard the EU as a capitalist club that is following a liberal agenda. This stance has caused problems with the PS, particularly on the question of budgetary priorities in the context of EMU and the requirement to curb spending and minimise deficit levels. The PCF has wanted more flexibility to increase expenditure levels and run a higher deficit. The Greens, too, have sometimes been hostile to Europe, although more recently their tone has softened. All told, European issues continue to divide the partners in the 'plural majority' and there is no doubt that further substantive moves towards European integration would bring these divisions very clearly to the surface. That said, on the right the European question has tended to be even more divisive and is, perhaps, currently the most public source of difference between the parties in this particular camp. So, for example, there have recently been splits within both the RPR (Rally for the Republic, Gaullist Party) and the UDF (Union for French Democracy) on this issue. In 1999 the anti-European RPF party was formed, bringing together Charles Pasqua and his supporters from the RPR and Philippe de Villiers' Mouvement pour la France Party, which itself had split from the UDF some years previously. Recent divisions, however, should not hide the fact that there have also been long-term problems between the RPR and the UDF on this issue. The UDF was founded to support Giscard d'Estaing, himself an ardent European, and it has always had a strong Christian Democratic element, whose pro-European mentality has often been at odds with the leaders of the RPR and, indeed, which continues to be so even after the exit of Pasqua and his supporters. The European question, therefore, poses problems for all of the traditional parties and their offshoots in the system. More than that, it has also provoked the formation of new parties altogether. Most notably, the formation and success of the Hunting–Fishing–Nature–Tradition party (CPNT) was at least partly the result of the campaign against EU legislation restricting the hunting season. In all these respects, therefore, issues associated with European integration have profoundly affected the cleavage structure of French party politics. More than that, elections to the European Parliament (EP) have themselves helped to redefine the dynamics of party competition in France. They have done so by offering a new electoral arena to parties otherwise excluded by the bipolar tendencies of the two-ballot majority system (see Chapter 6). Indeed, the emergence of the FN, the Greens and, more recently, the CPNT are all clear examples of how parties have exploited the opportunities created by EP elections to gain a foothold in the system.

Interest group politics, too, have been changed by developments at the European level. The increasing influence of the EU in national policy making, as well as the constraints arising from globalisation, have destabilised established patterns of policy making and provided new opportunities for political mobilisation (see Chapter 7). In agriculture, for example, the Uruguay Round of the GATT negotiations, in which the EU was a major participant, brought 'new' actors not usually associated with agricultural issues into the decision-making process and weakened the ties between agricultural trade unions and the French government. More explicitly, the Europeanisation of policy making has also offered interest groups new avenues of access to the decision-making process and allowed the traditional channels of domestic consultative procedures to be by-passed. Indeed, in a landmark case in the 1980s the travel agent, Nouvelles Frontières, was able to exploit the authority of the EC/EU to overcome the reluctance of both the French government and the state air company, Air France, to accept the full liberalisation of air transport and travel. Overall, there are now many more contacts between interest groups at the European level, a greater degree of lobbying by national and European-level groups of EU institutions and even the emergence of 'Euro-strikes' co-ordinated by interest group leaders at the European level with the participation of groups from many member states.

Policy issues

The range of policy areas in which the EU has a role has grown steadily and now encompasses almost all areas of decision making. In this respect, agriculture is perhaps the most Europeanised of all policy areas. The basic elements of the Common Agricultural Policy (CAP) were set out in the Treaty of Rome itself. Indeed, since the 1960s decisions that affect farmers most directly, such as intervention levels, import quotas and price controls, have been taken as a result of negotiations between member-state represen-tatives at the European level. More recently, additional policy areas, such as telecommunications, airlines, insurance, banking and competition policy, have also been increasingly subject to Europe-wide regulation, espe-cially since the passage of the Single European Act. More recently still, the introduction of EMU on 1 January 1999 has fundamentally altered the nature of economic and monetary policy in France. As noted above, the ECB now determines French interest rates. In addition, though, as a requirement of EMU membership, participating countries have been obliged to abide by the so-called 'Maastricht convergence critieria'. In effect, they have had to adopt a policy of economic rigour, keeping budgetary deficits low and maintaining a prudent mix of expenditure controls and fiscal management. All told, EMU countries, including France, have found that their margin for economic manoeuvre is less great than it was previ-ously.

This is not to say, though, that domestic actors are necessarily power-less. On the contrary successive French governments have found ways of managing the degree and the modality of the Europeanisation process. In this respect, the intergovernmental nature of the EC/EU is fundamental. Decision making at the European level usually consists of a long and complicated process of negotiations between representatives of member states. As Guyomarch *et al.* point out, the net result is that, even in the case of agricultural policy, decisions 'are made in Brussels, rather than by

Brussels' (1998, p. 141). In other words, domestic actors, both governmental and non-governmental, can still exert an influence on the policy-making process whatever the degree of Europeanisation. So, although French farmers have long complained about certain aspects of the CAP, particularly after the MacSharry reforms in 1992, France has long been able to use its influence so as to tailor policy in this area to help suit its own agricultural interests. In this way, agricultural policy is undoubtedly Europeanised, but domestic actors remain significant players in the policy-making game. Indeed, the same is true of other policy areas. On occasions French governments, like all of their EU counterparts, have done their best to oppose or delay European reforms. For example, in 1996 the French opposed an EU directive designed to liberalise postal services with the effect that France was allowed to delay the introduction of this reform until 2003. In the case of the state-owned electricity and gas companies, EDF and GDF, the EU's 1996 directive was translated into French law as late as 1999 and, moreover, the legislation was drafted in such a way that only the minimum provisions of the directive were met (see Cole, 1999). Thus, in some instances France, like the UK, can be portrayed as an 'awkward partner', promoting national self-interest at the expense of European co-operation.

Europe and the French policy-making style

This chapter examines the impact of the EC/EU on the French policy style. This begs the question, however, of exactly what is meant by the term 'policy style'. Richardson *et al.* (1981) have provided a useful definition of the concept. They equate it with the central characteristics of the policy process in any given country (Ibid., p. 1). Moreover, they are interested in examining the concept of a policy style not just in terms of how decisions are made, but also in terms of how they are implemented (Ibid., p. 2). To this end, they define a policy style as *'the interaction between (a) the government's approach to problem-solving and (b) the relationship between government and other actors in the policy process'* (Ibid., p. 13, emphasis in the original). This suggests that the study of a country's policy-making style is essentially concerned with an identification of the various arenas of decision making within that country, with an examination of the behaviour of the social and political actors that operate in those arenas and with an assessment of the policy outputs which emerge from the interrelationships of these different actors.

In this chapter, then, the concept of a policy-making style is designed in such a way that it captures the essential nature of the relationships between the various actors in the French political process in all of the arenas in which these actors operate and across the range of policies that are generated by them. The advantage of this approach is that it leaves open the question of whether France has its own, unique policy style or whether its policy style conforms with those in other countries. In other words, it does not prejudge the issue of whether policy styles are divergent or convergent from a cross-national perspective (Richardson *et al.*, 1981, p. 1). At the same time, it also allows a judgement to be made as to whether there is one policy style within France or many. That is to say, it encourages a debate about whether there is a single, dominant form of decision making or a sectorisation of the policy-making process (Ibid., p. 3).

Understood in this way, there are three main interpretations, or models, of the French policy-making style. These models capture the basic differences between the ways in which people think about and analyse the general nature of the policy process in France. The first model, the model of French exceptionalism, suggests that the main characteristics of the French policy-making process are unique. The second model, the model of French conformity, suggests that over time the French policy-making style has come to resemble its counterpart in other European countries. The third model, the model of bounded singularity, might be seen as a synthesis of the first two models in that it suggests that there are elements which are unique to the conduct of the French policy-making process but that there are other elements which closely resemble those to be found elsewhere.

Two points, however, should be noted right at the outset. The first is that in one sense at least the model of French exceptionalism and the model of French conformity might both be criticised as artificial constructs. This is so in that very few people who promote the former are likely to argue that France has always been exceptional in every respect. Similarly, equally few people who put forward the latter will be found to argue that the French policy style is now exactly the same as the policy style in every other EU country. In this way, there is a sense in which everyone, when pressed, is likely to support the model of bounded singularity. That said, there is a basic rationale for all three models including the models of exceptionalism and conformity. This can be found in the emphasis that people place on the arguments that they are making. So, those who stress above all the specific traits of the French system can reasonably be said to be promoting the exceptionalism model. Equally, those who stress more than anything else the comparative elements of the French process can justifiably be deemed to be asserting the conformity model. Finally, those who place the emphasis firmly and squarely on the mixed nature of the French policy style can be considered to be supporting the model of bounded singularity.

The second point concerns the relationship between Europeanisation and internationalisation, or globalisation. For the most part, the models presented in this chapter consider the French policy-making style from a wider perspective than simply Europe. For example, those who support the model of French exceptionalism usually wish to suggest that France is different from all other countries not just European ones. Similarly, those who propose the model of French conformity invariably argue that France is similar to other countries not just as a consequence of membership of the EC/EU but also as a result of wider developments in economic, social and political processes. In this chapter, therefore, we do stress the European aspect of the various models, but where appropriate we also consider international developments as well. After all, the EC/EU itself is by no means insulated from such developments. With these points in mind, each of the three models will now be considered in turn.

The model of French exceptionalism

French exceptionalism may be defined as the situation where the policy-making style in France is different from the equivalent style in any other EU country, or, indeed, from any other country at all. As such, this model might equally be known, for example, as the model of French specificity, the model of French distinctiveness, or the model of policy-making à la française. Whatever the terminology, this model is said by some to apply sectorally, meaning that in a particular issue area or institutional arena the policy-making process and/or the actual policy adopted will be different in France from the equivalent process and/or policy elsewhere. It is also said by others to be true more generally, meaning that the same point applies not just in individual policy areas and institutional arenas but more widely across a range of such areas and arenas as well. That said, what is common to all of those who put forward this model is that French politics and policy making can variously be described as unique, singular, distinctive, peculiar, specific and, hence, exceptional.

For one writer, 'the French exception was nowhere rigorously explained as a model of political behaviour' (Cole, 1998, p. 254). Leaving this question aside for the moment, it is undoubtedly a common perception that France is somehow politically unique both in a European context and from a wider perspective as well. This can be seen, for example, in the proliferation of newspaper articles that purport to identify particular manifestations of French exceptionalism. Indeed, even the most cursory glance at one newspaper can turn up a remarkable number of such reports in just a short space of time. These concern issues such as economic policy ('The double French exception', in *Le Monde Économie*, 10 February 1998, p. I), internet policy ('Internet: the French exception', in *Le Monde*, 28 March 1998), cultural policy ('The "cultural exception", a pessimistic consensus', in *Le Monde*, 7 April 1998) and racism ('Racism: the French exception', in *Le Monde*, 2 July 1998). In addition, the notion that France is unique can also be discerned in the work of many leading academics. Indeed, one writer argues that: 'In most of the comparisons between France and other modern democracies, France generally appears as an anomaly [sic]' (Ashford, 1982b, p. 3). In this context, some writers state very clearly that they are examining a particular aspect of French exceptionalism (see, for example, Cohen, 1998; Crozier, 1987; Godin, 1996;

Mazur, 1993; Sadran, 1997, pp. 53–94; and Smith, 1996). By contrast, others make the assumption more discretely or as part of a wider argument (see, for example, Hall, 1986; Hayward, 1982; and Williams, 1970, p. 3). All told, though, to the extent that at least some of these writers do not simply state that France is a special case but explain why this is so, then it may be argued that, contrary to the initial assertion, French exceptionalism has indeed been rigorously explained as a model of political behaviour.

There is seemingly plenty of evidence to suggest that the French policy style is unique in particular issue areas. For example, there was a widespread belief in the 1960s that French foreign policy was exceptional as France tried to chart an independent course between the two superpowers. Similarly, Hall has argued that in the post-war period French economic policy making has demonstrated peculiar characteristics (Hall, 1986). Equally, Mazur has argued that French sexual harassment policy is exceptional (Mazur, 1993). Indeed, she argues that it is exceptional not only in terms of its content (legislation takes account only of direct harassment of employees by their superiors) but also its timing (this issue was identified as a political problem much later in France than elsewhere) and approach (anti-harassment policy has taken the form of specific law rather than executive orders and case law as well) (Ibid.). In a similar vein, Bornstein has asserted that the Greenpeace affair (where French secret service agents sank the Greenpeace ship, the *Rainbow Warrior*, in 1985) suggests the 'persistence of important elements of French political exceptionalism' (Bornstein, 1987, p. 3). These include the mutual distrust between left-wing forces and the army; a centralisation of executive power; a political culture which is cynical towards politics and politicians; and a highly nationalistic view of France's role in the world (Ibid., p. 14). Along the same lines, Cohen has analysed the specific nature of changing state–society relations in France (Cohen, 1998). He argues that in the 1980s there was a peculiarly '*dirigiste* end to *dirigisme*' (Ibid., p. 42) and that France can still be discussed in terms of being a 'special case' (Ibid., p. 36). Finally, d'Arcy has argued that the French system of prefects remains quite exceptional (d'Arcy, 1996). Sadran, by contrast, contends more generally that the whole French system of local government is unique (Sadran, 1997). He argues that, unlike centre–periphery relations elsewhere, the French system has always been characterised by 'an extraordinary division of structures and a confusion of powers' (Ibid.). Indeed, Sadran makes the further argument that this sector is now also unique in the context of French public administration (Ibid.). This is because the policy-making style in other sectors has recently been subject to certain changes, such as the alternations in power in the 1980s and the increasingly important role of the Constitutional Council, which have brought about an end to French exceptionalism in these areas (Ibid.).

It is apparent, then, that a considerable degree of evidence can be gathered to back up the model of French exceptionalism. However, different factors are emphasised by different writers when accounting for the supposedly exceptional nature of French politics. For example, some people have stressed the social and cultural peculiarities of the French system. That is to say, some writers have tried to identify the essential elements of the French national character, arguing that the French possess certain personality traits that set them apart from other people in other countries both in Europe and elsewhere. These traits, it might then be argued, pervade the political process and result in a uniquely French system of decision making. So, for example, Waterman asserts that 'for all that there has been change, cultural patterns remain the primary stumbling block to the kind of "modern" politics which consensus has brought to other states with equivalent cultural homogeneity' (Waterman, 1969, p. 210). More particularly, Michel Crozier argues that the French fear face-to-face relations and have an in-built suspicion of authority (Crozier, 1967; 1970). As noted in Chapter 1, this has led to a highly bureaucratised system in which informal rules rather than interpersonal negotiation govern the relationship between the citizen and the state. Indeed, Crozier's model of French authority relations has been so influential that it has been explicitly adopted by a number of extremely influential writers (for example, Hoffman, 1967).

In addition to sociocultural arguments, some writers place a considerable degree of emphasis on France's historical trajectory and its concomitant impact on the political process. After all, by definition the country has a unique history and so, it might be argued, it is this historical uniqueness which has helped to create an exceptional policy style. For example, Rosanvallon argues that the singular character of the strong French state was caused by a number of historical factors (Rosanvallon, 1990, p. 274). Most notably, the secularisation of the political process occurred earlier and was more marked in France than elsewhere. Equally, the formation of the state in France preceded the creation of the nation which meant that the state had to assert its authority more comprehensively than was the case in other countries. In a similar vein, other writers have identified long-term historical trends that find expression in regional patterns of religiosity, occupational structures, educational attainment and leisure pursuits and that, for example, still help to shape voting behaviour from one geographical area to the next (Todd, 1990).

Complementing these approaches, some of those who set out to explain the exceptional nature of French policy making stress institutional factors (see, for example, Ashford, 1982a). Indeed, one writer has explicitly refused to adopt what she deems to be 'simplistic' explanations 'based on national character arguments' (Mazur, 1993) such as some of those presented above. In terms of institutional politics, Smith identified two specificities of the French system in his study of the relations between representatives of local government and decision makers at the European level (Smith, 1996, pp. 122–3). The first of these is the presence of the prefectoral system of field administration. Prefects are responsible for overseeing the implementation of EU policies and so occupy a strategic position from which to have an input into the decision-making process. The second is the role of elected politicians. The practice of multiple office-holding (*le cumul des mandats*) means that many politicians who hold office at the national level do so at the local level as well (see Chapter 4). This means that those in positions of authority at the local level have the opportunity to influence the European policy-making process by virtue of their national contacts and position. The result is a very French way of operating which is characterised, for Smith (like Sadran), by 'multiple structures of sub-national policy making' (Smith, 1996, p. 117).

In this vein, Muller outlined a further institutionally oriented version of French exceptionalism. In his earlier work he singled out three key character-istics of the French system (see Muller, 1992b, pp. 275–6). The first concerned the central role of the state in the policy-making process. The state dominated the policy agenda and was the only frame of reference in the policy process. The second pertained to the peculiarly French pattern of sectoral corporatism (see Chapter 7). The third related to the centralised nature of the French state that controlled the implementation of policy at the local level. In these ways, it is apparent that Muller's notion of French excep-tionalism is derived from some of the most long-standing features of French political life. As such, his model of policy making *à la française* is a combina-tion of a number of the most traditional models of politics that have been identified in this book. It should be noted, though, that Muller has since argued that these institutional features have been transformed and that the French policy process now resembles the same process in other European countries (Muller, 1992b, p. 297). In this way, Muller should now be identi-fied with one of the more contemporary models of the French policy style.

Finally, some of those associated with the model of French exception-alism extrapolate from their observations and build up a more general theory of French exceptionalism explicitly combining both institutional and sociocultural factors. For example, Mazur argues that the anomalies of the French policy towards sexual harassment are caused by the 'combined effect of three aspects of French politics and society' (Mazur, 1993). The first aspect is the statist pattern of policy formation, meaning that the policy process is state-centred and that the state only allows those whom it considers to be legitimate social actors to have an input into the policy-making process. The second is the operation of the legal system that relies not on precedent but on statutory penal codes and which has the effect of diluting the ability of feminist activists to litigate sexual harass-ment cases. The third consists of French attitudes towards sexual relations which means that the distinction between acceptable and unacceptable forms of behaviour at work is more blurred that in other countries.

A similar mode of analysis was adopted by Philip Williams. He argued that there were various reasons why there was such a French propensity towards political scandals (Williams, 1970, pp. 3–33). These included the deep social and ideological divisions in the country which meant that there was a considerable degree of mistrust between opposing political leaders (Ibid., p. 7). They also included the structure of government that 'makes it difficult to establish responsibilities and therefore facilitates the misdeeds which arouse public indignation' (Ibid.). In addition, he asserted that there were other relevant institutional factors, such as a venal press, lax court procedure, and underpaid and poor quality judges (Ibid., p. 8).

Finally, one the most comprehensive accounts of the French policy style has been provided by Hayward (1982). In more recent work, Hayward has revised his approach to French distinctiveness (see p. 190 below). However, his earlier analysis of the French policy style is a classic of its type. Here, Hayward is at pains to emphasise the difference between a country's normative policy style, meaning 'the principles that are supposed to govern the process' (Ibid., p. 111), and the behavioural policy style, meaning the 'practices that actually occur' (Ibid.). In the case of the latter, the likelihood is that a country will experience a range of policy styles both over time and across different issue areas at any one time (Ibid., p. 112). Nevertheless, Hayward does identify what he terms France's 'dual' policy style. For him, policy making in France is the result of both cultural and institutional elements. More particularly, it is the result of the particular institutional structure of the regime, the sociological bases of ideological cleavages and the psychological attitudes of insubordination and submissiveness (Ibid., p. 114). In this context, Hayward's argues that the French policy style is characterised on the one hand by a highly bureaucratised style which is reactive in character and which finds it difficult to bring about change by negotiation, and on the other by an assertive, active style which is caused by the informal networks and nucleus of executive power that exist at the summit of the French state (Ibid., pp. 114–16). Thus, there is 'a *capacity* for policy initiative, a *potential* for far-sighted planning and a *propensity* [for the state] to impose its will when this is necessary to obtain public objectives' (Ibid., p. 116, emphasis in the original). At the same time, there is no guarantee of state actors being able to assert their will successfully if politico-economic–administrative actors are resolutely opposed. In this case, a stalemate situation is likely to occur. As a result, in order to engage in successful policy making the state is obliged to bring interest groups on board (see Chapter 1). In this context, Hayward states that 'the mobilisation of private interests in the service of public ambitions is ... the salient element of the French policy style' (Ibid., p. 137). All told, while Hayward's argument is not explicitly expressed in terms of the model of French exceptionalism, the assumptions that are made and the context in which it appears encourage this classification.

Seemingly, therefore, there are plenty of examples to back up the model of French exceptionalism and plenty of reasons why these examples should manifest themselves. Indeed, it is apparent that there are definite connections between this model and some of the models which have been identified in previous chapters. At the same time, though, whatever the connections and whatever the evidence and arguments that can be marshalled more generally in its favour, it should also be noted that there are potential problems with the model of French exceptionalism. In this respect, three main points can be made.

First, it might be argued that this model is true but only trivially so. That is to say, there is no doubt that France has a unique history, singular social features and particular policy outputs. But, then, so too does every country, including France's closest European neighbours. According to this argument, therefore, the model can only be trivially true. That is to say, it is true only because of the mode of analysis rather than because of the validity of the evidence and the arguments which back it up.

Second, a different line of argument suggests that, even if this model was indeed once accurate, it has now passed into history. If at one time it did accurately describe the essential characteristics of the French policy-making process, then changes have since occurred, including the impact of Europeanisation, which now make it less salient. Indeed, it is apparent that many of those whose work is consistent with this model were writing in or about French politics in the period before the 1980s which was when the most significant changes in the political process occurred and when the pace of European integration was increased. Equally, it is also apparent that many of those whose work is more contemporary prefer to adopt a different model that takes account of these changes. So, while there may still be certain sectoral examples of French exceptionalism (see, for example, the model of bounded singularity), it might be argued that the general model of French exceptionalism no longer applies.

Third, it might also be argued that this model never really applied in the first place. The argument that France is exceptional is a comparative one. This is because by definition France can only be considered exceptional if its policy style is actually shown to be different from those of other countries. However, by and large those who promote the model of French exceptionalism are not comparativists but experts on France who base their arguments on in-depth country-specific studies of France alone. Indeed, most people who have argued that France is exceptional have invariably done so without anything but the most passing reference to other countries. And yet, just as French experts often consider France to be exceptional, there is a similar tendency for experts on other countries to consider the politics of their preferred country to be unique. So, British experts often consider Britain to be exceptional, Italian experts often consider Italy to be exceptional, German experts often consider Germany to be exceptional and so on. Consequently, those who are associated with the model of French exceptionalism may indeed have identified the most salient characteristics of the French policy style. However, it might be argued that if French politics is studied from a comparative perspective then many of these characteristics are in fact shared by other European countries (and were shared even prior to the beginning of the 1980s). According to this line of argument, then, the model of French exceptionalism is simply myopic.

The model of French conformity

In contrast to the previous model, the model of French conformity may be defined as the situation where the policy-making style in France is essentially the same as the equivalent style in other EU countries and, indeed, elsewhere as well. According to this model, the French policy process has increasingly been subject to the same economic, social and political pressures that have been present everywhere else. As a result, there has been a general convergence of policy styles both within the member states of the EU and across states more generally. As a result, the French policy process is now similar to the process in other countries and has lost its originality (*s'est banalisé*).

This model emerged in the late 1980s in the context of both the celebration of the bicentenary of the French Revolution and the moves towards greater European integration contained in the Single European Act and then the Maastricht Treaty. At this time, many of those who proposed this model couched their arguments in terms of a direct rebuttal of the model of French exceptionalism. That is to say, they almost invariably asserted not only that the French policy style now conformed to equivalent policy styles in other countries, but also that over time there had been a shift from the model of French exceptionalism to the model of French conformity (see, for example, Furet *et al.*, 1988; Hewlett, 1998; Imbert, 1989; Kuisel, 1995; Lesourne, 1998; Lovecy, 1992; Saint-Étienne, 1992; and Slama, 1995). Only rarely have writers argued that France has never been exceptional and even then such arguments have usually only been made in the context of a specific policy area (see, for example, Halimi, 1996). That said, there are a number of studies that stress the impact of the EU on the French political process and do so without directly evoking the end of French exceptionalism (see, for example, Dreyfus *et al.*, 1993; and Ladrech, 1994).

As with the exceptionalism model, there would appear to be plenty of evidence to back up the conformity model. For example, Imbert has underlined the changing ideological parameters of French foreign policy where there has been a move towards domestic political consensus most notably as the Gaullist Party has relaxed its 'often stormy nationalism' (Imbert, 1989, p. 53; see also Rouban, 1990). By contrast, others who put forward this theme stress the extent to which it has affected France more generally. So, Hewlett argues that France has become more consensual (Hewlett, 1998). He argues that since the beginning of the 1980s there has been a convergence of ideological opinion and, although protest does still occur, it now tends to be perpetrated by groups who aim to defend the status quo 'rather than constituting positive action in favour of radical, often socialist-inspired change, as was often the case in the 1960s and 1970s' (Hewlett, 1998, p. 84). For Hewlett, this does not necessarily mean that France now conforms to 'any sort of perfect liberal democratic model' (Ibid.), but it does indicate that France now shares some of the most basic characteristics of its nearest neighbours. Similarly, Machin argues that in the 1980s France became more and more Europeanised. He points out that French monetary policy followed the German line and that in the areas of agriculture, industry, taxation, transport, public procurement and international economic relations policy making was determined at the European level (Machin, 1990, p. 1). This leads him to state that: 'French politics and policy making are intrinsically and increasingly part of a greater European whole' (Ibid., p. 2). Finally (and in a slight contrast to Hewlett's argument), Furet asserts that France now manifests the characteristics of other democratic societies which are based on prosperity, education, the standardisation of class and morals and the public acceptance of the organisation of political power (Furet, 1988, p. 54). Thus, he states that: 'the French political theatre of the exceptional has closed and the country has entered the common-law ranks of other democracies' (Ibid.; see also Lesourne, 1998).

Whether France now conforms to other countries in particular areas or more generally, what is common to most of the above writers and others is that France has lost elements of its distinctive identity and with it its political exceptionalism as well. Thus, Furet *et al.* state that 'what we are currently going through is quite simply the end of French exceptionalism' (Furet *et al.*, 1988, p. 11). In a similar, but more melancholy, vein, Kuisel laments:

> This *fin de siècle* France is different from the France of 1900 or even 1950 because its boundaries (economic, social and cultural) are porous. Because its society now appears to be ethnically divided. Because key institutions and ways of life that identified Frenchness, such as the Catholic Church, the peasantry, linguistic purity and prestige, a bourgeois society, and a paternalistic State have faded. Because society and culture have become, to a degree, Americanized. Because the economy is more embedded in Europe and the world than even before.
>
> (Kuisel, 1995, pp. 45–6)

Indeed, this tone is adopted by many of those who write on this theme. So, for example, Saint-Étienne begins by painting a sombre picture of the loss of French values, stating *à la* Furet *et al.* that 'the political theatre of exceptionalism is closed' (Saint-Étienne, 1992, p. 29), and then goes on to propose a blueprint for French society, which he believes will allow new forms of French exceptionalism to re-emerge.

The proponents of the model of French conformity can point to three particular reasons why the country's policy style has changed. The first concerns the transformation of French social and cultural life (see Lesourne, 1998, chapters IV–V). This theme is cogently presented by Mendras (Mendras, 1994; Mendras with Cole, 1991). He argues that France has undergone a social revolution which began in the 1960s (Ibid., pp. 5–12). He points out that the period from 1944 to 1965 was marked by tremendous economic growth, a demographic explosion, rural depopulation, the decline of the peasantry and the rise of the salaried classes. Thereafter, though, social and economic trends were more contradictory: the birth rate fell, immigration increased, as did unemployment, whereas the number of women in employment actually rose. Also after 1965, the Fifth Republic's institutions matured, the Catholic Church modernised, hypermarkets started to appear and permissiveness was on the increase. For Mendras, these changes and others marked the beginning of the second French Revolution. The social, economic and political rules of the game were transformed. There was a decline in the revolutionary tradition, an acceptance that economic objectives were more important than social or political ones and the end of the clerical/anti-clerical division. It should be noted that Mendras's analysis is almost exclusively Franco-French. However, he does note that the same, or equivalent, changes occurred in roughly the same period elsewhere and so their net effect has been to propel France in the direction of other countries (Mendras, 1994, pp. 434–43). Thus, the second French Revolution may indeed have resulted in the situation where end-of-century France is 'scarcely recognisable even from the vantage point of the 1980s' (Mendras with Cole, 1991, p. 12). At the same time, though, it is clearly the case that at the end of the 1990s socially and culturally France is remarkably similar to counterparts in Europe and the wider world.

The second reason why the French policy style has changed concerns the impact of the EC/EU more specifically. For example, Ladrech states that: 'Europeanization is an incremental process reorienting the direction and shape of politics to the degree that EC political and economic dynamics become part of the organizational logic of national politics and policy-making' (Ladrech, 1994, p. 69). The implication is that all EU countries are experiencing this phenomenon and that the policy styles in EU countries are, therefore, converging. So, while Ladrech argues that the EU has changed two particular aspects of the French policy style, he also notes that these changes are 'indicative of trends found in other EC Member States' (Ibid., p. 70). The first change that he identifies concerns constitutional and parliamentary developments. Here, constitutional amendments, such as those necessitated by the Maastricht Treaty, have both weakened the French concept of citizenship (Ibid., p. 74), whereby previously citizenship was restricted to French nationals (i.e., members of a specific social community), and revived the concept of parliamentary democracy (Ibid., p. 76) in the sense that the legislature can now vote on EU resolutions rather than simply expressing an opinion. The second change deals with the territorial bases of decision making. Ladrech suggests that the impact of the EU has resulted in a more deconcentrated and decentralised process in which regions and departments now have greater input into traditional policy networks (Ibid., p. 80). As a result of these, and other, changes, it is reasonable to suggest, as Machin does, that domestic politics in France 'are increasingly normal, in the sense of resembling those of France's similar-sized European neighbours, West Germany, Britain and Italy' (Machin, 1990, p. 2).

The third reason for the transformation of the French policy style concerns the trend towards the internationalisation of economic, social and political life. This trend has affected not just France but all EU countries as well as other liberal democracies more generally (Lesourne, 1998, chapter II). In the French context, two manifestations of this trend are often underlined. The first is quite specific and concerns the Americanisation of French life (Kuisel, 1995, pp. 37–9). The cultural hegemony of the US has fed into the French system, changing the language, the content of television programmes, leisure pursuits, eating patterns and a host of other lifestyle issues. Overall, it has created the situation where the French now supposedly 'revel in the comforts and attractions of consumer society and mass culture' (Ibid., p. 39). It might also be argued that this has helped to reinforce changing political values, such as ideological consensus and the end of anti-Americanism as a pillar of foreign policy. The second aspect of this trend is more general and concerns the internationalisation of economic policy. The world economy has opened up. There has been a growth of multinational companies, the liberalisation of financial capital and the rise of world trade agreements. In this context, the decision-making autonomy of national governments has declined. The net result is that decision makers now only have a very restricted set of policy options between which to choose. Thus, convergence becomes inevitable. In the French case, perhaps the most notable consequence of this trend has been the decline of state-directed economic planning (Maclean, 1997, p. 226). Indeed, the main lesson to be learnt from the experience of the socialist government from 1981 to 1984 was that decision makers in France no longer have the capacity to buck the world economic trend and go it alone.

As with the previous model, the model of French conformity does appear to have plenty of evidence to back it up and a strong set of arguments to underpin it intellectually. As before, though, there are also potential criticisms of this model. In this case, two may be singled out for particular attention.

The first criticism begins by acknowledging that change has occurred.

There has clearly been a profound transformation of French economic, social and political life since the beginning of the 1980s (and even since the 1960s and 1970s). It can also be acknowledged that this transformation naturally encourages the interpretation that there has also been a complete reorientation of the French policy style. However, this criticism then suggests that change is not something that has just occurred recently. Instead, social transformation has been a consistent feature of the French system for at least two centuries. Thus, if the policy-making style in the period prior to the current wave of change was consistent with the model of French exceptionalism, then there is no logical reason why the policy-making style should not also be consistent with this model during and even after the current period of change. So, even though the form of the changes in the current period may be time-specific (the development the EU and so on), the experience of change is nothing new. As such, just as economic, social and political transformations in the 1800s and early 1900s may have resulted in an exceptional French policy style, so similar transformations at the end of the twentieth century may just have maintained an equally exceptional style.

The second criticism also begins by acknowledging that change has occurred. Here, though, the argument can then be made that the pace of change, particularly the pace of European development, has been uneven. So, whereas in some areas there has indeed been an upheaval of the traditional French policy style, in others the basic elements of the older system remain. So, although European integration has shaped the content of policy in certain areas (agriculture, competition and monetary policy, for instance), elsewhere the basic patterns of decision making have been less affected (pensions, taxation and labour relations). This, then, suggests neither that the French policy style is still exceptional (if it ever was) nor that it is simply the same as can be found elsewhere. Instead, it suggests that the model of bounded singularity is more appropriate.

The model of bounded singularity

The model of bounded singularity may be defined as the situation where the French policy-making style shows both similarities with and differences from policy styles in other European countries. This model can be considered as an intermediate model which combines the essential assumption of each of the two previous models. So, in line with the model of French conformity, here the policy-making style is said to have undergone change in recent years. At the same time, consistent with the model of French exceptionalism, the policy style is also deemed still to exhibit distinctive traits. According to this model, then, there are many features of the French policy process that are recognisable in policy styles elsewhere. At the same time, though, there are also aspects of the French process which continue to differ markedly from the experience of other countries.

As with the previous model, the model of bounded singularity has emerged only relatively recently. Those who propose it insist that France maintains certain singular features even if it has lost others. Thus, like the previous model, it is often put forward by those who believe that France is no longer exceptional, even though it once was. Moreover, it is also supported by those who believe that, although France has changed, it still maintains elements of its long-standing distinctiveness. The meso-level nature of this argument means that there are clear links between this model and some of the models examined in the previous chapters which emphasised the multifaced, differentiated nature of the French polity. Indeed, Guyomarch *et al.* provide an indication of these links when they stress the complexity of the contemporary policy-making process in France and argue that the impact of the European Union on French politics has resulted in a situation where there are now 'numerous and overlapping multi-level territorial and sectoral networks' (Guyomarch *et al.*, 1998, p. 240) which, by implication, militate against macro-level accounts of the French policy-making style. All told, the bounded singularity model is characterised by the degree of emphasis that writers place on both the similarities and differences of the French policy style when compared with other countries. In this context, those who may be associated with the model of bounded singularity include Boyer, 1992; Cole, 1998; Hayward, 1986; 1988; Hoffman, 1987; Hollifield, 1991; Kassim, 1997; Rémond, 1993; Ross, 1991; Suleiman, 1995; and Wright, 1989; 1997.

As might be expected, there is plentiful evidence to support the model of bounded singularity. For example, Boyer has argued that the last twenty years have seen a transformation of French industry and yet he also concludes that, even if the dominant mode of French production is similar to other countries, France still maintains distinctive characteristics (Boyer, 1992). He states that: 'a certain erosion of French particularism is ongoing, but it would be premature to conclude from this that there has been a complete and definitive convergence on a single model' (Boyer, 1992, p. 23). Similarly, Wright has insisted that the French model of state-directed economic planning (*dirigisme*) has been reshaped as a function of ideological and political changes, budgetary constraints, globalisation, Europeanisation and technological transformation (Wright, 1997, p. 151). As such, he argues that the reshaping of *dirigiste* policies has meant a partial end to French exceptionalism (Ibid., p. 152). At the same time, though, he also states that: 'in spite of convergence, France retains a distinctive fiscal system, industrial relations and wage bargaining systems, labour market regulations, educational and training systems, and financial and corporate governance' (Ibid.). He then adds: 'These distinctive features of France have resulted in different timing and pace as well as extent and nature of the implementation of the new economic orthodoxy' (Ibid.). Thus, he suggests that there has been a sectorisation of the French policy style that is consistent with the model of bounded singularity. In making this point, he is elaborating on a previous argument that stressed both the international constraints on public policy making and the peculiarly domestic set of political, administrative and constitutional factors (Wright, 1989, p. 348).

Over and above this sector-specific evidence, other writers have stressed the themes of bounded singularity more generally. For example, Cole argues that 'France has certainly changed' (Cole, 1998, p. 260), but immediately adds that it 'has not quite become a nation like the others' (Ibid.). To back up his argument, Cole argues that France maintains a degree of specificity in terms of its foreign policy and its self-perceived cultural mission (Ibid.). Suleiman, too, emphasises the changes that France has undergone but notes that these have taken place within the context of a singularly French policy style. The result is that 'the change of values remains fragile and reliant on more long-term trends' (Suleiman, 1995, pp. 21–2). Hoffman makes a similar argument. He notes that 'Much to the regret of many students of French uniqueness, France has become very much more *comme les autres*' (Hoffman, 1987, p. 350). The normalisation of French politics manifests itself in freer television channels, more rights for workers in enterprises, more local self-government, more habeas corpus, the meltdown of the Communist Party, the *aggiornamento* of the Socialist Party and the more pragmatic concerns of the French electorate. At the same time, Hoffman also notes that there are 'many features that remain distinctive' (Ibid., p. 351). These include the continuing strength of the state, the organisational weakness of French society, the persistent failures of party representation, the nature of French authority relations, the educational system, the jacobin conception of national identity and France's foreign policy. Finally, the overall theme of Hollifield and Ross (1991) is that France has changed economically, socially and politically, but that a new equilibrium situation has not yet been established. As such, Ross asserts that 'France is unquestionably quite a bit less like it was a quarter-century ago and rather more like its neighbours' (Ross, 1991, p. 15) and Hollifield concludes that 'As France faces the twenty-first century, it does so with a familiar admixture of the new and the old' (Hollifield, 1991, p. 293).

A similar argument is made in the later work of Jack Hayward (1986; 1988). He argues that France did have a distinctive 'dual' policy style (see p. 182 above). However, he also states that international pressures have now affected the fundamental nature of this style. Thus, he argues that French policy making can still be distinctively 'heroic' (Hayward, 1988, p. 101), but that it is now more difficult to generalise across policy areas (Ibid., p. 92). More specifically, he argues that French policy making may still be unique in intention, meaning that decision makers continue to champion French-specific solutions but that outcomes have become less distinctive as a result of international constraints and commitments (Ibid., p. 107). Thus, French policy making is now an example of 'Prometheus bound' (Hayward, 1988, p. 222), or the situation where what survives of French distinctiveness is the way in which the country adapts to general trends (Hayward, 1988, p. 114). As Hayward puts it, France cannot lead but 'she can at least follow in her own way' (Ibid.).

A final example of the bounded singularity model has been provided by Kassim (1997). He considers the impact of the EU on French policy making. He argues that France was scarcely affected by the EU until the mid-1980s, but that since this time there has been a considerable degree of Europeanisation (Ibid., p. 167). However, he also argues that it is impor-tant not to exaggerate 'either the influence of the Union as an impetus to policy change, the impact of the EU as a constraint on the French state, or the powerlessness of French governments' (Ibid., p. 168). Instead, the EU's impact has been uneven, meaning that there is a considerable degree of sectoral differentiation from one policy area to another. Thus, overall there has been a 'dissipation of the national' (Ibid., p. 179) but not a complete effacement of the French policy style.

In explaining the presence of bounded singularity, different writers emphasise different points. For example, Rémond makes a quite particular argument (Rémond, 1993). He contends that the nature of French politics has changed not because of the Europeanisation of the political process but as a result of social changes which have been occurring both within France and in countries more generally (Ibid., p. 204). The domestic focus of his argument leads him to conclude that recent changes are likely to find expres-sion in new and original ways of behaviour that will remain quintessentially French (Ibid., p. 209) rather than a loss of French originality altogether. In a similar way, Suleiman argues that, despite the changes that the French policy style has recently undergone, the singular traits which remain are caused by the unique nature of the country's culture and history (Suleiman, 1995, p. 360). Thus, he asserts that 'Culture and history neither imprison a society nor prevent it from changing, but remain present, even if they are less and less noticeable' (Ibid.). Again, therefore, bounded singularity is caused by dom-estic reasons based on culture and historical trajectory.

A slightly different argument is provided by Cole (1998). This argument is more general, explaining bounded singularity in terms of internal institu-tional reasons and external factors as well. He argues that three factors have served to render the changes to French exceptionalism 'more visible' (Cole, 1998, p. 254) than elsewhere. These are: the role of France as a leading European nation with the concomitant responsibilities that this status implies; the particular state tradition which implies state-directed intervention in the policy process; and the country's historical legacy which shapes attitudes and beliefs (Ibid.). At the same time, the influence of these elements is such that the 'case for a weakening of the French exception should not be overstated' (Ibid., p. 260). In conclusion, he argues that 'the policy responses adopted by French governments will continue to combine particular patterns of governing inherited from French history, with necessarily flexible responses to the changing circumstances of policy making in the twenty-first century' (Ibid., p. 261).

As with the other models of the French policy-making style, the model of bounded singularity would appear to be quite persuasive. There is apparently good evidence to demonstrate it and seemingly coherent arguments to support it. As with these other models, though, there are certain problems. However, as a result of the very nature of the model, these problems merely echo points that were made previously. So, two particular concerns might be voiced.

First, as in the case of the model of French exceptionalism, it might be argued that the model of bounded singularity is true but only trivially so. That is to say, it is quite apparent that the French policy style varies from one sector to another. However, it is bound to do so and it would be naive to suggest that it could otherwise be the case. Thus, any model that stresses the sectoralisation of policy making is true but such a model adds little or nothing to our understanding of the system as a whole.

Second, if it is accepted that the model of bounded singularity is only valid if it applies generally rather than sectorally, then the counterargument is simply that the extent of change has been either overestimated or underestimated depending on the point of view. So, those who support the model of French exceptionalism might suggest that the degree of change has been overestimated, whereas those who support the model of French conformity might indicate that the degree of change has been underestimated. Thus, it might be argued, the fact that the model of bounded singularity takes an intermediate stand between the two other models merely means that it lies in an academic no man's land and not that it provides a more 'realistic' picture of the French policy scene.

Conclusion

It is clear, then, that there is an ongoing debate about the main features of the French policy-making style especially in relation to the equivalent features in other countries (see Table 8.1). What is also clear is that in many respects the controversies surrounding this debate are similar to those surrounding many of the other debates in this book. So, there are various competing alternatives from which to choose. Is France unique, or is it simply a country like any other? Is political life quintessentially French, or is the French political process remarkable for its unremarkability? Alternatively, is the policy process a mix of both traits? Do certain distinctively French features coexist alongside other more comparatively normal aspects of the French political scene? As before, these alternatives are incompatible. The acceptance of one must involve the rejection of the others. In this vein, it is apparent that writers have tended to gravitate towards the third of these options. So strong is the notion that France is exceptional that it is difficult for many authors to suggest that there has

Table 8.1 Models of the French policy-making style

	French exceptionalism	French conformity	Bounded singularity
Definition/key assumptions	1 The French policy-making style is different from anywhere else 2 French politics and policy making is unique, singular, peculiar and specific	1 The French policy-making style is the same as other countries, particularly in EU 2 For most writers, this is a recent development	1 The French policy-making style shows both similarities with and differences from other countries 2 The policy style varies from one issue area to another
Proponents	Cohen (1998), Godin (1996), Hall (1986), Hayward (1982), Mazur (1993), Sadran (1997), Smith (1996), Williams (1970)	Furet et al. (1988), Hewlett (1998), Imbert (1989), Kuisel (1995), Lesourne (1998), Lovecy (1992), Saint-Étienne (1992), Slama (1995)	Boyer (1992), Cole (1998), Hoffman (1987), Hollifield (1991), Rémond (1993), Ross (1991), Suleiman (1995), Wright (1997)
Argument/evidence	France is historically, socially, culturally and institutionally unique. Evidence: economic policy and sexual harassment policy	France has been affected by Europeanisation and internationalisation Social and cultural life has been transformed Evidence: foreign policy and state/society relations	Economic, social and political change, but no new equilibrium situation Evidence: economic planning
Criticisms	1 The model is only trivially true 2 Model is now outdated 3 Model was never applicable as cross-national studies showed	1 Change is not new, so the current period of change does not have to bring about conformity 2 Pace of change is uneven so there are areas of specificity and conformity	1 The model is only trivially true 2 Some say change is underestimated 3 Others say change is overestimated

been a complete *banalisation* of French political life. At the same time, so overwhelming has been the influence of international and European pressures that it is difficult to conclude that France remains wholly sheltered from the economic, social and political transformations that have occurred elsewhere. Once more, we are overwhelmingly confronted with a picture of French politics that emphasises complexity, disaggregation and differentiation. The student must decide whether or not this particular interpretation is the most accurate portrayal of the French policy-making style.

9 Conclusion

In the Preface we stated that this book was born out of both passion and frustration. We hope that our passion for French politics has come to the fore. We also hope that we have worked out some of our frustration. In particular, we hope that the models we have presented constitute a significant value-added to the student of French politics – undergraduate, postgraduate and academic alike. In the past, we have been stimulated by the debates that we have encountered. At the same time, we have also been frustrated in the cases where scholars have taken assumptions as given and where these assumptions have been treated as if they were uncontestable. We hope that we have brought some of these hidden assumptions out into the open so perhaps allowing for more direct and clear-cut debates to occur in the future.

Whatever our personal motivation, throughout this book our fundamental concern has been to show that people disagree with each other. These disagreements come about because writers make varying assumptions about the topic in question and because they provide particular examples to back up these assumptions. True, there are overlaps between the work of different people. For example, if the writers associated with two separate models make three fundamental assumptions and two of these assumptions are the same in both cases, then their work is bound to contain certain similarities. Even so, the basic point still stands. Writers choose to make some assumptions and not others. They also choose to emphasise particular pieces of evidence at the expense of others, or at least they choose to interpret the same piece of evidence in different ways. In this way, academic debates of the sort considered in this book are all about making intellectual judgements and justifying those judgements with empirical evidence.

For any given topic, therefore, the task of the student of French politics is to identify the particular assumptions that are being made and to judge whether or not the proposed evidence confirms the validity of these assumptions. So, for example, with regard to Europe and the French policy-making style, the nature of the debate was quite clear. Different writers made different assumptions about the uniqueness of French policy making. Some argued that it was peculiarly French. Others said that it was Europeanised. Others still suggested that it was a mixture of both. The student must decide which of these judgements is the most convincing on the basis of the best available evidence. The student must determine which of these alternatives most accurately captures the fundamental characteristics of the French policy-making style.

Moreover, this point applies not just to the controversies in individual chapters but to debates in French politics more generally. Across the range of different topics in this book we have tried to show that people disagree with each other quite consistently. In other words, the disagreements that are apparent in one particular chapter are often closely related to the disagreements that are apparent in other chapters. This situation occurs because the assumptions upon which a certain model is based are often related to wider aspects of the political process. This means that there are links between the models in different debates. For example, if a writer believes that the presidency is virtually all-powerful, then that writer is likely to support both the monocratic government model of executive politics and the presidentialised party model of party politics. It also means that there are links between models more generally. For example, if a writer believes that the state sector is in the process of a profound transformation, then he or she is likely to support not only the model of the disoriented state but also the model of the fragmented bureaucracy, the model of local governance, the policy network model of interest group activity and the bounded singularity model of the French policy-making style. Thus, academic debates are not only about making choices, they are about making consistent choices. The student must decide not only which choices most accurately capture the fundamental characteristics of a particular debate, but also whether these choices are consonant with the assumptions that have been made in other debates as well.

In addition to reporting the various debates in French politics, in this book we have also tried to chart the development of these debates. What we have endeavoured to show is that for any given topic the terms of the debate have changed over time. So, for example, the pluralist model of interest group activity was challenged by the corporatist model, which was then countered by both the untidy reality model and, more recently, by policy network accounts of state/society relations. In line with the point in the previous paragraph, what we also wish to show is that the development of these individual debates is related to developments in the study of French politics more generally. In this context, it is useful to classify the development of French politics into three distinct periods.

The first period is characterised by a dominant intellectual paradigm that was established in the early years of the Fifth Republic. So, we find that the principal points of reference at this time were the model of the strong state, the monocratic government or, arguably, the segmented government model of executive politics, the technocracy model of the bureaucracy, the agent model of local government, the presidentialised party model of party politics, the sociocultural model of voting behaviour, the pluralist model of interest group politics and, finally, the model of French exceptionalism. What we also find was that many of these models were based on an historical institutionalist account of French politics. They tended to focus on the historical relationship between institutions; they tended to privilege the legal and constitutional aspects of this relationship; and they tended to assume that the French state was a strong, monolithic and highly centralised entity.

The second period is characterised by a reaction to this dominant paradigm. For the most part this reaction occurred in the 1970s or early 1980s. In some cases, it was inspired by empirical observations. For example, the inability of the sociocultural model of voting behaviour to predict the result of the 1978 and, particularly, the 1988 election led to the development of the model of the 'new' voter. Equally, the development of the party influence model of party politics was largely inspired by the role of the Socialist Party after its victory in 1981. Similarly, the conformity model of the French policy-making style emerged following observations about the increasing influence of the EU and the internationalisation of political and economic life more broadly. In other cases, however, the reaction to the dominant paradigm was brought about both by the development of more complex institutional accounts of the French system and by the application of assumptions from other intellectual disciplines, notably sociology and economics, to the study of political life. The complex institutional accounts tended to attack the dominant paradigm on its own terms and, more often than not, suggested that the French state was not simply as strong, monolithic or highly centralised as people had previously assumed it to be. These accounts can be associated with the model of the weak state, the shared government account of executive politics, the administration and politics model of the bureaucracy, the institutional variant of the cross-regulation model of local government and the corporatist model of interest group politics. The sociology-inspired accounts tended to privilege the personal and social context within which institutional relationships were played out. This line of thought led to the power elite model of the bureaucracy and the sociological variant of the cross-regulation model of local government. Finally, economics-related accounts tended to apply assumptions about individual rationality to political behaviour, resulting in econometric models of French voting behaviour. All in all, by the mid-1980s the study of French political life was intellectually much richer than it had been two decades previously and some very clear debates in French politics had emerged.

The third period is ongoing and is characterised by the current scholarly trend towards micro-level and sector-specific analysis. This line of reasoning became intellectually fashionable in the mid-1980s and has emerged as the dominant paradigm in the 1990s. It privileges differentiated accounts of political life. It rejects what its proponents consider to be over-generalisations about the political process. It presents what might be deemed to be more realistic accounts of French politics. Accordingly, this type of analysis is consistent with the disoriented model of the French state, the fragmented model of the bureaucracy, the interactive school of voting behaviour, the untidy reality and policy network models of interest group politics and the bounded singularity model of the French policy style. Indeed, it might also be consistent with the ministerial government model of executive politics, although as noted in Chapter 2 this model remains largely unexplored as yet. All told, therefore, the current trend in political analysis is towards intellectual deconstructionism and correspondingly disaggregated accounts of the political process.

The question that remains, therefore, is where is the study of French politics likely to go? How are the debates considered here going to develop in the foreseeable future? In the individual chapters of the book we have suggested a number of answers to these questions. More broadly, though, we would like to signal two potentially fruitful lines of inquiry for the future.

The first is a response to the problems associated with the various disaggregated accounts of French political life identified above. The current trend towards micro-level, differentiated accounts of the French polity is not without its critics. As noted in the various chapters, these models provide a reassuringly complex picture of the political process that avoids the pitfalls of the some of the more caricatural accounts that preceded them. For example, the model of the disoriented state is undoubtedly more convincing than a number of the rather one-dimensional examples of the strong state model. At the same time, these models can sometimes slip into mere description and *reportage*. In short, they can fail to discriminate between the relative importance of the different independent variables with which they are concerned. So, no doubt the state shows elements of both strength and weakness as the model of the disoriented state implies, but is this observation sufficient to build up a theory of power that can be used to predict the state's capacity to shape social forces? If not, then a more fruitful line of inquiry might be one which reworks the more traditional and discriminating models of French politics so as to maintain their original emphasis, but in a way which makes them consistent with contemporary developments. Arguably, the example that already comes closest to this line of reasoning was encountered in the chapter on local government. Here, it is clear that at least some of the examples of the local governance model are potentially consistent with the seemingly outdated agent model of centre/periphery relations. Thus, what may emerge in the future is an account that is premised on the assumption that there are many types of centre/periphery relations, but also stresses the generally predominant role of the central state. All told, there is room for future debates in French politics to develop by way of an imaginative synthesis of some of the models that have already been constructed so far rather than the development of new paradigms altogether.

The second potentially fruitful line of inquiry is quite different. As students of French politics ourselves, we have been repeatedly struck by the Franco-French nature of French political studies. As Chapter 8 amply demonstrates, there is a long and continuing tradition of French exceptionalism or at least bounded singularity. Equally, other chapters have shown that many of the debates in French politics revolve around specifically French controversies, such as whether or not there is a French power elite, or whether the sociocultural model provides a convincing explanation of voting behaviour. And yet, political science is a global discipline. True, the influence of Anglo-American, particularly US, scholarship is preponderant, but political inquiry occurs in all academic contexts across the world. Moreover, there are many types of such inquiry: theoretical and empirical, comparative and country-specific, qualitative and quantitative, to name but a few. What we would suggest is that there is great scope for more of this work to be applied to the French case. Indeed, the approach adopted in this book was itself largely inspired by two such pieces of work (Dunleavy and O'Leary, 1987; and Dunleavy and Rhodes, 1990). In particular, there is room for more rational choice accounts of French political life, for more of the public policy literature to be considered in the French context and for more concepts from comparative politics generally to be applied to the French case. This is not to say, of course, that Franco-French models have no merits. In fact, we would also argue that there is considerable potential for such models to be exported elsewhere and for them to be tested in other country-specific contexts. Moreover, this is also not to say that comparative politics paradigms have not been applied to the French case. Indeed, many of the disaggregated accounts of French political life have their intellectual roots outside the hexagon. It is simply to suggest that some of the more sterile debates in French politics, or aspects of them, might be transformed by the infusion of paradigms from the study of politics elsewhere. Indeed, we would argue that the party government model in Chapter 5 is a good example of this principle at work. If this suggestion is followed up, then there are many different ways in which the various debates on French politics may evolve.

This book was written in the hope that it would stimulate debates in French politics. To this end, we hope that we have also indicated a number of ways in which these debates might move forward. Indeed, the success of this book will at least partly be determined by the speed at which the debates as we have reported them become obsolete and are replaced by new paradigms and alternative interpretations of French politics.

Bibliography

Ardant, P. (1991) *Le Premier Ministre en France*, Paris: Montchrestien.

Ashford, D.E. (1982a) *British Dogmatism and French Pragmatism: Central–Local Policymaking in the Welfare State*, London: George Allen and Unwin.

—— (1982b) *Policy and Politics in France. Living with Uncertainty*, Philadelphia: Temple University Press.

Atkinson, M.A. and Coleman, W.D. (1989) 'Strong states and weak states: sectoral policy networks in advanced capitalist economies', in *British Journal of Political Science* 19 (1): 47–67.

Avril, P. (1979) 'Ce qui a changé dans la Ve République', in *Pouvoirs* 9: 53–70.

—— (1982) 'Le Président, le parti et le groupe', in *Pouvoirs* 20: 115–26.

—— (1986) 'Présidentialisme et contraintes de l'exécutif dual', in J-L. Seurin (ed.) *La Présidence en France et aux Etats-Unis*, Paris: Economica, pp. 237–245.

—— (1994) 'La majorité parlementaire?' in *Pouvoirs* 68: 45–53.

Badie, B. and Birnbaum, P. (1983) *The Sociology of the State*, Chicago: Chicago University Press.

Balme, R. (1998) 'The French region as a space for public policy', in P. Le Galès and C. Lequesne (eds) *Regions in Europe*, London: Routledge, pp. 181–98.

Balme, R. and Jouve, B. (1996) 'Building the regional state: Europe and territorial organization in France', in L. Hooghe (ed.) *Cohesion Policy and European Integration. Building Multi-Level Governance*, Oxford: Clarendon Press, pp. 219–55.

Balme, R., Garraud, P., Hoffmann-Martinot, V., Le May, S. and Ritaine, E. (1994) 'Analysing territorial policies in Western Europe. The case of France, Germany, Italy and Spain', in *European Journal of Political Research* 25: 389–411.

Baumgartner, F.R. (1996) 'The many styles of policymaking in France', in J.T.S. Keeler and M.A. Schain (eds) *Chirac's Challenge. Liberalization, Europeanization and Malaise in France*, London: Macmillan, pp. 85–101.

Baumgartner, F.R. and Walker, J. L. (1989) 'Educational policymaking and the interest group structure in France and the United States', in *Comparative Politics* 21 (3): 273–88.

Bell, D. and Criddle, B. (1988) *The French Socialist Party*, Oxford: Oxford University Press.

Birnbaum, P. (1982a) *The Heights of Power. An Essay on the Power Elite in France*, Chicago: University of Chicago Press.

—— (1982b) *La logique de l'État*, Paris: Fayard.

Birnbaum, P., Barucq, C., Bellaiche, M. and Marié, A. (1978) *La classe dirigeante française*, Paris: Presses Universitaires de France.

Blondel, J. (1977) 'Types of governmental leadership in Atlantic countries', in *European Journal of Political Research* 5: 33–51.

—— (1980) *World Leaders*, London: Sage.

—— (1984) 'Dual leadership in the contemporary world: a step towards executive and regime stability?' in D. Kavanagh and G. Peele (eds) *Comparative Government and Politics. Essays in Honour of S. E. Finer*, London: Heinemann, pp. 73–91.

—— (1995) 'Toward a systematic analysis of government–party relationships', in *International Political Science Review* 16 (2): 127–43.

Blondel, J. and Cotta, M. (1996) 'Introduction', in J. Blondel and M. Cotta (eds) *Party and Government*, London: Macmillan, pp. 1–21.

Borella, F. (1990) *Les partis politiques en France d'aujourd'hui*, Paris: Seuil.

Bornstein, S.E. (1987) 'An end to French exceptionalism? The lessons of the Greenpeace affair', in *French Politics and Society* 5 (4): 3–16.

Bourdieu, P. and Passeron, J.-C. (1964) *Les héritiers*, Paris: Éditions de Minuit.

Boy, D. and Dupoirier, E. (1993) 'Is the voter a stategist?' in D. Boy and N. Mayer (eds) *The French Voter Decides*, Ann Arbor: University of Michigan Press, pp. 149–65.

Boy, D. and Mayer, N. (1993) 'The changing French voter', in D. Boy and N. Mayer (eds) *The French Voter Decides*, Ann Arbor: University of Michigan Press, pp. 167–84.

—— (1997a) 'Que reste-t-il des variables lourdes?' in D. Boy and N. Mayer (eds) *L'électeur a ses raisons*, Paris: Presses de la FNSP, pp. 101–38.

—— (1997b) 'Conclusion', in D. Boy and N. Mayer (eds) *L'électeur a ses raisons*, Paris: Presses de la FNSP, pp. 327–45.

Boyer, R. (1992) 'Vers l'érosion du particularisme français', in *French Politics and Society* 10 (1): 9–24.

Bréchon, P. (1997) 'Is there religious voting in France?' *La Lettre de la Maison française d'Oxford* 8: 5–29.

Briquet, J.-L. and Sawicki, F. (1989) 'L'analyse localisée du politique', in *Politix* 7–8: 6–16.

Burdeau, G. (1959) 'La Conception du Pouvoir selon la Constitution Française du Octobre 1958', in *Revue Française de Science Politique* 9 (1): 87–100.

—— (1977) *Droit constitutionnel et institutions politiques*, 18th edn, Paris: LGDJ.

Burin des Roziers, É (1990) 'Les rapports entre le Président de la République et le Premier ministre, janvier 1962–juillet 1967', in *De Gaulle et ses Premiers ministres 1959–1969*, Paris: Plon, pp. 81–9.

Capdevielle, J. *et al.* (1981) *France de gauche vote à droite*, Paris: Presses de la FNSP.

Carcassonne, G. (1988) 'France (1958): The Fifth Republic after thirty years', in V. Bogdanor (ed.) *Constitutions in Democratic Politics*, Aldershot: Gower, pp. 241–56.

Castells, M. and Godard, F. (1974) *Monopolville, l'État urbain*, Paris-La Haye: Mouton.

Cawson, A., Holmes, P. and Stevens, A. (1987) 'The interaction between firms and the state in France: the telecommunications and consumer electronics sectors', in S. Wilks and M. Wright (eds) *Comparative Government–Industry Relations*.

Western Europe, the United States and Japan, Oxford: Clarendon Press, pp. 10–34.

Cayrol, R. *et al.* (1997) 'Le modèle économique électoral de l'Iowa: fiabilité, limites et complementarité', in *Revue Politique et Parlementaire* 989: 65–9.

Chabal, P. and Fraisseix, P. (1996) 'Déclin et renouveau de la présidence française dans le contexte de l'élection de 1995', in *Revue française de droit constitutionnel* 25: 35–71.

Chagnollaud, D. and Quermonne, J.-L. (1996) *Le gouvernement de la France sous la Ve République*, Paris: Fayard.

Chantebout, B. (1989) *Droit constitutionnel et science politique*, 9th edn, Paris: Armand Colin.

Charlot, J. (1971) *The Gaullist Phenomenon*, London: George Allen and Unwin Ltd.

—— (1986) 'Le Président et le parti majoritaire', in M. Duverger (ed.) *Les régimes semi-présidentiels*, Paris: PUF, pp. 313–30.

Chodak, S. (1989) *The New State. Etatization of Western Societies*, Boulder: Lynne Rienner.

Cohen, E. (1998) 'A *Dirigiste* End to *Dirigisme?*' in M. Maclean (ed.) *The Mitterrand Years. Legacy and Evaluation*, London: Macmillan, pp. 36–45.

Cohen, E. and Bauer, M. (1985) *Les grandes manoeuvres industrielles*, Paris: Belfond.

Cohen, S. (1985) 'L'immédiate primauté présidentielle', in O. Duhamel and J.-L. Parodi (eds) *La Constitution de la Cinquième République*, Paris: Presses de la FNSP, pp. 91–100.

—— (1986) *La monarchie nucléaire*, Paris: Hachette.

Cohen-Tanugi, L. (1993) *La métamorphose de la démocratie française. De l'État jacobin à l'État de droit*, Paris: Gallimard.

Cole, A. (1989) 'The French Socialist Party in transition', in *Modern and Contemporary France* 37: 14–23.

—— (1993) 'The Presidential Party and the Fifth Republic', in *West European Politics* 16 (2): 49–66.

—— (1994) *François Mitterrand. A Study in Political Leadership*, London: Routledge.

—— (1998) *French Politics and Society*, London: Prentice Hall.

—— (1999) 'The *service public* under stress', in *West European Politics* 22 (4).

Cole, A. and John, P. (1995) 'Local policy networks in France and Britain: policy co-ordination in fragmented political sub-systems', in *West European Politics* 18 (4): 89–109.

Coleman, W.D. (1993) 'Reforming corporatism: the French banking policy community, 1941–1990', in *West European Politics* 16 (2): 122–43.

Colliard, J.-C. (1994) 'Que peut le Président?' in *Pouvoirs* 68: 15–29.

Converse, P.E. and Pierce, R. (1986) *Political Representation in France*, London: The Belknap Press of Harvard University Press.

Cox, A. and Hayward, J. (1983) 'The inapplicability of the corporatist model in Britain and France. The case of labor', in *International Political Science Review* 4 (2): 217–40.

Criddle, B. (1987) 'France. Parties in a presidential system', in A. Ware (ed.) *Political Parties. Electoral Change and Structural Response*, Oxford: Blackwell, pp. 137–57.

Crozier, M. (1967) *The Bureaucratic Phenomenon*, Chicago: University of Chicago Press.

—— (1970) *The Stalled Society*, New York: Viking.

—— (1987) *État modeste, État moderne. Stratégie pour un autre changement*, Paris: Fayard.

—— (1994) *La société bloquéé*, 3rd edn, Paris: Seuil.

Crozier, M. and Freidberg, E. (1977) *L'acteur et le système*, Paris: Seuil.

Crozier, M. and Thoenig, J.-C. (1975) 'La régulation des systèmes organisés complexes. Le cas du système de décision politico-administratif local en France', in *Revue Française de Sociologie* 16 (1): 3–32.

Culpepper, P.D. (1993) 'Organisational competition and the neo-corporatist fallacy in French agriculture', in *West European Politics* 16 (3): 295–315.

Dagnaud, M. and Mehl, D. (1989) 'L'élite rose confirmée', in *Pouvoirs* 50: 141–50.

d'Arcy, F. (1996) 'L'administration territoriale de la République ou le maintien de la spécificité française', in F. d'Arcy and L. Rouban (eds) *De la Ve République À l'Europe*, Paris: Presses de Sciences Po, pp. 203–225.

de Baecque, F. (1976) *Qui gouverne la France?* Paris: Presses Universitaires de France.

—— (1981) 'L'interpénétration des personnels administratifs et politiques', in F. de Baecque and J.-L. Quermonne (eds) *Administration et politique sous la Cinquième République*, Paris: Presses de la FNSP, pp. 19–60.

—— (1986) 'Le partage des moyens entre la présidence de la République et le premier ministre', in J.-L. Seurin (ed.) *La Présidence en France et aux Etats-Unis*, Paris: Economica, pp. 282–306.

de Baecque, F. and Quermonne, J.-L. (eds) (1981) *Administration et politique sous la Cinquième République*, Paris: Presses de la FNSP.

Debbasch, C. (1986) 'Les pouvoirs du Président de la République française et de ses conseillers face à ceux du Premier ministre', in J.-L. Seurin (ed.) *La Présidence en France et aux Etats-Unis*, Paris: Economica, pp. 201–5.

de Monricher, N. (1995) 'Decentralization in France', in *Governance* 8 (3): 405–18.

Denni, B. (1993) 'Les élites en France', in D. Chagnollaud (ed.) *La vie politique en France*, Paris: Seuil, pp. 418–31.

Dorandeu, R. (1994) 'Le cercle magique. Quelques remarques sur les élites de la République', in *Pouvoirs* 64: 111–23.

Dreyfus, F.-G., Morizet, J. and Peyrard, M. (1993) *France and EC Membership Evaluated*, London: Pinter.

Duhamel, A. (1980) *La République giscardienne*, Paris: Grasset.

Duhamel, O. (1987) 'The Fifth Republic under François Mitterrand. Evolution and perspectives', in G. Ross, S. Hoffman and S. Malzacher (eds) *The Mitterrand Experiment*, Cambridge: Polity Press, pp. 140–60.

Dunleavy, P. and O'Leary, B. (1987) *Theories of the State*, London: Macmillan.

Dunleavy, P. and Rhodes, R.A.W. (1990) 'Core executive studies in Britain', in *Public Administration* 68, Spring: 3–28.

Dupoirier, É. (1986) 'Chassés-croisés électoraux', in É. Dupoirier and G. Grunberg (eds) *Mars 1986: la drôle de défaite de la gauche*, Paris: Presses Universitaires de France, pp. 167–88.

Dupuy, F. (1985) 'The politico-admininstrative system of the département in France', in Y. Mény and V. Wright (eds) *Centre–Periphery Relations in Western Europe*, London: Allen and Unwin, pp. 79–103.

Dupuy, F. and Thoenig, J.-C. (1983) *Sociologie de l'Administration française*, Paris: Armand Colin.

—— (1985) *L'administration en miettes*, Paris: Fayard.

Duran, P. and Thoenig, J.-C. (1996) 'L'État et la gestion publique territoriale', in *Revue Française de Science Politique* 46 (4): 580–623.

Duverger, M. (1974) *La Monarchie républicaine*, Paris: Robert Laffont.

—— (1996) *Le système politique français*, 21st edn, Paris: Presses Universitaires de France.

Eberlein, B. (1996) 'French center–periphery relations and Science Park Development: local policy initiatives and intergovernmental policymaking', in *Governance* 9 (4): 351–74.

Ehrmann, H.W. (1971) *Politics in France*, 2nd edn, Boston: Little, Brown and Co.

Elgie, R. (1993) *The Role of the Prime Minister in France, 1981–91*, London: Macmillan.

—— (1996) 'The institutional logics of presidential elections', in R. Elgie (ed.) *Electing the French President, The 1995 Presidential Election*, London: Macmillan, pp. 51–72.

—— (1996a) 'The French Presidency – conceptualizing presidential power in the Fifth Republic', in *Public Administration* 74 (2): 275–91.

—— (1997a) 'Models of executive politics: a framework for the study of executive power relations in parliamentary and semi-presidential regimes', in *Political Studies* 45 (2): 217–31.

—— (1997b) 'The twin-headed executive in France', in J.M. Shafritz (ed.) *Encyclopaedia of Public Policy and Administration*, vol. 4, Boulder: Westview Press, pp. 2292–6.

—— (1997c) 'Two-ballot majority electoral systems', in *Representation* 34 (2): 89–94.

—— (1998) 'The classification of democratic regime types: conceptual ambiguity and contestable assumptions', in *European Journal of Political Research* 33 (2): 219–38.

Elgie, R. and Griggs, S. (1991) 'À quoi sert le PS? The influence of the Parti socialiste on public policy since 1981', in *Modern and Contemporary France* 47: 20–9.

Elgie, R. and Thompson, H. (1998) *The Politics of Central Banks*, London: Routledge.

Epstein, P.J. (1997) 'Beyond policy community: French agriculture and the GATT', in *Journal of European Public Policy* 4 (3): 355–72.

Faure, A. (1994) 'Les élus locaux à l'épreuve de la décentralisation. De nouveaux chantiers pour la médiation politique locale', in *Revue Française de Science Politique* 44 (3): 462–79.

Favier, P. and Martin-Roland, M. (1990) *La Décennie Mitterrand. 1. Les ruptures*, Paris: Seuil.

Feigenbaum, H.B. (1985) *The Politics of Public Enterprise. Oil and the French State*, Princeton: Princeton University Press.

Fontaine, J. (1996) 'Public policy analysis in France: transformation and theory', in *Journal of European Public Policy* 3 (3): 481–98.

Frears, J. (1981) *France in the Giscard Presidency*, London: Allen and Unwin.

Furet, F. (1988) 'La France unie', in F. Furet, J. Julliard and P. Rosenvallon, *La république du centre. La fin de l'exception française*, Paris: Calmann-Lévy.

Furet, F., Julliard, J. and Rosenvallon, P. (1988) *La république du centre. La fin de l'exception française*, Paris: Calmann-Lévy.

Gaffney, J. (1989) 'Introduction: presidentialism and the Fifth Republic', in J. Gaffney (ed.) *The French Presidential Elections of 1988*, Aldershot: Dartmouth, pp. 2–36.

Gerstlé, J. (1996) 'L'information et la sensibilité des électeurs à la conjoncture', in *Revue Française de Science Politique* 40 (5): 731–52.

Gicquel, J. (1995) *Droit constitutionnel et institutions politiques*, 14th edn, Paris: Monchrestien.

Giuliani, J.-D. (1991) *Marchands d'influence. Les lobbies en France*, Paris: Seuil.

Godin, E. (1996) 'Le néo-libéralisme à la française: une exception?' in *Modern and Contemporary France* 4 (1): 61–70.

Goguel, F. (1981) *Chroniques électorales. La Quatrième République*, Paris: Presses de la FNSP.

—— (1983) 'The evolution of the institution of the French presidency, 1959–1981', in F. Eidlin (ed.) *Constitutional Democracy: Essays in Comparative Politics*, Boulder: Westview Press, pp. 49–61.

Grémion, P. (1976) *Le pouvoir périphérique: Bureaucrates et notables dans le système public français*, Paris: Seuil.

Groux, G. and Moriaux, R. (1996) 'The dilemma of unions without members', in A. Daley (ed.) *The Mitterrand Era. Policy Alternatives and Political Mobilization in France*, London: Macmillan, pp. 172–85.

Grunberg, G. (1985a) 'France', in I. Crewe and D. Denver (eds) *Electoral Change in Western Democracies: Patterns and Sources of Electoral Volatility*, London: Croom Helm, pp. 202–29.

—— (1985b) 'L'instabilité du comportement électoral', in D. Gaxie (ed.) *Explication du vote*, Paris: Presses de la FNSP, pp. 418–46.

Guyomarch, A., Machin, H. and Ritchie, E. (1998) *France in the European Union*, London: Macmillan.

Haas, P.M. (1992) 'Introduction: epistemic communities and international policy coordination', in *International Organization* 46 (1): 1–36.

Habert, P. (1990) 'Les élections européennes de 1989. Le temps des mutations', in *Commentaire* 13 (49): 17–30.

—— (1992a) 'Le vote éclaté', in *Le vote éclaté. Les élections régionales et cantonales des 22 et 29 mars 1992*, Paris: Département d'études politiques du *Figaro* et Presses de la FNSP, pp. 21–30.

—— (1992b) 'Le choix de l'Europe et la décision de l'électeur', in *Commentaire* 15 (60): 871–80.

Habert, P. and Lancelot, A. (1988) 'L'émergence d'un nouvel électeur?' in *Élections législatives 1988*, Paris: *Le Figaro* Études politiques, pp. 16–23.

Hadas-Lebel, R. (1992) 'Président de la République et Premier ministre: dyarchie au sommet?' in *De Gaulle et son siècle*, vol. 2, Paris: Plon/La Documentation Française, pp. 206–20.

Halimi, S. (1996) 'Less exceptionalism than meets the eye', in A. Daley (ed.) *The Mitterrand Era. Policy Alternatives and Political Mobilization in France*, London: Macmillan, pp. 83–96.

Hall, P.A. (1986) *Governing the Economy: The Politics of State Intervention in Britain and France*, Cambridge: Polity Press.

—— (1990a) 'Pluralism and pressure politics', in P.A. Hall, J. Hayward and H. Machin (eds) *Developments in French Politics*, London: Macmillan, pp. 77–92.

—— (1990b) 'The state and the market', in P.A. Hall, J. Hayward and H. Machin (eds) *Developments in French Politics*, London: Macmillan, pp. 171–87.

Hayward, J. (1982) 'Mobilising private interests in the service of public ambitions: the salient element of the dual policy style', in J. Richardson (ed.) *Policy Styles in Western Europe*, London: George Allen and Unwin, pp. 111–40.

—— (1986) *The State and the Market Economy. Industrial Patriotism and Economic Intervention in France*, Brighton: Wheatsheaf.

—— (1988) 'From fashion-setter to fashion-follower in Europe: the demise of French distinctiveness', in J. Howorth and G. Ross (eds) *Contemporary France. A Review of Interdisciplinary Studies. Volume Two*, London: Pinter, pp. 89–116.

—— (1990) 'Conclusion: political science, the state and modernisation', in P.A. Hall, J. Hayward and H. Machin (eds) *Developments in French Politics*, London: Macmillan, pp. 282–97.

Hayward, J.E.S. (1983) *Governing France: The One and Indivisible Republic*, 2nd edn, London: Weidenfeld and Nicolson.

Hewlett, N. (1998) *Modern French Politics. Analysing Conflict and Consensus since 1945*, Cambridge: Polity Press.

Hoffman, S. (1967) 'Heroic leadership: the case of modern France', in L.J. Edinger (ed.) *Political Leadership in Industrialized Societies*, New York: John Wylie and Sons, Inc., pp. 108–54.

—— (1987) 'Conclusion', in G. Ross, S. Hoffman and S. Malzacher (eds) *The Mitterrand Experiment*, Cambridge: Polity Press, pp. 341–53.

Hollifield, J.F. (1990) 'Immigration and the French state. Problems of policy implementation', in *Comparative Political Studies* 23 (1): 56–79.

—— (1991) 'Conclusion: still searching for the New France', in J.F. Hollifield and G. Ross (eds) *Searching for the New France*, London: Routledge, pp. 275–97.

Hollifield, J.F. and Ross, G. (eds) (1991) *Searching for the New France*, London: Routledge.

Howorth, J. (1993) 'The President's special role in foreign and defence policy', in J. Hayward (ed.) *De Gaulle to Mitterrand, Presidential Power in France*, London: Hurst, pp. 150–89.

Imbert, C. (1989) 'The end of French exceptionalism', in *Foreign Affairs* Fall: 48–60.

Jobert, B. (1989) 'The normative frameworks of public policy', in *Political Studies* 37: 376–86.

—— (1996) 'L'actualité des corporatismes', in *Pouvoirs* 79: 21–34.

Jobert, B. and Muller, P. (1987) *L'État en action. Politiques publiques et corporatismes*, Paris: Presses Universitaires de France.

Josselin, D. (1995) 'Policy networks and the making of EC policy: the case of financial services in France and the UK, 1987–1992', unpublished PhD thesis, University of London: London School of Economics.

Jouve, B. (1995) 'Réseaux et communautés politiques', in P. Le Galès and M. Thatcher (eds) *Les réseaux de l'action publique*, Paris: L'Harmattan, pp. 121–39.

Kassim, H. (1997) 'French autonomy and the European Union', in *Modern and Contemporary France* 5 (2): 167–80.

Katz, R.S. (1987) 'Party government and its alternatives', in R.S. Katz (ed.) *Party Governments: European and American Experiences*, Berlin: Walter de Gruyter, pp. 1–26.

Katz, R.S. and Mair, P. (1995) 'Changing models of party organization and party democracy', in *Party Politics* 1 (1): 5–28.

Keating, M and Hainsworth, P. (1986) *Decentralisation and Change in Contemporary France*, Aldershot: Gower.

Keeler, J.T.S. (1981) 'Corporatism and offical union hegemony: the case of French agricultural syndicalism', in S.D. Berger (ed.) *Organising Interests in Western Europe. Pluralism, Corporatism and the Transformation of Politics*, Cambridge: Cambridge University Press, pp. 185–205.

—— (1985) 'Situating France on the pluralism–corporatism continuum. A critique of and an alternative to the Wilson perspective', in *Comparative Politics* 17 (2): 229–49.

—— (1987) *The Politics of Neo-corporatism in France*, Oxford: Oxford University Press.

—— (1993) 'Executive power and policy-making patterns in France: Gauging the impact of the Fifth Republic institutions', in *West European Politics* 16 (4): 518–44.

Kesler, J.-F. (1997) 'L'énarchie n'existe pas', in *Pouvoirs* 80: 23–41.

King, A. (1976) 'Modes of executive–legislative relations; Great Britain, France, and West Germany', in *Legislative Studies Quarterly* 1 (1): 11–36.

Kuhn, R. (1998) 'The state and the broadcasting media: all change?' in M. Maclean (ed.) *The Mitterrand Years. Legacy and Evaluation*, London: Macmillan, pp. 287–99.

Kuisel, R.F. (1995) 'The France we have lost: social, economic and cultural discontinuities', in G. Flynn (ed.) *Remaking the Hexagon. The New France in the New Europe*, Boulder: Westview, pp. 31–48.

Ladrech, R. (1994) 'Europeanization of domestic politics and institutons: the case of France', in *Journal of Common Market Studies* 32 (1): 69–88.

Lafont, R. (1971) *Décoloniser la France*, Paris: Gallimard.

—— (1973) *La révolution régionaliste*, Paris: Gallimard.

Lancelot, A. (1981) 'Préface', in J. Capdevielle *et al.*, *France de gauche vote à droite*, Paris: Presses de la FNSP, pp. 9–13.

—— (1985) 'L'orientation du comportement politique', in M. Grawitz and J. Leca (eds) *Traité de Science Politique. 3. L'action politique*, Paris: Presses Universitaires de France, pp. 367–428.

—— (1986a) *1981: Les Elections de l'Alternance*, Paris: Presses de la FNSP.

—— (1986b) 'France: où en est la sociologie électorale?' in *1986 Universalia*, Paris: Encyclopedia Universalis, pp. 257–60.

Lancelot, A. and Lancelot, M.-T. (1987) 'The evolution of the French electorate: 1981–86', in G. Ross, S. Hoffman and S. Malzacher (eds) *The Mitterrand Experiment*, Cambridge: Polity Press, pp. 77–99.

Lavau, G.E. (1958) 'Political pressures by interest groups in France', in H.W. Ehrmann (ed.) *Interest Groups on Four Continents*, Pittsburgh: University of Pittsburgh Press, pp. 60–95.

—— (1986) 'L'électeur devient-il individualiste?' in P. Birnbaum and J. Leca (eds) *Sur l'individualisme*, Paris: Presses de la FNSP, pp. 301–29.

Lavigne, P. (1982) 'Retour au "régime des partis" sous la Cinquième République', in G. Conac, H. Maisl and J. Vaudriaux (eds) *Itinéraires. Études en l'honneur de Léo Hamon*, Paris: Economica, pp. 415–27.

Lawson, K. (1983) 'Corporatism in France: The Gaullist contribution', in F. Eidlin (ed.) *Constitutional Democracy. Essays in Comparative Politics*, Boulder: Westview, pp. 344–75.

Le Galès, P. (1995) 'Du gouvernement des villes à la gouvernance urbaine', in *Revue Française de Science Politique* 45 (1): 57–95.

Le Galès, P. and Harding, A. (1998) 'Cities and states in Europe', in *West European Politics* 21 (3): 120–45.

Lesourne, J. (1998) *Le modèle français. Grandeur et décadence*, Paris: Odile Jacob.

Lewis-Beck, M.S. (1983) 'Economics and the French voter: A microanalysis', in *Public Opinion Quarterly* 47: 347–60.

—— (1993) 'The French voter – steadfast or changing?' in D. Boy and N. Mayer (eds) *The French Voter Decides*, Ann Arbor: University of Michigan Press, pp. 1–13.

—— (1997) 'Le vote du "porte-monnaie" en question', in D. Boy and N. Mayer (ed.) *L'électeur a ses raisons*, Paris: Presses de la FNSP, pp. 239–62.

Loughlin, J. and Mazey, S. (1995) 'Introduction', in J. Loughlin and S. Mazey (eds) *The End of the French Unitary State? Ten Years of Regionalization in France (1982–1992)*, London: Frank Cass, pp. 1–9.

Lovecy, J. (1992) 'Comparative politics and the Fifth French Republic', in *European Journal of Political Research* 21: 385–408.

Mabileau, A. (1985) 'Les institutions locales et les relations centre-périphérie', in M. Grawitz and J. Leca (eds) *Traité de Science Politique. 2. Les régimes politiques contemporains*, Paris: Presses Universitaires de France, pp. 553–98.

—— (1989) 'Local government in Britain and local politics and administration in France', in A. Mabileau, G. Moyser, G. Parry and P. Quantin (eds) *Local Politics and Participation in Britain and France*, Cambridge: Cambridge University Press, pp. 17–33.

—— (1991) *Le système local en France*, Paris: Montchrestien.

—— (1997) 'Les génies invisibles du local. Faux semblants et dynamiques de la décentralisation', in *Revue Française de Science Politique* 47 (3–4): 340–76.

—— (1998) 'La région à l'épreuve des relations intergouvernementales', in E. Dupoirier (ed.) *Régions. La croisée des chemins. Perspectives françaises et enjeux européens*, Paris: Presses de Sciences Po, pp. 53–65.

Machin, H. (1977) *The Prefect in French Public Administration*, London: Croom Helm.

—— (1979) 'Traditional patterns of French local government', in J. Lagroye and V. Wright (eds) *Local Government in Britain and France. Problems and Prospects*, London: George Allen and Unwin, pp. 28–41.

—— (1981) 'Centre and periphery in the policy process', in P.G. Cerny and M.A. Schain (eds) *French Politics and Public Policy*, London: Frances Pinter, pp. 125–41.

—— (1989) 'Stages and dynamics in the evolution of the French party system', in *West European Politics* 12 (4): 59–81.

—— (1990) 'Introduction', in P.A. Hall, J. Hayward and H. Machin (eds) *Developments in French Politics*, London: Macmillan, pp. 1–12.

—— (1993) 'The president, the parties and parliament', in J. Hayward (ed.) *De Gaulle to Mitterrand, Presidential Power in France*, London: Hurst, pp. 120–49.

Machin, H. and Wright, V. (1985) 'Economic policy under the Mitterrand Presidency, 1981–1984: an introduction', in H. Machin and V. Wright (eds) *Economic Policy and Policy-Making under the Mitterrand Presidency, 1981–1984*, London: Frances Pinter, pp. 1–43.

Maclean, M. (1997) 'Privatisation, *dirigisme*, and the global economy: An end to French exceptionalism?' in *Modern and Contemporary France* 5 (2): 215–28.

Marceau, J. (1981) 'Power and its possessors', in P.G. Cerny and M.A. Schain (eds) *French Politics and Public Policy*, London: Methuen, pp. 48–78.

Marsh, D. and Rhodes, R.A.W. (eds) (1992) *Policy Networks in British Government*, Oxford: Oxford University Press.

Massot, J. (1988) 'La pratique présidentielle sous la Ve République', in *Regards sur l'Actualité* no. 139.

—— (1993) *Chef de l'État et chef du Gouvernement. Dyarchie et hiérarchie*, Paris: La Documentation Française.

Maus, D. (1985a) *Les grands textes de la pratique institutionnelle de la Ve République*, Paris: La Documentation Française.

—— (1985b) 'La constitution jugée par sa pratique', in O. Duhamel and J.-L. Parodi (eds) *La Constitution de la Cinquième République*, Paris: Presses de la FNSP.

Mayer, N. (1986) 'Pas de chrysanthèmes pour les variables sociologiques', in É. Dupoirier and G. Grunberg (eds) *Mars 1986: la drôle de défaite de la gauche*, Paris: Presses Universitaires de France, pp. 149–65.

—— (1995) 'Elections and the left–right division in France', in *French Politics and Society* 13 (1): 36–44.

—— (1996) 'Acteurs et comportements politiques. Les modèles d'analyse des comportements électoraux', in Y. Léonard (ed.) *Découverte de la science politique*, Paris: La Documentation Française, pp. 41–50.

—— (1997) 'Introduction', in N. Mayer (ed.) *Les modèles explicatifs du vote*, Paris: l'Harmattan, pp. 10–18.

Mayer, N. and Perrineau, P. (1992a) 'Why do they vote for Le Pen?' in *European Journal of Political Research* 22: 123–41.

—— (1992b) *Les comportements politiques*, Paris: Armand Colin.

Mazey, S. (1986) 'Public policy-making in France: The art of the possible', in *West European Politics* 9 (3): 412–28.

—— (1990) 'Power outside Paris', in P.A. Hall, J. Hayward and H. Machin (eds) *Developments in French Politics*, London: Macmillan, pp. 152–67.

—— (1995) 'French regions and the European Union', in J. Loughlin and S. Mazey (eds) *The End of the French Unitary State? Ten Years of Regionalization in France (1982–1992)*, London: Frank Cass, pp. 132–57.

Mazur, A.G. (1993) 'The formation of sexual harassment policy in France: another case of French exceptionalism?' in *French Politics and Society* 11 (2).

Méchet, P. and Witkowski, D. (1996) 'Abécédaire de l'opinion', in O. Duhamel, J. Jaffré and P. Méchet (eds) *L'état de l'opinion 1996*, Paris: Seuil, pp. 299–327.

Mendras, H. (1994) *La Seconde Révolution française 1965–1984*, Paris: Gallimard.

Mendras, H. and Cole, A. (1991) *Social Change in Modern France. Towards a Cultural Anthropology of the Fifth Republic*, Cambridge: Cambridge University Press.

Mény, Y. (1983) *Centre et périphéries: le partage de pouvoir*, Paris: Economica.

—— (1987a) 'France: The construction and reconstruction of the centre, 1945–86', in *West European Politics* 10 (4): 52–69.

—— (1987b) 'France', in E.C. Page and M.J. Goldsmith (eds) *Central and Local Government Relations. A Comparative Analysis of West European Unitary States*, London: Sage, pp. 88–106.

—— (1989a) 'Le nouvel espace politique français', in Y. Mény (ed.) *Idéologies, partis politiques et groupes sociaux*, Paris: Presses de la FNSP, pp. 147–57.

—— (1989b) 'The national and international context of French policy communities', in *Political Studies* 37: 387–99.

—— (1992) *La Corruption de la République*, Paris: Fayard.

Meynaud, J. (1962) *Nouvelles études sur les groupes de pression en France*, Paris: Armand Colin.

—— (1968) *Technocracy*, London: Faber and Faber.

Michel, H. (1998) 'Government or governance? The case of the French local political system', in *West European Politics* 21 (3): pp. 146–69.

Michelat, G. (1993) 'In search of left and right', in D. Boy and N. Mayer (eds) *The French Voter Decides*, Ann Arbor, University of Michigan Press, pp. 65–90.

Michelat, G. and Simon, M. (1977) *Classe, réligion et comportement politique*, Paris: Presses de la FNSP.

Morel, L. (1996) 'France: party government at last?', in J. Blondel and M. Cotta (eds) *Parties and Governments*, London: Macmillan, pp. 40–60.

Muller, P. (1992a) *L'Administration française est-elle en crise?* Paris: L'Harmattan.

—— (1992b) 'Entre le local et l'Europe, La crise du modèle français des politiques publiques', in *Revue Française de Science Politique* 42 (2): 275–97.

Müller, W. (1994) 'Models of government and the Austrian cabinet', in M. Laver and K.A. Shepsle (eds) *Cabinet Ministers and Parliamentary Government*, Cambridge: Cambridge University Press, pp. 15–34.

O'Leary, B. (1991) 'An Taoiseach: The Irish Prime Minister', in *West European Politics* 14 (2): 133–62.

Parodi, J.-L. (1983) 'Dans la logique des élections intermédiaires', in *Revue Politique et Parlementaire* 903: 42–70.

Percheron, A. (1989) 'Peut-on encore parler d'héritage politique en 1989', in Y. Mény (ed.) *Idéologies, partis politiques et groupes sociaux*, Paris: Presses de la FNSP, pp. 71–88.

Pierce, R. (1995) *Choosing the Chief. Presidential Elections in France and the United States*, Ann Arbor: University of Michigan Press.

Portelli, H. (1989) 'Les partis et les institutions', in *Pouvoirs* 49: 57–68.

Powell, E.R. (1997) 'The TGV project: a case of technico-economic *dirigisme*?', in *Modern and Contemporary France* 5 (2): 199–214.

Quermonne, J.-L. (1980) 'Pouvoir présidentiel et pouvoir partisan sous la Ve République', in *Projet* 150: 1177–88.

—— (1981) 'Politisation de l'administration ou fonctionnarisation de la politique?' in F. de Baecque and J.-L. Quermonne (eds) *Administration et politique sous la Cinquième République*, Paris: Presses de la FNSP, pp. 329–60.

—— (1986) 'Le cas français: le Président dominant la majorité', in M. Duverger (ed.) *Les régimes semi-présidentiels*, Paris: PUF, pp. 183–208.

—— (1991) *L'appareil administratif de l'État*, Paris: Seuil.

Reif, K. (1987) 'Party government in the Fifth French Republic', in R.S. Katz (ed.) *Party Governments: European and American Experiences*, Berlin: Walter de Gruyter, pp. 27–77.

Rémond, R. (1982) *Les droites en France*, Paris: Aubier.

—— (1993) *La politique n'est plus ce qu'elle était*, Paris: Calmann-Lévy.

Rhodes, R.A.W. (1997) *Understanding Governance. Policy Networks, Governance, Reflexivity and Accountability*, Buckingham: Open University Press.

Richardson, J., Gustafsson, G. and Jordan, G. (1981) 'The concept of policy style', in J. Richardson (ed.) *Policy Styles in Western Europe*, London: George Allen and Unwin.

Ridley, F.F. (1966) 'French technocracy and comparative government', in *Political Studies* 14 (1): 34–52.

Ridley, F.F. and Blondel, J. (1964) *Public Administration in France*, London: Routledge and Kegan Paul.

Rigaud, J. (1986) 'Pouvoir et non-pouvoir du ministre', in *Pouvoirs* 36: 5–14.

Rogers, V. (1998) 'Devolution and economic development in France', in *Policy and Politics* 26 (4): 417–37.

Rohr, J.A. (1996) 'What a difference a state makes. Reflections on governance in France', in G.L. Wamsley *et al. Refounding Democratic Public Administration*, London: Sage, pp. 114–40.

Rondin, J. (1985) *Le sacre des notables. La France en décentralisation*, Paris: Fayard.

Rosa, J.-J. and Amson, D. (1976) 'Conditions économiques et élections. Une analyse politico-économetrique (1920–1973)', in *Revue Française de Science Politique* 26 (6): 1101–19.

Rosanvallon, P. (1990) *L'État en France. De 1789 à nos jours*, Paris: Seuil.

Ross, G. (1991) 'Introduction: Janus and Marianne', in J.F. Hollifield and G. Ross (eds) *Searching for the New France*, London: Routledge, pp. 1–16.

Rouban, L. (1990) 'La modernisation de l'État et la fin de la spécificité française', in *Revue Française de Science Politique* 40 (4): 521–44.

—— (1998) *La fin des technocrates?*, Paris: Presses de Sciences Po.

Sabatier, P. (1988) 'An advocacy coalition framework of policy change and the role of policy-oriented learning therein', in *Policy Sciences* 21: 129–69.

Sadran, P. (1997) *Le système administratif français*, 2nd edn, Paris: Montchrestien.

Safran, W. (1991) *The French Polity*, 3rd edn, London: Longman.

Saint-Étienne, C. (1992) *L'exception française*, Paris: Armand Colin.

Schmidt, V.A. (1990) *Democratizing France. The Political and Administrative History of Decentralization*, Cambridge: Cambridge University Press.

—— (1996) *From State to Market? The Transformation of French Business and Government*, Cambridge: Cambridge University Press.

—— (1997) 'Running on empty: the end of *dirigisme* in French economic leadership', in *Modern and Contemporary France* 5 (2): 229–41.

Schmitter, P. (1974) 'Still the century of corporatism?' in F.B. Pike and T. Strich (eds) *The New Corporatism*, Notre Dame: University of Notre Dame Press, pp. 85–131.

Schonfeld, W.R. (1992) 'De Gaulle et le paradoxe entre ses idées sur le rôle des partis et l'évolution de la pratique constitutionnelle française', in *De Gaulle et son siècle. 2. La République*, Paris: Plon/La Documentation Française, pp. 277–87.

Servais, M. (1997) 'Les modèles économétriques du vote', in N. Mayer (ed.) *Les modèles explicatifs du vote*, Paris: l'Harmattan, pp. 133–53.

Slama, A.-G. (1995) 'Democratic dysfunctions and republican obsolescence: The demise of French exceptionalism', in G. Flynn (ed.) *Remaking the Hexagon. The New France in the New Europe*, Boulder: Westview, pp. 49–65.

Smith, A. (1996) 'The French case: The exception or the rule?' in *Regional and Federal Studies* 6 (2): 117–30.

—— (1997) 'Studying multi-level governance. Examples from French translations of the structural funds', in *Public Administration* 75, Winter: 711–29.

Stevens, A. (1978) 'Politiciation and cohesion in the French administration', in *West European Politics* 1 (3): 69–80.

—— (1996) *The Government and Politics of France*, 2nd edn, London: Macmillan.

Stoffaës, C. (1986) 'Industrial policy in the high-technology industries' in W.J. Adams and C. Stoffaës (eds) *French Industrial Policy*, Washington DC: The Brookings Institution, pp. 36–62.

Suleiman, E.N. (1974) *Politics, Power and Bureaucracy in France*, Princeton: Princeton University Press.

—— (1978) *Elites in French Society. The Politics of Survival*, Princeton: Princeton University Press.

—— (1980) 'Presidential government in France', in E.N. Suleiman and R. Rose (eds) *Presidents and Prime Ministers*, Washington DC: American Enterprise Institute, pp. 94–138.

—— (1987a) *Private Power and Centralisation in France. The Notaires and the State*, Princeton: Princeton University Press.

—— (1987b) 'State structure and clientelism: The French state versus the "Notaires"', in *British Journal of Political Science* 17 (3): 257–79.

—— (1994) 'Presidentialism and political stability in France', in J.J. Linz and A. Valenzuela (eds) *The Failure of Presidential Democracy*, Baltimore: The Johns Hopkins University Press, pp. 137–62.

—— (1995) *Les ressorts cachés de la réussite français*, Paris: Seuil.

Tarrow, S. (1977) *Between Centre and Periphery*, New Haven: Yale University Press.

Thiébault, J.-L. (1993) 'Party leadership selection in France', in *European Journal of Political Research* 24: 277–93.

—— (1994) 'The political autonomy of cabinet ministers in the French Fifth Republic', in M. Laver and K.A. Shepsle (eds) *Cabinet Ministers and Parliamentary Democracy*, Cambridge: Cambridge University Press, pp. 139–49.

Thoenig, J.-C. (1973) *L'ère des technocrates. Le cas des Ponts et Chaussées*, Paris: Les éditions d'organisation.

—— (1979) 'Local government institutions and the evolution of contemporary French society', in J. Lagroye and V. Wright (eds) *Local Government in Britain and France. Problems and Prospects*, London: George Allen and Unwin, pp. 74–104.

—— (1987) 'Pour une approche analytique de la modernisation administrative', in *Revue Française de Science Politique* 37 (4): 526–38.

—— (1992) 'La décentralisation, dix ans après', in *Pouvoirs* 60: 5–16.

Todd, E. (1990) *The Making of Modern France. Politics, Ideology and Culture*, Oxford: Blackwell.

Turpin, D. (1992) *Droit constitutionnel*, Paris: Presses Universitaires de France.

Waterman, H. (1969) *Political Change in Contemporary France. The Politics of an Industrial Democracy*, Columbus, Ohio: Charles E. Merrill Publishing Company.

Waters, S. (1998a) 'New social movements in France: une nouvelle vague citoyenne?' in *Modern and Contemporary France* 6 (4): 493–504.

—— (1998b) 'New social movement politics in France: The rise of civic forms of mobilization', in *West European Politics* 21 (3): 170–86.

Williams, P. (1964) *Crisis and Compromise*, London: Longman.

—— (1968) *The French Parliament 1958–67*, London: George Allen and Unwin.

—— (1970) *Wars, Plots and Scandals in Post-War France*, Cambridge: Cambridge University Press.

Williams, P.M. and Harrison, M. (1971) *Politics and Society in de Gaulle's Republic*, London: Longman.

Wilsford, D. (1988) 'Tactical advantages versus administrative heterogeneity: the strengths and the limits of the French state', in *Comparative Political Studies* 21 (1): 126–68.

—— (1991a) *Doctors and the State: The Politics of Health Care in France and the United States*, Durham: Duke University Press.

—— (1991b) 'Running the bureaucratic state: the administration in France', in A. Farazmand (ed.) *Handbook of Comparative Development and Public Administration*, New York: Marcel Dekker, pp. 611–24.

Wilson, F.L. (1982) 'Alternative models of interest intermediation: the case of France', in *British Journal of Political Science* 12 (2): 173–200.

—— (1983) 'French interest group politics: pluralist or neo-corporatist?' in *American Political Science Review* 77 (4): 895–910.

—— (1987) *Interest-group Politics in France*, Cambridge: Cambridge University Press.

Worms, J.-P. (1966) 'Le préfet et ses notables', in *Sociologie du Travail* 8 (3): 249–75.

Wright, V. (1974) 'Politics and administration under the French Fifth Republic', in *Political Studies* 22 (1): 44–65.

—— (1989) *The Government and Politics of France*, 3rd edn, London: Unwin Hyman.

—— (1997) 'Introduction: la fin du *dirigisme?*' in *Modern and Contemporary France* 5 (2): 151–3.

Ysmal, C. (1994) 'The history of electoral studies in France', in *European Journal of Political Research* 25 (3): 367–85.

Zuckerman, A.S. (1989) 'The bases of political cohesion. Applying and reconstructing crumbling theories', in *Comparative Politics* 21 (4): 473–95.

Zysman, J. (1983) *Governments, Markets and Growth. Financial Systems and the Politics of Industrial Change*, Ithaca: Cornell University Press.

Index